ROUSSEAU AND DIGNITY

Rousseau

AND

Dignity

ART SERVING HUMANITY

EDITED BY Julia V. Douthwaite

UNIVERSITY OF NOTRE DAME PRESS

NOTRE DAME, INDIANA

University of Notre Dame Press
Notre Dame, Indiana 46556
www.undpress.nd.edu

The University of Notre Dame Press gratefully acknowledges the support of the Institute
for Scholarship in the Liberal Arts of the College of Arts and Letters
of the University of Notre Dame in the publication of this book.

Library of Congress Cataloging-in-Publication Data
Names: Douthwaite, Julia V., editor.
Title: Rousseau and dignity : art serving humanity / edited by Julia V. Douthwaite.
Description: Notre Dame : University of Notre Dame Press, 2016. | Includes index.
Identifiers: LCCN 2016039864| ISBN 9780268100360 (hardcover : alk. paper) |
ISBN 0268100365 (hardcover : alk. paper)
Subjects: LCSH: Rousseau, Jean-Jacques, 1712-1778. | Dignity.
Classification: LCC B2137 .R6785 2016 | DDC 179/.9--dc23
LC record available at https://lccn.loc.gov/2016039864

CONTENTS

ILLUSTRATIONS

ACKNOWLEDGMENTS

We would like to thank the following people and departments for their support of the Rousseau 2012/DIGNITY events celebrated at the University of Notre Dame in January–March 2012. For hosting distinguished guests during their visits to campus, thanks go to Gina Costa, Tom Kselman, Olivier Morel, Alison Rice, Steve Reifenberg, Holly Rivers, Sharon Schierling, and Michael Zuckert. For the initial funding that allowed the project to take flight, we are grateful for a grant from the Henkels Lecture Fund, Institute for Scholarship in the Liberal Arts, College of Arts and Letters, University of Notre Dame. Additional support was provided by the Department of Romance Languages and Literatures; the Kellogg Institute for International Studies; the Program in Liberal Studies; the Department of Political Science; the Department of History; the Center for Social Concerns; the Undergraduate Minor in Poverty Studies; the Program in Gender Studies; the Department of American Studies; and the Ph.D. Program in Literature. Thanks also go to the Nanovic Institute for European Studies for the research funding that supported the trip to Paris where I first saw the exhibit in the company of Andrew Kelly and where we first hatched the idea of bringing DIGNITY to campus. As volume editor, I would like to express gratitude to Matthew Dowd at the University of Notre Dame Press for his patience and good humor.

Part of chapter 9, by Christopher Kelly, is drawn from his article, "Rousseau and the Bad Calculations of the Philosophers," in *Rousseau et les philosophes*, Studies on Voltaire and the Eighteenth Century 2010:12, edited by Michael O'Dea, 57–66. We thank Oxford University and the editors of the SVEC series for permission to reprint here.

Thanks especially to Chuck Loving of the Snite Museum and Stephen Little of the University of Notre Dame Press for believing in the project from beginning to end.

NOTE ON EDITIONS, TRANSLATIONS, AND ABBREVIATIONS

All references to the works of Jean-Jacques Rousseau designate the following translations and are made as parenthetical notations in the text. A list of works and the abbreviations used in the text are found below. The first item on the list is the book series in which all the other items appear.

CW   The Collected Writings of Rousseau (series). Hanover, NH, and London: Dartmouth College and the University Press of New England. 1992–.

Abstract   *Abstract of Monsieur the Abbé de Saint-Pierre's Plan for Perpetual Peace.* CW, vol. 11. Edited by Christopher Kelly. Translated by Judith R. Bush and Christopher Kelly. 2005.

Conf   *The Confessions.* CW, vol. 5. Edited by Christopher Kelly, Roger D. Masters, and Peter G. Stillman. Translated by Christopher Kelly. 1995.

D'Alembert   *Letter to D'Alembert and Writings for the Theater.* CW, vol. 10. Translated and edited by Christopher Kelly, Allan Bloom, and Charles Butterworth. 2004.

Dialogues   *Rousseau Judge of Jean-Jacques: Dialogues.* CW, vol. 1. Edited by Roger D. Masters and Christopher Kelly. Translated by Judith R. Bush, Roger D. Masters, and Christopher Kelly. 1992.

DOI   *Discourse on the Origin and Foundations of Inequality among Men.* CW, vol. 3. Edited by Roger D. Masters and Christopher Kelly. Translated by Judith R. Bush, Roger D. Masters, Christopher Kelly, and Terence Marshall. 1992.

DSA   *Discourse on the Sciences and Arts.* CW, vol. 2. Edited by Roger D. Masters and Christopher Kelly. Translated by Judith R. Bush, Roger D. Masters, and Christopher Kelly. 1992.

Emile	*Emile, or, On Education.* CW, vol. 13. Translated and edited by Christopher Kelly and Allan Bloom. 2010.
GM	*Geneva Manuscript* (first version of *Social Contract*). CW, vol. 4. Edited by Roger D. Masters and Christopher Kelly. Translated by Judith R. Bush, Roger D. Masters, and Christopher Kelly. 1994.
Judgment	*Judgment of the Plan for Perpetual Peace.* CW, vol. 11. Edited by Christopher Kelly. Translated by Judith R. Bush and Christopher Kelly. 2005.
Julie	*Julie, or, The New Heloise: Letters of Two Lovers Who Live in a Small Town at the Foot of the Alps.* CW, vol. 6. Edited by Roger D. Masters and Christopher Kelly. Translated by Philip Stewart and Jean Vaché. 1997.
Moral Letters	"Moral Letters." In *Autobiographical, Scientific, Religious, Moral, and Literary Writings.* CW, vol. 12, 175–203. Edited and translated by Christopher Kelly. 2007.
Or	"Funeral Oration for His Most Serene Highness Monseigneur the Duke of Orléans." In *Autobiographical, Scientific, Religious, Moral, and Literary Writings.* CW, vol. 12, 252–63. Edited and translated by Christopher Kelly. 2007.
PE	*Discourse on Political Economy.* CW, vol. 3. Edited by Roger D. Masters and Christopher Kelly. Translated by Judith R. Bush, Roger D. Masters, Christopher Kelly, and Terence Marshall. 1992.
Reveries	*The Reveries of the Solitary Walker.* CW, vol. 8. Edited by Christopher Kelly. Translated by Charles E. Butterworth, Alexandra Cook, and Terence E. Marshall. 2000.
SC	*Social Contract.* CW, vol. 4. Edited by Roger D. Masters and Christopher Kelly. Translated by Judith R. Bush, Roger D. Masters, and Christopher Kelly. 1994.
SOW	*The State of War.* CW, vol. 11. Edited by Christopher Kelly. Translated by Judith R. Bush and Christopher Kelly. 2005.

Introduction to Rousseau 2012 and DIGNITY at Notre Dame

Julia V. Douthwaite

> *In order to be fair, to justify its existence, critical writing has to be partial, impassioned, and political.*
> —Charles Baudelaire (French poet and art critic, 1821–67)

> *Whether it is a question of the living or the dead, impartiality is just indifference.*
> —Jules Simon (French philosopher and statesman, 1814–96)

This is not a commemorative volume. Rather, this is an account of a series of events held in the name of Jean-Jacques Rousseau's tercentennial in 2012, a testimonial by some of the people who took part in those events, and a reminder of the work that lies ahead. Our aim is not to commemorate Rousseau in the ordinary sense of the term, that is, to celebrate or solemnly preserve his memory through eulogistic or honorable mention.[1] We aim on the contrary to retrieve his work in all its imperfection, to subject it to updated critical inquiry, and put it back into circulation for what it can do today: help us remember how to use our talents and skills to be fully human. As Rousseau reminds readers of *Emile, or, On Education* (1762): "To live is not to breathe; it is to act; it is to make use of our organs, our senses, our faculties, of all the parts of ourselves, which give us the sentiment of our existence. The man who has lived the most is not he who has counted the most years but he who has most felt life" (*Emile*, CW, 13:167). That is a tall order to be sure and the author himself made it even harder.

The life and writings of Jean-Jacques Rousseau (Geneva, 1712–Paris, 1778) exemplify the fascinating contradictions of the Enlightenment and show how the eighteenth century transformed the ferment of Renaissance humanism into the rough-and-tumble political struggles of modernity. Rousseau was a self-made man. Although his mother died in childbirth and his father, an unsuccessful watchmaker, abandoned him at age twelve, young Jean-Jacques acquired a vast knowledge of Western philosophy through his own readings. His first books—the *Discourse on the Sciences and Arts* (1750) and the *Discourse on the Origin and Foundations of Inequality among Men* (1755)—launched this nobody into fame and made him sought-after by the aristocrats of the Parisian intelligentsia. But his ideas actually attacked the interests of his benefactors! The *Discourse on the Origin of Inequality* includes many now-famous quotes that seem designed precisely to make the wealthy squeamish, such as: "Do you not know that a multitude of your brethren die or suffer from need of what you have in excess?" (*DOI*, CW, 3:53). Moreover, by pointing out that no one can "own" the earth (an idea that later inspired Karl Marx), Rousseau denounced the mainstay of capitalism, that is, private property: "The first person who, having fenced off a plot of ground, took it into his head to say *this is mine* and found people simple enough to believe him, was the true founder of civil society" (*DOI*, CW, 3:43). These quotes, and the love-hate emotions that characterized Rousseau's relations with powerful people, make him hard to fathom.

Contradictions form a prominent theme in Rousseau's life and works. An unhappy and tormented man, Rousseau refused to raise the five children borne by his illiterate common-law wife Thérèse and abandoned them to their fate in an orphanage.[2] Yet his book *Emile* laid down the fundaments for our modern understanding of the distinct phases of childhood and adolescence. Maria Montessori (1870–1952) drew heavily on Rousseau's works in creating her method of child-centered education; these principles are still well respected and practiced by teachers today. During his tempestuous life, which took him from Geneva to Italy to a long sojourn in Paris, before state-sponsored persecution drove him back to Switzerland and to England, Rousseau was a prolific writer whose works were translated instantly into the major European languages. He is often held up as the first modern autobiographer for his poignant *Confessions* (first ed. 1782), where he explores the oddities of his psyche and expresses a sense of exultation with the natural world that resonated profoundly with writers of the Romantic age (1790–1830). Based on his lyrical descriptions of Alpine scenery and his awareness of how nature is everywhere threatened by human industry, some claim that Rousseau was the first green thinker.

Rousseau was also a religious renegade whose staunch refusal of orthodoxy has made him notorious among Catholics, Protestants, and organized religions in general. Although born in Calvinist Geneva, he converted to Roman Catholicism at age fifteen and later eschewed both approaches to the divine in *Emile*'s controversial chapter on the Savoyard Vicar. There he demands a more personal, Deist approach to worship that is similar to the writings of Thomas Jefferson and Joseph Priestley. It was this work—which was banned by the Catholic Church upon its publication in 1762— that forced Rousseau into the exile of his later life.

At times celebrated by the high and mighty across Europe, at other times outcast by all but a few tolerant souls, Rousseau was a thorn in the side of authority. In *On the Social Contract* (1762), he laid out the concepts of the social contract and the popular will, declaring for instance that: "Man is born free, and everywhere he is in chains," "force does not make right," and that "one is only obligated to obey legitimate powers" (*SC*, CW, 4:131, 134). These ideas inspired the leaders of the French Revolution to seek an alternative to absolute monarchy. Despite the fact that he died well before the tumult began, Rousseau's writings have become notorious for generating the populist spirit of 1789 and serving as guiding light to Robespierre and the Jacobins whose hopes for national reform eventually degenerated into terrorist tactics. His utopian vision of a state led by a single will, with clear and luminous maxims and no contradictory interests, has been interpreted as leading to totalitarianism. Yet it also arguably contributed to the demand for democratic forms of government in Europe and South America that marked the nineteenth century and continue to drive social progress in our world. Indeed the slogan of the Amnesty International Demand Dignity campaign ("We are all born free and equal in dignity and rights—yet everywhere, these rights are being denied") has a distinctly Rousseauian feel to it.

The tercentennial of Rousseau was a huge undertaking that was planned far in advance by the city of Geneva. Thanks to the Rousseau for All website, over the course of 2012 one could track the philosopher's impact around the globe.[3] Alongside lectures and scholarly gatherings in Switzerland and France, events included an opera in São Paulo, Brazil; conferences from Turkey to Tokyo; a soccer tournament in the village of Bohicon, Bénin; and a rowing regatta in Saint Petersburg, Russia. The efforts detailed in this volume were somewhat different because they sought to make Rousseau 2012 into a platform that might create intergenerational teachable moments, experienced not in a world capital or cultural haven but rather in provincial France and the heartland of the United States.

The events in South Bend, Indiana, came about by chance. In May 2010, Andrew Kelly (ND '11) and I were in Paris on research and happened to visit the DIGNITY show during its opening at the Hôtel de Ville when the photographers were present. Based on our enthusiasm for the exhibit and our sense of its relevance to Notre Dame's Catholic mission, we started making plans to bring the show to the United States; these plans culminated nineteen months later in tandem with an exploration of Rousseau's tercentennial.

In January–March 2012, a program entitled Rousseau 2012/DIGNITY brought scholars, photojournalists, and the exhibit to the town of South Bend, Indiana, and the campus of the University of Notre Dame. Over five thousand people from various walks of life joined in events to learn why one should keep reading Rousseau through the lens of enduring concerns such as political justice, power relations, and religious liberty. An important visual component of the Notre Dame project was the large photographic exhibit created by Amnesty International to launch its Demand Dignity campaign in France, and which was housed in the Snite Museum of Art during its American debut. DIGNITY shows what poverty looks and feels like through formal portraits and reportage of people telling their stories from five countries: Egypt, India, Macedonia, Mexico, and Nigeria. As readers will find below, the catalog includes not only these people's names, ages, and hometowns, it also provides the text of their testimonials as recorded by the five photographers: Philippe Brault, Guillaume Herbaut, Jean-François Joly, Johann Rousselot, and Michaël Zumstein. The fact that all these people are named, and that they are our contemporaries, elicited strong reactions. Sympathetic observers had the feeling of walking in the shoes of some of the world's dispossessed, if only for a while. Others were annoyed by the demands that DIGNITY seemed to be making on their conscience via the pitiful conditions of those portrayed. Some of the more graphic images brought to mind photography's potential to exploit relations between viewer and image or to subtly manipulate the truth—to transform a supposedly objective snapshot into a staged experience. This ambivalence over truth and representation has inspired scholars Serge Margel's and Philip Stewart's contributions on Rousseau's strange "dialogues" recorded in *Rousseau Judge of Jean-Jacques*, as well as Gabrielle Gopinath's foray into relational aesthetics—a form of art based on one-on-one artist-viewer interaction. By reprinting the words and images of the exhibit alongside some reactions to it, and framing the whole in a sustained reflection on issues such as the truth-value of art, the multiple motivations behind altruism, and the cyclical nature of injustice and poverty—that is, concerns passed down to us from Rousseau—this volume aims to serve as a teaching tool.

Although the connection may seem tenuous at first, the linkage between the DIGNITY exhibit and Rousseau's thought was not lost on the college students who visited the exhibit, some of whose reflections are included here, nor on the scholars involved in the lecture series and this volume. Written by some of the foremost experts in the academy today, the essays do not rehash traditional disputes or indulge in micro-analyses, rather they revisit the man's work with an eye for his relevance to modern-day problems both sociopolitical and psychological in nature. Fayçal Falaky reminds us of one main difference between Rousseau and us, and that is his scorn for the very term "dignity." The man refused to use that word and bristled at the very concept of privilege all the while enjoying many luxuries conveyed by such *dignités*. Conversely, his fear of *indignités*, Philip Stewart argues, drove much of the author's angst in the *Rousseau Judge of Jean-Jacques* where he rails against unfair criticism. Other topics include the equivocal morality of cosmopolitanism in Rousseau's political thought (Andrew Billing), Rousseau's philosophy of human misery and advice for achieving happiness (Christopher Kelly), and the strains running through his utopian literature and social theory, as translated into the Occupy Wall Street movement of 2011–12 (Christie McDonald). Margel and Stewart address the existential dilemma of seeing oneself objectified in the gaze of another, a dilemma that

Rousseau tried to address in his political writings as well as in his autobiography, with mixed results. Providing the connective tissue between DIGNITY and the philosopher's paradoxical views on art, Gopinath is sure to spark debate with her frank embrace of subjective photography. In her interpretation of Guillaume Herbaut's photograph of Raúl Lucas Lucía (fig. 9), for example, she argues that the sympathy between sitter and artist "affirms the value of a humanist ethics vested . . . in the righteousness of the authentic, individual conscience." This "relational" aesthetic is akin to Rousseau's ideal of human communion as found in his autobiographical writings as well as his political theory; Gopinath argues that it constitutes a "spiritual heirloom" left by Rousseau and trumps objectivity with its power to persuade. Finally, some heartfelt reactions to the debate were penned by schoolchildren from South Bend, members of a photography club in a nearby community center for the underprivileged, and college students, whose words and pictures are found at the end of this volume.

Meanwhile, on the other side of the Atlantic, a film was being made with a similar approach to commemorating Rousseau. *Entre nous Jean-Jacques* was designed as a community outreach program in Compiègne, France (a city of forty-one thousand people, forty miles north of Paris), and culminated in the creation of a fifty-six-minute documentary shown at the philosopher's three-hundredth-birthday party at the Parc Jean-Jacques-Rousseau in Ermenonville. Created by a young director with modest financial backing from a nonprofit film institute and the regional offices of the Oise and Picardie departments, *Entre nous Jean-Jacques* unfolded over the course of winter–spring 2011–12 as filmmakers, teachers, and caregivers collaborated to explain the relevance of Rousseau's writing to one-hundred-some people ages ten to ninety-two years old. Participants in Notre Dame events became aware of *Entre nous Jean-Jacques* thanks to the research of Monica Townsend, then a senior in college. As Townsend explains, the spirit behind the two events was rather different: organizers of the American events tackled the question of Rousseau's relevance head-on by declaring, "Rousseau was a pioneer of humanitarian thought!" and juxtaposing readings to a militant art exhibit on human rights. Organizers of the French event were less directive and elicited more intimate, idiosyncratic responses from participants. In the video letters that constitute *Entre nous Jean-Jacques* (many of which are reprinted in the Teach This! section), some people identify primarily with the man's self-doubt and loneliness or connect with his day-dreamy reveries in nature, while others seethe with frustration over his limited understanding of the stakes involved in their attempts to get justice from an indifferent state. Like Gopinath, film director Delphine Moreau explains how the subjective lens she chose for her work was not only an artistic choice, it was also a philosophical expression of compassion for her sitters. She orchestrated the film as a composite of individual voices speaking their own, uncensored views and compiled the whole in homage to the human spirit. Although the two programs unfolded simultaneously with no knowledge of each other, they both aimed to prompt today's audiences to find new insights into Rousseau. This volume focuses primarily on the events that transpired in South Bend, but because of the common cause that unites us, we felt it only fitting to include some of the words and images brought to life through *Entre nous Jean-Jacques*.

The core goal of both programs—and of this volume of essays and art—is the cultivation of what Rousseau called "seeds of humanity" through realization of our "common miseries."[4] The Rousseauian ideal is a liberating education that resists certain truths held self-evident in Western society today. It is centered not on social conditioning or technical training but on nurturing self-determining people: people who see through the blandishments of financial capitalism and manage to lead fulfilling lives despite the economic pressures that weigh on them. It involves fostering appreciation for humility and commiseration, "all the attractive and sweet passions naturally pleasing to men," as Rousseau wrote in *Emile*, and that have their origins in empathy.[5] The project is intimately linked to educating the young because, as *Emile* points out: "The first sentiment of which a carefully raised young man is capable is not love; it is friendship. The first act of his nascent imagination is to teach him that he has fellows [*semblables*]; and that the species affects him" (*Emile*, CW, 13:371). It is also crucial to forming active citizens: an ongoing concern in our day when voter turnout tends to be disappointingly low (ranging from 40–60 percent in the United States, and 60–70 percent in France).[6] Rousseau hit that nail on the head when he wrote in the preface to the *Social Contract*, "Born a citizen of a free State, and a member of the sovereign, the right to vote there is enough to impose on me the duty of learning about public affairs, no matter how feeble the influence of my voice may be" (*SC*, CW, 4:131). The author was not unaware of the pitfalls of such idealism, however, and his own life story as recounted in *The Confessions, Rousseau Judge of Jean-Jacques*, and *The Reveries* gives ample evidence of weakness, contradiction, and cowardice. Readers of the Sixth Walk (*Reveries*), for instance, may be excused for smirking when they discover that this author—so famous for his discourses on pity and fellow-feeling—admits that his daily walks were ruined by the presence of a little lame boy who always asked him for alms. Although initially amused by the boy's flattery and efforts to befriend him, Rousseau eventually found it bothersome, so much so that he began taking long detours to avoid running into him, even if it meant that he thereby broke his own rules on charity.[7]

Given the philosopher's imperfect record as a father, husband, and person, critics may well ask why we chose to invest so much time and energy on him. Surely such a problematic character should not be held up as a model? The answer lies in interpretation, of course. Rousseau is vast; perhaps we can pardon a writer for contradicting himself now and then when we realize that his collected writings form sixteen volumes and his vast correspondence adds up to fifty-two more.[8] But it also lies in our interest in the civic morality and soul-searching that Rousseau strove to exemplify and which have often been misunderstood. One critic blasted Rousseau for opposing what we see as the central project in *The Discourse on Inequality*, *Emile*, and *The Social Contract*, that is, "the urgent need for a reawakened awareness of personal character and responsibility as the basis of civilized society. The individual must be encouraged to face the hard and primary obligations of the here and now, chief of which is improvement of self and doing right by 'neighbor.'"[9] Where Claes Ryn interpreted Rousseau as an irresponsible "Jacobin" for his role as spiritual leader of the French Revolution (1789–94), we focus on the issues of justice, human development, and psychological integrity that Rousseau tried to address. He may not have succeeded 100 percent, but his innovative concepts of the social contract that binds us to our neighbors, the universality of suffering and its helpmeet compassion, and the benefits of child-centered education are still good food for thought.

Whatever one's opinion on Rousseau's thought, it remains potent. The issues raised here may be anchored in eighteenth-century circumstances, but they remain urgent. Which members of the population should be allowed to join policy debates? At what point does strong leadership verge into dictatorship, and how can one arrest such a development? How should democratic entities balance the loyalties that people feel they owe to other identities—religious, ethnic, or regional? Under what conditions must a state punish its own citizens, and what constitutes a fair punishment? These are tough questions, as a glance at any daily newspaper will show; and Rousseau's answers are only partly satisfactory, as the testimonials in *Entre nous Jean-Jacques* make clear. Delving into the ways that these questions were visualized by the DIGNITY photographers and were debated by scholars and students may provide some perspective.

> *Photography actualizes Rousseau's otherwise impossible dream: it renders the invisible visible.*
> —Gabrielle Gopinath

Visitors to the DIGNITY show were struck by the beauty of the photographs and the way that they captured destitute people in a manner that seemed serious and respectful. Consider the portrait of *Rasheed Ajaï* of Jakonde, Nigeria, by Michaël Zumstein (fig. 45). Although he is perched on a rock in a street flooded with waste water and sewage, Mr. Ajaï, a baker, stands with regal assurance. (Zumstein affectionately calls him *The Floating Baker*.) His upright posture and sober gaze compel viewers to appreciate the abject reality of his slum, yet the play of light and shadow running between the blues and greys of the buildings, reflected in the water, makes for a soothing image not unlike a seascape. None of the people in DIGNITY are crying or bleeding or prostrate with grief; the exhibit refrains from what Susan Sontag has qualified as "the indecency of such co-spectatorship."[10] But it was not the first exhibit to resist that temptation; artists have long fought against the tendency to dehumanize the poor and unfortunate. In order to put DIGNITY into dialogue with that tradition, the Snite Museum of Art organized a sister exhibit that was displayed in the same room, and which gathered together works by artists such as Francisco de Goya, Jean-François Millet, and Félix Nadar from its permanent collection of eighteenth- to twentieth-century art. Viewers thus realized that: (1) poverty is not a new topic in art, and (2) artists from much earlier times devised their own strategies to confer dignity on the dispossessed.

Some works incite compassion through clever compositions that skew the observer's perspective. In Pier Leone Ghezzi's *The Alms Giver* (eighteenth century; fig. 1), for example, a well-dressed priest placed center-stage looks off indifferently as a beggar pleads for help from below. The traditional full-body portrait of the alms giver contrasts with the truncated portrait of the beggar who is represented only by his feet and crutches lying on the ground. Crammed into the corner of the frame, cut off by the border of the paper, this pauper's presence is literally forced into the margins and forms a wry commentary on the self-satisfied gaze of the clergyman. Similarly, by magnifying the pathos of *Überfahren (Run Over)* (1910–13, fig. 2) in what appears to be an under-sized frame, Käthe Kollwitz forces viewers to acknowledge the scene's silent, workaday horror. In this image of a dead child being carried by two hunched adult figures, a crowd of children anxiously follows the parents and seems to squeeze onto the page, in mimicry of their close tenement quarters. The flowing lines of the woman's black dress and the horizontal composition conjure up a feeling of movement, as if the procession were going by in front of your eyes. The people's lowered heads and the dead girl's white gown sanctify the scene and demand a respectful response.

Compassion is also conjured up by the photographs of Guillaume Herbaut. A lowered gaze and sense of sadness mark the portrait of *Modesta Cruz Victoriano* (fig. 11) although the significance of the picture in her hands is unclear. The red and black of her clothing (symbolizing blood and death), and the stark white lines of her cottage wall, which form a cross behind her, place her in an aura of gravity. What is different here, as compared to Kollwitz's etching, is the scene's pressing actuality. In the testimonial recorded by Herbaut, Modesta Victoriano explains that she is holding a photo of her late husband Lorenzo Fernández Ortega's dead body. Ortega was assassinated in 2008 at the age of thirty-nine after being kidnapped and tortured for his activism on behalf of their people, the Me'phaa. His murder was a deliberate reprisal by the army against the Me'phaa community. Through Victoriano's portrait, the photographer explicitly shames the Mexican government and demands a response. Where Kollwitz's image describes the agony of nameless witnesses to a tragic event, and stirs observers with what she called the "full force of the proletarian's fate," Herbaut's work names specific perpetrators, explains the deliberate malevolence of the violence, and calls on viewers to demand reparation for the victim.[11] Since visitors to DIGNITY could know who she is and where she lives, and that a respected NGO is working on her behalf, they could feel that this photo may actually get results.[12]

Figure 1. *The Alms Giver*. Engraving by Pier Leone Ghezzi, eighteenth century. Courtesy of Snite Museum of Art, University of Notre Dame.

Figure 2. *Überfahren (Run Over)*. Soft ground etching by Käthe Kollwitz, 1910–13. Courtesy of Snite Museum of Art, University of Notre Dame.

Or they might feel manipulated by the emotional blackmail that such art wraps around the viewer. Neither reaction is wrong or unexpected. As the photographers stated in their interviews, the art makes no claim to objectivity; rather, it tries to involve the viewer. Young viewers were especially sensitive, and frequently sought more information on the sitters or voiced a desire to "make a difference" in some way. Will their wishes translate into action?

When my student assistants and I filmed interviews of the DIGNITY team members talking about their work, we were struck by a recurrent theme: each man expressed a drive to make his photos into a form of humanitarian statement, yet with their long experience of working in these countries, none harbored any illusions about their impact.[13] The connection they felt to their subjects, the time they spent learning and listening to people's stories, and the artwork they created to communicate those stories were worth it in themselves. Students were impressed by the candid views on photojournalism expressed by Johann Rousselot and Philippe Brault during their visits to campus; they underlined the difficult material issues posed by a profession caught between the global slump in newspaper production and competition with the Internet. Brault surprised us when he revealed the very few shots that he typically took during the days he spent in the slums of Cairo. In order to create the stunning portraits such as *Ihaab on Her Wedding Day* (fig. 33), he used older equipment with slower shutter speeds and made it a habit to join the sitters for a few—or sometimes several—hours. He preferred to sit quietly and listen, waiting for an opportune moment to capture a telling shot, rather than snapping hundreds of photos indiscriminately with a digital camera and editing afterwards. As a result, he sometimes took as few as five photos a day.

Another striking feature of DIGNITY and *Entre nous Jean-Jacques* was their portrayal of people whose plight mirrored the plight of viewers' own acquaintances, either through analogy or because they actually are neighbors. South Bend, Indiana, is a rust belt city of 101,000 inhabitants located ninety miles east of Chicago with high rates of unemployment and crime. The percentage of residents living in poverty is approximately 27.9 percent, and a disproportionate number are people of color (40.7 percent for Black residents, 41.8 percent for Hispanic or Latino residents, as opposed to 20.3 percent for White non-Latino residents). More than one-third of the children under eighteen in South Bend live in poverty.[14] Their household distress puts these children at a disadvantage to learn: a recent report ranked two-thirds of our public elementary schools as below average or failing.[15] Such urban ills may be one reason why the linkage between DIGNITY and Rousseau's political writings hit home; some parts of our town do not look so different from certain photos of Skopje, Macedonia, and Festac Town, Nigeria.

> In a world where there is so much wealth, so many resources to feed everyone, it is unfathomable that there are so many hungry children, that there are so many children without an education, so many poor persons. Poverty today is a cry.
> —Pope Francis

Catholicism may lie beneath the exhibit's appeal in South Bend. As Daniel Philpott writes below, "That a Catholic university would host the DIGNITY project was fitting. . . . The Church's love for the poor resonates with the beautiful, poignant, and provocative pictures featured." A strong tradition of community activism lives on at Notre Dame, and many students take to heart the social justice teachings of the church to work with the poor. The university's Center for Social Concerns and the Law School's Center for Civil and Human Rights lent significant support to our efforts. But Rousseau's relationship to church dogma was complicated. The combination of humanitarian reflection, Rousseauian philosophy, and Catholicism makes for a potent brew.

Empathy for the marginal of her town sparked the work of Delphine Moreau as well. Like the director behind the camera, viewers of *Entre nous Jean-Jacques* in Ermenonville are touched by the struggles with the French language articulated by recent immigrants from Africa and Southeast Asia and the loneliness described by the elderly. In short, a heightened sensitivity to humanity runs through both programs. But empathy for the poor and the aged does not explain it all.

It is my contention that these events succeeded because they broke with academic mainstays that often go unspoken, and it is our hope that this volume will achieve a similar goal. Instead of intimidating readers with Rousseau's complexities or obliging them to learn enough about twenty-first-century economics to understand the dilemma of foreign aid, the writers gathered here invite readers to interact with the material on their own terms, just as viewers to the exhibit and participants in the film were able to do. By linking Rousseau with photojournalism and filmmaking, writing and art, we seek to invite teachers, students, schoolchildren, and the elderly to explore the meaning of his writings for their lives.

Photographer Jean-François Joly made a powerful connection between Rousseau and the visual arts by noting how the gaze or *le regard* divides people. Rousseau describes mankind's descent into modern society and unhappiness in *The Discourse on Inequality* by noting how people began looking at each other differently once they began living in proximity and comparing their relative beauty, wealth, talent, and so forth: "Each one began to look at the others and to want to be looked at himself, and public esteem had a value. . . . From these first preferences were born on one hand vanity and contempt, on the other shame and envy; and the fermentation caused by these new leavens eventually produced compounds fatal to happiness and innocence" (*DOI*, CW, 3:47). In his photographs of the Roma people from Macedonia, Joly created sober close-ups of great intensity where sitters look directly into the camera and thereby challenge the judgments of a society based on money and status. As he explained in his interview: "I think that poverty is directly tied to the *regard* [or gaze] that is cast upon these people. Even [in Paris] when you take the metro or the RER [interurban train], as soon as you see somebody coming around begging, observe how people look at him. Either they don't look at him, or else by the way that they look at him, they push him deeper into failure. So for me, as a photographer, it's also a way to re-integrate these people in the regard of others. . . . Dignity, that's it, it's the fact of standing up."[16] The double meaning of the word "regard" neatly sums up the connection between Rousseau and Joly. By putting his subjects—most of whom are homeless, nationless outcasts—at eye-level with viewers in the exhibit, Joly's photos give them some modicum of the dignity they deserve. He frees them from the contemptuous gaze of daily life in Skopje for a while. But Joly's practice also involves self-discovery and examination: since his photographs were made with Polaroid film, he was able to share the results with sitters immediately after the picture was taken. For some people, it was the first self-portrait they had ever seen.

Cynics may counter that these little gestures—of looking people in the eye, helping them to tell their story, or offering them a picture of themselves—are unworthy of the humanitarian label. After all, the problems faced by the long-term unemployed of South Bend and Compiègne, like the Roma of Macedonia and the other people in the DIGNITY exhibit, are rooted in intractable structural issues. Having the right attitude toward the poor is a first step, but by itself it does not solve most problems. History suggests that neither Rousseauian nor any other political ideology holds a monopoly of wisdom on the noxious cycles of deprivation, hopelessness, and violence.

Nevertheless, one must start somewhere with the young people in our care. Consider what psychologist David DeSteno has done in the social science laboratory. DeSteno's experiments have succeeded by orchestrating simple actions among total strangers: by tapping their hands in synchrony, people reported feeling more similar and having more compassion for each other's situation. The events of Rousseau 2012 worked differently—in an art museum and a film shoot—but the ultimate results were similar, as are the goals for this book. By reflecting on a text by Rousseau and then looking into the camera to talk to him, or reading a person's testimonial and then gazing into his eyes in the DIGNITY exhibit, participants may feel kinship with a hitherto-unknown subject. As DeSteno notes, "the compassion we feel for others is not solely a function of what befalls them: if our minds draw an association between a victim and ourselves—even a relatively trivial one—the compassion we feel for his or her suffering is amplified greatly. . . . Simply learning to mentally re-categorize one another in terms of greater commonality would generate greater empathy among all of us."[17]

Some visitors to DIGNITY translated its message into a personal or professional commitment to do things differently. Consider the work of MIT Poverty Lab pioneer Esther Duflo. In her essay below, she issues a charge to economists seeking to diminish inequality, writing that the fight against poverty "requires bold solutions and systematic experimentation," including micro-lending schemes with first-time borrowers. Although she admits the imperfection of such methods, she also captures the urgency to try different approaches. Despite the possibility of errors that arise in any venture, "making choices based on experimental methods, and using the most efficient results, is the only practical means we have to start making respect for human rights a worldwide reality."

A similar urgency ran through the words of Notre Dame political scientist Steve Reifenberg. In a lecture presented during the Rousseau 2012/DIGNITY events, Reifenberg quoted book 2 of *Emile*, "Men, be kind to your fellow-men; this is your first duty. . . . What wisdom can you find that is greater than kindness?" to illustrate the concept of accompaniment, and prodded policy makers and students to acknowledge the web of humanity that binds us together.[18] Accompaniment provides insights on "how to promote—in an operational way—dignity in the real world," he said. Tracing the long history of human rights back to Rousseau, Reifenberg reminded us that despite the 1948 United Nations Universal Declaration of Human Rights, its adoption in 1966 and ratification in 1976, there are several countries that have refused to ratify, including the United States. "Accompaniment connects the core of who we are and what we do with one another," he explained. "The word has its origins in Latin—*ad cum panis*—'breaking bread together.' It's less about personal efficacy than an intense attentiveness, a partnership in close rhythm with the other."[19] This theological concept is now commonplace in development studies. Witness Harvard professor Paul Farmer who, in a now-famous essay from *Foreign Affairs* (2011), stated that: "Accompaniment is about sticking with the task until it's deemed completed, not by the *accompagnateur* but by the person accompanied."[20] While it is employed here in talking about foreign-aid policy rather than religion, this discourse nevertheless blurs lines between giver and receiver, donor and recipient, in ways that echo Pope Francis.

Some younger visitors expressed responses to Rousseau 2012/DIGNITY that were powerful too, such as the nine-year-old who captured the alienation of the industrial workplace in stark simplicity. Gazing at Johann Rousselot's photograph of a working man pushing a tire through the mud in Juruli, India (fig. 19), he wrote: "Long ago there was a man doing his job which is taking a tire back. He doesn't like the job. That was the only job there was." Or contemplate the enthusiasm emanating from the twelve-year-old who simply wrote, "Let's make a change in our world!"[21] Some older audience members were dubious about the combination of commemoration and activism, however. A few grumbled about the irrelevance of Occupy Wall Street in a lecture on Rousseau and human rights. Another protested the university's partnership with Amnesty International, which he erroneously labeled a pro-abortion organization.

Such disagreement did not end in 2012. It also characterizes some of the essays collected here. Dignity itself comes under the microscope in the essay by Fayçal Falaky, who reminds us that the concept did not connote life-giving empathy and equality in Rousseau's day, but rather suggested privilege, status, and rank. The philosopher might have rankled at seeing his name associated with it, at least in this traditional usage. Other contradictions between the philosopher's theory and practice are revealed in the chapters by Billing, who tackles the uncertain opposition between cosmopolitanism and nationalism in Rousseau, and Stewart, who shows how the autobiographical texts both appeal to and refuse connection with readers. Or consider Philpott's essay, which reveals the religious intolerance of the man we are touting as a champion of humanity. These contradictions were never reconciled in Rousseau's work, and they still have the power to perplex. That is why they are useful. Because the ultimate goal of the events, as for this volume, was not simply to produce more Rousseau scholarship or to force agreement on the best ways to solve the world's problems, but rather to reveal how the philosopher's complex legacy lives on. So that all viewers have to judge its value for themselves.

EDITOR'S POSTFACE, MAY 2016

Now that the excitement is long over, one might ask if it was worth it. Organizing a lecture series and an art exhibit, like making a documentary film, is a huge amount of work, and its impact may be short-lived. Forgetting is natural in the transient world of teaching. Yet there are signs that the project's spirit endures. Out of the sixteen students in the class on "Humanitarian Thought, from Rousseau to the Present" that I taught in spring 2012, one has chosen to become a teacher. A second volunteered with me on a weekly basis from September 2012 to May 2015 in a story-writing workshop for kids that we led at the public library. Her goal upon graduation from law school was to defend children from abuse, possibly as a state prosecutor. The dramatic, seemingly intractable conflicts visualized in the DIGNITY exhibit between human rights and self-interest seem to be more on the mind of college students, as seen in the rising popularity of fields such as behavioral economics, public policy, and conflict resolution. Business faculty have even taken up the torch. Consider Yale Economics professor Robert J. Shiller who in *Finance and the Good Society* presents concrete ways to balance people's drive for material wealth and success with strategies on how to live a humane, meaningful life by democratizing finance and supporting more small businesses.[22] Some say this public spirited attitude is spreading beyond the academy to sustain positive new connections between colleges and their local communities.[23]

Working with the DIGNITY photojournalists and seeing how we formed common cause was energizing. This affected all of us, I think. Johann Rousselot was so interested in the South Bend mentoring program that he joined my mentee (then age twelve) and me for lunch at her school one day. Although he never did get her to talk, it was doubtless eye-opening for him to meet an African American schoolgirl on her own turf. In the drive we took afterwards through her neighborhood of abandoned houses and garbage-strewn vacant lots, Rousselot saw what poverty looks and feels like in the United States.

Understanding how photojournalists do their work prompted me to seek other ways to use my skills too. Since 2012, I have been teaching language arts in a program for local high school students called the Upward Bound summer academy. Through daily contact over our time together each summer, I've begun to glimpse the challenges faced by people whose lives are not so different from the DIGNITY photos: adolescents growing up in American ghettos. Thanks to books such as Paul Tough's *How Children Succeed* and the publications of the 826 National network, founded by Dave Eggers, I was inspired to create the "Write YOUR Story" workshop.[24] We write stories and create altered books for the kids to display their stories in, in a class held for free at the public library. Evidence suggests that a small commitment from a reliable mentor can mean a lot to children and their families. (Plus it is fun for all involved.)

Some of the writings produced by students of my Upward Bound classes are raw; they tell of loved ones being shot on the streets of South Bend in execution-style murders or drive-by gunfire, and their descriptions of violence and discrimination are appallingly realistic. Equally real, however, was the satisfaction that I have seen on their faces when they managed to weave that knowledge into a beautiful illustrated book, or to use their outrage to analyze how race prejudice comes across in American art. In one of the "Write YOUR Story" groups, there was a boy who could barely make out the simplest writing. His chaotic home situation doubtless affected his low reading level and drove him to quit after one semester too. But during his involvement with the group, his imagination and vocabulary took flight. In one book we created, *Oscar Saves the Day*, a kindly doctor ocelot cures an epidemic in his town by making medicine out of mangoes and bat guano, that is, local, renewable resources instead of high-cost, imported chemicals. The children's (unconscious?) choice of a multi-colored protagonist to channel their ambitions is interesting, as is the environmentally astute solution they came up with to heal the sick people. With kids like these in town, and college students like the contributors to this volume, one cannot help but feel some optimism for the future.

NOTES

I would like to thank the following people for commenting on an earlier draft: Tobias Boes, John Deak, Robert Fishman, Tom Kselman, Alex Martin, Pierpaolo Polzonetti, Yasmin Solomonescu, and Lesley Walker. Thanks to Chuck Loving and the team at the Snite Museum of Art who made the DIGNITY art exhibit happen on the Notre Dame campus. Gratitude is also due to Marthe-Marie Meadows who in the course of summer–fall 2012 gave me the library of her late husband, Professor Paul Meadows, a distinguished *Rousseauiste* and professor of French. It was a pleasure to put Rousseau's works back into circulation through this project, and discovering Professor Meadows's notes in the margins of his books made it even more meaningful. Biggest thanks go to Alexa Craig for teaching "Write YOUR Story" with me in South Bend from 2012 to 2015, and to Anna Bourbonnais and Kirstyn Ruiz, who have done so in 2015–16.

1. "Commemoration, n." OED Online, available at www.oed.com.

2. Not to excuse this uncharitable act, but there is some debate over whether those children were actually his and whether his long-winded admissions of fault might not have been a smokescreen to protect Thérèse and her less-than-ideal family. See for example Françoise Bocquentin, *Jean-Jacques Rousseau, femme sans enfants? Essai sur l'analyse des textes autobiographiques de J.J. Rousseau à travers sa "langue des signes"* (Paris: Harmattan, 2003), and V.L., *J.-J. Rousseau infirme n'a jamais eu d'enfants* (Nice: Imprimerie Honoré Robaudi, 1912).

3. "Rousseau pour tous," available at http://www.ville-ge.ch/culture/rousseau/.

4. "It follows . . . that we are attached to our fellows less by the sentiment of their pleasures than by the sentiment of their pains, for we see far better in the latter the identity of our natures with theirs and the guarantees of their attachment to us. If our common needs unite us by interest, our common miseries unite us by affection" (*Emile*, CW, 13:372–73).

5. Rousseau conceived of pity as an essential human trait, "a natural feeling which, moderating in each individual the activity of love of oneself, contributes to the mutual

preservation of the entire species." From there he extrapolated the principle of enlightened self-interest, writing: "Instead of that sublime maxim of reasoned justice, *Do unto others as you would have them do unto you*, [pity] inspires Men with this other maxim of natural goodness, much less perfect but perhaps more useful than the preceding one: *Do what is good for you with the least possible harm to others*" (*DOI*, CW, 3:37).

6. Arend Lijphart, "Unequal Participation: Democracy's Unresolved Dilemma," *American Political Science Review* 91, no. 1 (March 1997): 1–14.

7. *Reveries*, CW, 8:49. On the dark humor running through this passage and others in the *Reveries*, see Julia V. Douthwaite, "Is Charity for Schmucks? The Legitimacy of *Bienfaisance*, ca. 1760–82 and ca. 2013–15," *The Eighteenth Century: Theory and Interpretation* 57, no. 1 (Spring 2016): 1–21.

8. Rousseau, *Collection complète des œuvres de J. J. Rousseau*, 16 volumes (Geneva and Paris: Chez Volland, 1790–91); Rousseau, *Correspondance complète de Jean-Jacques Rousseau*, edited by R. A. Leigh, 52 volumes (Geneva: Institut et Musée Voltaire, 1965–98).

9. Claes G. Ryn, *The New Jacobinism: Can Democracy Survive?* (Washington, DC: The National Humanities Institute, 1991), 94.

10. Susan Sontag, *Regarding the Pain of Others* (New York: Picador, 2003), 60.

11. Kaethe Kollwitz, *The Diary and Letters of Kaethe Kollwitz*, ed. Hans Kollwitz, trans. Richard Wilson and Clara Wilson (Evanston, IL: Northwestern University Press, 1988), 43. Thanks go to Brenda Rix of the Art Gallery of Ontario for her help in interpreting this image.

12. In October 2010, the Inter-American Court of Human Rights issued a ruling that greatly aids the fight for justice being waged by Inés Fernández Ortega, also featured in a portrait by Guillaume Herbaut in the Mexico section. For more information on her case, see the Amnesty International human rights blog: http://blog.amnestyusa.org/

13. The team included Lea Malewitz and Lauren Wester, who also assisted with the translation of the DIGNITY catalog, and Elizabeth Kelly as camerawoman and editor extraordinaire. The interviews were filmed in October 2011 and remain available at https://www.youtube.com/user/DignityND.

14. As of March 2012, the unemployment rate in South Bend was 11.2 percent (as compared to the U.S. average—with seasonal adjustment—of 8.1 percent). Poverty data is from 2009. The city's crime rate was as follows in 2010: 6 murders, 52 rapes, 339 robberies, 349 assaults, 2,216 burglaries, and 3,411 cases of theft. With a composite index of 521.7, this placed South Bend well above the national average of 319. Data gathered from http://www.city-data.com/city/South-Bend-Indiana.html, http://www.gallup.com/poll/153761/unemployment-declines-march.aspx on September 9, 2012, and U.S. Census Bureau, American Community Survey, 2010, Table S1701, accessed thanks to the "Community Conversation about Poverty, Inequality, and Economic Injustice" organized by the Community Forum for Economic Development and held at Indiana University South Bend, September 15, 2012.

15. Of the eighteen primary schools in South Bend, six received Ds (below average) and six received Fs (failing). Kim Kilbride, "State Grades Schools," *South Bend Tribune*, November 1, 2012, A1–2.

16. Interview with Jean-François Joly, filmed on October 21, 2011 in Saint-Denis, France; my translation. The interview is available at https://www.youtube.com/watch?v=T3Y0VWuwcxo.

17. David DeSteno, "Compassion Made Easy," *New York Times*, July 15, 2012, SR BW 12.

18. Jean-Jacques Rousseau, *Emile*, translated by Barbara Foxley (London: J. M. Dent, 1938), 43. Although lovely, the Foxley translation is actually not a faithful rendition of the original phrase, "Hommes, soyez humains, c'est votre premier devoir. . . . Quelle sagesse y a-t-il pour vous hors de l'humanité?" The Kelly translation captures the original: "Men, be humane. This is your first duty. . . . What wisdom is there for you save humanity?" (*Emile*, CW, 13:209).

19. Steve Reifenberg, "Dignity, Human Rights, and Accompaniment" presented at Reflecting on Dignity and Human Rights: A Panel Discussion with Notre Dame Internationalists (University of Notre Dame Hesburgh Center for International Studies, February 23, 2012).

20. Paul Farmer, "Partners in Help," *Foreign Affairs* (July 29, 2011) http://www.foreignaffairs.com/articles/68002/paul-farmer/partners-in-help. This article was originally part of Farmer's commencement speech to students of the John F. Kennedy School of Government (Harvard University) in May 2011.

21. Quotes are from participants in workshops held for the Robinson Community Learning Center (February 24, 2012) and the general public (March 3, 2012) at the Snite Museum of Art, University of Notre Dame.

22. Robert J. Shiller, *Finance and the Good Society*, 2nd ed. (Princeton: Princeton University Press, 2013), ix–xviii, 8–14, 177, 187–239. That such hopes involve a precarious balancing act, or may only come to fruition late in a person's life, is a sobering reality here. Also sobering is Shiller's reduction of the United Nations's Universal Declaration of Human Rights to a "well-intentioned" document that raises expectations too high for what he calls "entitlements" for the poor (such as education and health), without considering who will finance those activities (149). Instead, he writes, "We need to reframe the wording of 'universal human rights' so that they represent the rights of *all* people to a fair compromise— to financial arrangements that share burdens and benefits effectively" (150).

23. Julie Ellison, "The New Public Humanists," *PMLA* 128, no. 2 (March 2013): 289–98.

24. See Paul Tough, *How Children Succeed: Grit, Curiosity, and the Hidden Power of Character* (Boston: Houghton, Mifflin, Harcourt, 2012). 826 National is a nonprofit organization that provides strategic leadership, administration, and other resources to ensure the success of seven writing and tutoring centers nationwide. The 826 National books include: *Don't Forget to Write for the Secondary Grades: 50 Enthralling and Effective Writing Lessons*, ed. Jennifer Traig (San Francisco: Jossey-Bass, 2011), and *Don't Forget to Write for the Elementary Grades: 50 Enthralling and Effective Writing Lessons*, ed. Jennifer Traig (San Francisco: Jossey-Bass, 2011). See http://826national.org/about/ and http://jdouthwa.wixsite.com/writeyourstory1.

Part One

SETTING THE STAGE IN SOUTH BEND AND COMPIÈGNE

CHAPTER 1

Remembering Rousseau in 2012
A Franco-American Comparison

Monica Townsend

Jean-Jacques Rousseau played many roles in his life: he was a writer, a philosopher, an anthropologist, and a composer; he wrote about religion, politics, and humanism, and he offered insights that were as complex as they were varied. During the year 2012, the three-hundredth anniversary of his birth, the world remembered this man and his legacy. How should one remember a man whose contributions are so varied and sometimes controversial? I propose two ways. The first, Rousseau 2012/DIGNITY, presents an adaptation of Rousseau's philosophy for a modern audience on the subject of humanitarianism and inequality. The second, *Entre nous Jean-Jacques*, is a film from the "Fête de Rousseau 2012, Tricentenaire" in the Oise department of France that links Rousseau's philosophy to the local population. These two events, rather than be confined to the safety and familiarity of the "traditional" scholarly audience that might participate in the commemoration of a historic figure, instead take on a fresh approach to Rousseau. These approaches unknowingly shared common themes as their organizers sought to cast a new light on Jean-Jacques Rousseau. Both Rousseau 2012/DIGNITY and *Entre nous Jean-Jacques* developed innovative approaches using various media to reach a new demographic; the projects quite literally bring Rousseau "home" by introducing his philosophy and his legacy to the residents of South Bend, Indiana, and Compiègne, France. The use of photography and film media allows for the depiction of the modern world in a way that is reminiscent of Rousseau's philosophy. The ability of these projects to bring the philosophy of Rousseau off the pages of his discourses and out of the lecture hall to the "real world" in 2012 distinguishes them from more traditional commemorations. This essay seeks to highlight their unique presentations and the motivations of their creators. Additionally, after comparing these two cases of "nontraditional" commemoration, I explore the potential and dangers of their techniques. For example, the use of photos of poor people for an activist cause, as DIGNITY does, is controversial; these photos possess the potential to incite the viewer to react, but they risk exploiting their subjects. Furthermore, in choosing certain Rousseauian themes to show the public, the organizers of these two commemorations could appear biased. Nonetheless, I conclude that it is necessary to take these risks in order to accomplish a unique and creative commemoration that engages the public. The efficacy of these two commemorations derives from the link that they create between a historic man and a modern public.

2012 is not the first time that intellectuals have commemorated Rousseau. In 1978, the *Rousseauistes* of the world united for a conference at Trinity College, Cambridge, entitled "Rousseau après deux cents ans: bilan d'une vie et d'une œuvre" (Rousseau after Two Hundred Years: Assessing His Life and Works). Their ambitious goal was difficult to attain because, as organizer R. A. Leigh explained, "Rousseau is too vast and too elusive a subject for convenient encapsulation. Indeed, it is unlikely that a completely satisfactory account of him and his work will ever be given."[1] Despite the enormity of this task, the fact remains that these scholars tried to commemorate Rousseau and highlight his influence—and this is exactly the same thing that was done in 2012 by the University of Notre Dame and the department of Oise. Why commemorate this man at all? Leigh gives one reason when he calls attention to the tendency to assign "paternity" to Rousseau's ideas. Rousseau is supposedly the father of romanticism, the father of subjectivism in religion, the father of the French Revolution, and so forth. Rousseau's influence is vast, both in history and in modern times; it seems that there exist millions of elements of his legacy that one could commemorate.

ROUSSEAU AND DIGNITY:
COMMEMORATING ROUSSEAU AS A HUMANIST

At the University of Notre Dame, organizers chose a less well-known theme of Rousseau's and explored it through association with current affairs. This theme, humanitarianism and human rights, was linked with Amnesty International's DIGNITY exhibit in order to create an event that revealed the dreadful situation of the poor in developing countries. Rousseau's philosophy of human rights emerges from two texts: *Discourse on the Origin and Foundations of Inequality among Men* (or *Second Discourse*, 1755) and *On the Social Contract* (1762). While it seems that these works promote contradictory ideas—the former promotes individualism by critiquing society and the latter promotes collectivism by creating an ideal society for everyone—they actually complement each other. As Hartley Alexander has noted, Rousseau looks to show how man is inherently good in both works.[2] This optimistic view about the goodness of man suggests that, according to Alexander, compassion and pity are at the heart of mankind, and the capacity to help others is born from this pity. The humanitarian side of Rousseau is most evident in his critique of inequality. He claims that inequality, a negative product of society, runs against the laws of nature: "moral inequality. . . is contrary to Natural Right whenever it is not combined in the same proportion with Physical inequality" (*DOI*, CW, 3:67). Rousseau implicates his compatriots because they allow this inequality to continue, saying: "Do you not know that a multitude of your brethren die or suffer from need of what you have in excess?" (*DOI*, CW, 3:53). If man is inherently good and if all men are equal by nature, it is necessary to treat them reasonably. For Rousseau, the only solution is to introduce a contract; as he explains: "What man loses by the social contract is his natural freedom and an unlimited right to everything that tempts him and that he can get; what he gains is civil freedom and the proprietorship of everything he possesses" (*SC*, CW, 4:141). It is in this advocacy for both equality and civil freedom that Rousseau's humanitarian convictions are most evident, and most conflicted.

Three hundred years later, there is a modern movement that is indirectly (one might even say accidentally) championing Rousseau's ideas on human rights. The photographic exhibit *DIGNITÉ: Droits humains et pauvreté* (DIGNITY: Human Rights and Poverty) is part of the "Demand Dignity" campaign launched by Amnesty International in 2009. In its introduction to the original exhibit catalog, Amnesty International asserts that "The world-wide phenomenon of poverty incarnates a flagrant disregard for human rights."[3] DIGNITY is an attempt to gain buy-in from decision makers in economics and politics because such buy-in is "crucial to breaking the chain between societal exclusion, rights infringements, and the poverty that results." DIGNITY plays a role in this campaign by "bypassing the usual recourse to statistics and figures" and conferring "individual human faces and a sense of dignity to each of the testimonials recounted here. They ask only for the respect that all of us, as human beings, owe to each other."[4] While Rousseau represents perhaps the first *thinker* on the causes of inequality, the modern approach of Amnesty International is rather that of an *activist* wishing to eliminate those disparities and focusing on the results of economic inequality.

The connection between Rousseau and DIGNITY was highlighted by the lecture series at Notre Dame, which created a fusion between the commemoration of Rousseau's tercentennial and a call for public action on behalf of human rights. Its organizer, Julia Douthwaite, said that she was frustrated by the typical ways in which universities present historic figures like Rousseau, and she decided to organize an event that might make more of an impact. She explains: "I wanted to try and make a much larger audience understand the interest of Rousseau for our times. The Rousseau who is the most interesting for our day is Rousseau the pioneer of humanitarianism."[5] One of the DIGNITY photographers, Johann Rousselot, praised

Douthwaite for making this connection, which he considered an "excellent" idea that made him remember key themes of Rousseauian philosophy that he had studied in school.[6] In fact, the link made him realize that his own collection portrayed a very Rousseauian take on the ideals of humanitarianism. When looking at his photos in retrospect, he found that they represented the phases of human society in its unhappy evolution toward modernity and industrialization. They begin with idyllic scenes of an Indian village (figs. 16–18) that resonate with Rousseau's poetic depiction of primitive society and man's natural state. Next, his photos represent the introduction of industry (figs. 19–20), which are juxtaposed with images that underline the tragic results of industry: human alienation, sickness, and environmental devastation (figs. 21–24). Just as Rousseau's *Social Contract* held out hope for humanity through collective political action, however, Rousselot's exhibit ends on a positive note too. The last scenes portray some activists speaking to the local community and show the people's desire to band together against adversity (figs. 25–26). In at least one village, Kucheipadar (Kashipur), this kind of grassroots activism seems to be working to keep the multinational corporations at bay.

It was not just an interest in Rousseau that inspired Douthwaite to create this project; she also sought to touch people who are not often included in university symposiums: "The idea was to avoid 'life as usual,'" she explained, "of doing just another conference on Rousseau with eighteenth-century scholars and discussing his work in fastidious detail. No. I wanted to include students and a different audience." This public included people from the South Bend community, high school students, and schoolchildren, who were given the opportunity to see the DIGNITY photos within the context of Jean-Jacques Rousseau's philosophy.

ROUSSEAU IN OISE: THE PHILOSOPHY THAT AFFECTS DAILY LIFE

Rousseau's philosophy affects many academic subjects and belongs to almost every facet of daily life: such was the guiding principle behind the "Fête Rousseau 2012" that was held in Oise, the region north of Paris where the philosopher lived his last days. The organizers thus sought to prove the relevance of Rousseau for our time and to create a connection between ordinary people and the philosopher. In order to do so, they foregrounded not only Rousseau's works but also his interesting biography, and echoed the approach of scholars such as Leo Damrosch, who has argued that "As powerful as Rousseau's legacy as a thinker has been, it is still more his example that has influenced those who have come after, including many who have never read him. Above all he is a questing personality, unwilling to settle for what life seems to have dealt him and yearning for something deeper than mere success, which he achieved and then rejected."[7]

This type of analysis tries to find the Rousseau behind the texts and to answer questions such as: where does his inspiration come from, what events formed his life, and how do these elements manifest themselves in his legacy? Damrosch notes, for example, the importance of Rousseau's wandering years and how powerful ideas came to him in his daydreams along country roads and mountain paths. Perhaps we can learn just as much from the example of Rousseau's life as we can from his works.

In celebrating Rousseau's vast philosophy and his life, the "Fête de l'Oise" presented a more personal mode of commemoration than the academic paradigm and allowed exploration of many famous topics of Rousseau's philosophy: this is its primary difference from Rousseau 2012/DIGNITY. The fête, a series of creative activities that took place throughout the year in various towns of the Oise department, culminated in the long weekend of Rousseau's three-hundredth birthday party in June, when numerous films and cultural events were staged in the Parc Jean-Jacques Rousseau at Ermenonville. A highlight of events was the documentary, *Entre nous Jean-Jacques* (Between Us Jean-Jacques), directed by Delphine Moreau, that focuses on the people of Compiègne and their connection to Rousseau. This project was inspired by the same idea as the Notre Dame commemoration: what makes Rousseau relevant to people today?

According to director Delphine Moreau, the project represented a logical way to commemorate a man whose thoughts are ever-present. As she explains in her essay below, autobiography and intellect are inextricably linked in both documentary films and in the work of Rousseau. What this meant in practice is that Moreau's team tried to connect Rousseau to contemporary society by working with four groups in the city of Compiègne: schoolchildren, high-schoolers, immigrants or unemployed people, and the elderly. When I interviewed her, she stressed her conviction that Rousseau "underlined questions and ideas that echo issues in our own society today," and the film organized each group within a specific theme to bring out those echoes.[8] For the schoolchildren, it was the importance of nature; for the elderly, it was the pursuit of happiness as Rousseau presented it in *Emile* and *The Reveries of the Solitary Walker*; for the immigrants and unemployed, it was the concept of social justice from *The Social Contract*. The high-schoolers were given their own choice.

The connection between past and present was most evident in the work of the high school students. Prompted by Moreau's instructions, students chose topics as varied as education, love, nature, God, child abandonment, the relation between mother and child, and the role of women. Students presented their ideas in myriad ways, by reading a poem they wrote about nature, for instance, or by bringing in their own mothers to dialogue with Rousseau on maternity.[9] For the elderly, the task was slightly more difficult. Since the organizers had chosen the theme of happiness, they invited the participants from the retirement home—all of them women—to speak abstractly about the importance of happiness for them. Rousseau's concept of happiness can be appreciated in Christopher Kelly's essay below and in quotes such as this one from *Emile*: "You must be happy, dear Emile. . . . That is the first desire which nature has impressed upon us, and the only one which never leaves us" (*Emile*, CW, 13:630). Moreau adapted Rousseau's ideas into questions, such as: "How have you found happiness in your life?" and "What symbolizes happiness for you?" The results were mixed. One woman decided to use two pictures: a photo of her granddaughter playing in the mountains and a painting of the countryside that she has kept since her childhood: both depict natural places where she found happiness.[10] Another woman showed a box of drawings, photos, and letters that she has kept for her entire life, and drew on them in a way that reverberated with the Rousseau of *The Reveries*. In that work, his last, the philosopher noted the paradoxical nature of happiness: its source lies not in events that happen, but rather in our own minds. Reminiscing about his earlier years, the author often found himself feeling happiness almost despite himself: "In wanting to recall so many sweet reveries, instead of describing them, I fell back into them" (*Reveries*, CW, 8:9–10). These women thus connected with Rousseau in a more subtle manner than the high school students.

COMMEMORATION: ITS POTENTIAL AND DANGERS

Rousseau 2012/DIGNITY and *Entre nous Jean-Jacques* were unusual commemorations: in lieu of adopting the traditional university approach to celebrating a historical figure, organizers produced creative events that put Rousseau's philosophy into easy reach for diverse audiences. Their approaches have certain limitations, however, and raise potential problems. First of all, one must admit that the media used—photography and film—run the risk of exploiting their subjects. The risk of visual exploitation is perhaps most explicit in DIGNITY, where the subjects of the photos are all impoverished—whether victims of political violence or marginalized people living in developing countries. Susan Sontag has warned that the invention of photography produced a culture in which it is normal to be the spectator of major calamities, and, as spectators, we run the risk of becoming apathetic to even the most horrific images.[11] Moreover, political photos that wish to stir up emotions against injustice, like those in DIGNITY, can prove useless if the observer does not recognize how to react. As Sontag notes, "Compassion is an unstable emotion. It needs to be translated into action, or it withers. The question is what to do with the feelings that have been aroused, the knowledge that has been communicated."[12] Not only does this emotion need to be harnessed, but it must be made relevant to the individual. As Andrew Billing points out in his contribution to this volume, Rousseau admitted that it is human nature to disregard those we consider removed from ourselves. Witness this quote from the *Discourse on Political Economy*: "It seems that the sentiment of humanity evaporates and weakens as it is extended over the whole world, and that we can't be moved by calamities in Tartary or Japan as we are by those of a European people. Interest and commiseration must in some way be confined and compressed to be made active" (*PE*, CW, 3:151). In this regard, the organizers of DIGNITY faced two key challenges: how to convert raw emotion into meaningful action and how to make the subject meaningful to an audience a world away.

The photos of suffering and misery in DIGNITY were so sad that some viewers may have devolved into sorrowful reflection instead of hearing the call to collective action intended by organizers. As critic Michelle Bogre explains, however, there is still an enormous potential in photography to examine situations from a social, cultural, and psychological perspective.[13] According to Bogre, the photographic genre has the ability to provoke the emotion essential for activism, but it is also "uniquely suited to being able to balance intellectual and sensory understanding." We must not consider activist photography as an end in itself but rather as the beginning of a response to humanitarian crises: photos uncover the emotion that is necessary to mobilize people.[14] This makes sense for DIGNITY: it is a start rather than an end for its viewers. The photos incite strong feelings, feelings to which the observer must find a way to react.

A second liability of these unusual kinds of commemoration lies in forcing a personal message upon viewers. Both Moreau's and Douthwaite's projects could be held guilty of this because both directed the thoughts of the audience to some extent. For example, in proposing Rousseau's writings in the context of DIGNITY, an exhibition with a unilateral message calling for humanitarian action, there is the risk of only depicting a single side of Rousseau. In this context, the viewer *must* see Rousseau as a humanitarian. That problem was alleviated by the lectures that accompanied the exhibit and which were not limited to Rousseau's humanitarianism: they touched upon various subjects including politics, the pursuit of happiness, and religious liberty. *Entre nous Jean-Jacques* faced a similar problem because the filming was done after several weeks of workshops. The subjects' connections to Rousseau might not be as organic as one might think; rather they may have resulted from lessons taught in the workshops. This problem underlies the documentary as a genre: all films are necessarily the product of editorial decisions regarding who and what is included or excluded. Moreover, the documentary lends itself to the impression that viewers are seeing the authentic truth. *Entre nous Jean-Jacques* gives a very positive portrayal of the philosopher and lacks a substantive critique of his work, thereby running the risk of disseminating an overly idealized image.

Clearly, these two commemorative projects faced difficulties. Nevertheless they shared a unique philosophy that distinguished them from other efforts, and that reminds us that it does not suffice to *remember* a man; one must go further to discover his interest to the modern day. Therein lies the greatest potential: public engagement. Through the efforts of Julia Douthwaite and Delphine Moreau, audiences were not mere spectators of a celebration of Rousseau's legacy but instead active participants in the translation of philosophical principles into daily life. The ability to engage allowed for emotions to be transformed into tangible experience. In the case of Rousseau 2012/DIGNITY, the injustices of the developing countries were revealed to the eyes at the same time that the philosophy of Rousseau on inequality penetrated the mind. Hopefully, this created a desire to learn more and take action. This project therefore encourages the projection of compassion and indignation outward and away from oneself through action, replacing the egocentric self-pity that Rousseau sometimes presented in his desire to excuse his own actions or inaction. In the case of *Entre nous Jean-Jacques*, viewers discover that the thoughts of an eighteenth-century man are extremely pertinent to seemingly every aspect of modern life: Rousseau's philosophy echoes back to us through the speakers' experiences.

Furthermore, the two commemorations distinguished themselves by involving children and adolescents: a public that is not often targeted by academic conferences. This demographic is one that is often the most receptive to new ideas and could fully experience the philosophy of Rousseau and the message of DIGNITY in a way that was devoid of preconception. One could consider this a sort of response to Rousseau's own conviction that people become set in their ways:

> Peoples, like men, are docile only in their youth. As they grow older they become incorrigible. Once customs are established and prejudices have become deeply rooted, it is a dangerous and vain undertaking to want to reform them. The people cannot abide having even their evils touched in order to eliminate them, just like those stupid and cowardly patients who quiver at the sight of a physician. (*SC*, CW, 4:105)

What better way to reach past preconceived notions than by engaging the most honest among us—children? *Entre nous Jean-Jacques* made Rousseau's philosophy accessible to elementary school children by asking them to write or draw their feelings about nature after having visited the Parc Jean-Jacques Rousseau in Ermenonville. While the children did not understand everything that they read, by including them in the discussion, surprisingly pertinent insights came to light. This sentiment was shared by Douthwaite after she presented the DIGNITY exhibit to children in South Bend; she spoke of being stunned by the optimism and compassion that the children demonstrated while viewing DIGNITY (and which are reproduced below in part 4 of this volume, "Teach This!"). Although they may not yet have read Rousseau, they clearly understood the project's goal.

The engagement of the general public, especially of children, in Rousseau 2012/DIGNITY and *Entre nous Jean-Jacques* is the element that distinguishes these projects from other commemorations. In this sense, I believe that they achieved a much more profound impact than most events of their kind. They created a vibrant and living Rousseau, a Rousseau that we can still find everywhere. Both took risks, but the potential of finding a much larger audience to share in the philosophy and thoughts of this man made it worth it.

NOTES

1. R. A. Leigh, "Introduction," in *Rousseau After 200 Years: Proceedings of the Cambridge Bicentennial Colloquium*, ed. Leigh (Cambridge: Cambridge University Press, 1978), vii.

2. Hartley Burr Alexander, "Rousseau and Political Humanitarianism," *The Journal of Philosophy, Psychology and Scientific Methods* 14, no. 22 (1917): 600.

3. Amnesty International, "Plus de droits, moins de pauvreté," in *DIGNITÉ: Droits humains et pauvreté; Un document de l'Œil public et d'Amnesty International* (Paris: Éditions Textuel and Amnesty International, 2010), 6. My translation.

4. Ibid., 5–6.

5. Julia Douthwaite, personal interview at the University of Notre Dame, March 2, 2012.

6. Johann Rousselot, personal interview at the University of Notre Dame, February 10, 2012.

7. Leo Damrosch, *Jean-Jacques Rousseau: Restless Genius* (Boston: Houghton Mifflin, 2005), 3.

8. Delphine Moreau, personal interview in Compiègne, France, March 12, 2012.

9. Examples taken from observations of filming of *Entre nous Jean-Jacques* in Compiègne, March 12, 2012.

10. Examples taken from observations of filming of *Entre nous Jean-Jacques*, March 12, 2012.

11. Susan Sontag, *Regarding the Pain of Others* (New York: Picador, 2004), 18.

12. Ibid., 101.

13. Michelle Bogre, *Photography as Activism: Images for Social Change* (Waltham, MA: Elsevier, 2012), 6.

14. Ibid., 7, 72.

CHAPTER 2

Entre nous Jean-Jacques
A Project of Documentary Film-Making

DELPHINE MOREAU
Translated by Julia V. Douthwaite

Before becoming a documentary filmmaker, I loved studying philosophy and history. I loved the way they allowed me to visit long-ago times and to learn how to think differently, to understand things "from the inside out" and to inhabit multiple, distant perspectives on life's perennial questions. I wanted to share that experience with other people, and I've found that the documentary medium makes it possible. I have some expertise in historical and archival film-making, but the idea of making a philosophical documentary was daunting. How can one take others on a mental journey, or make the mind of another person come alive in a visual medium? Because of its concrete, graphic nature, the moving picture seems worlds away from the solitary meanderings of thought.

Since my grandparents are from Ermenonville, I grew up in symbolic proximity to Jean-Jacques Rousseau. Rousseau died in the "Philosophical Gardens" of Ermenonville in 1778, just two centuries before my birth. When the Oise department announced that funding was available to underwrite projects to celebrate the philosopher's tercentennial, I jumped at the chance to make a philosophical film that would nevertheless be anchored in the lived experience of ordinary people. Based on an ambitious proposal that involved workshops led by four filmmakers and the collaboration of one-hundred-some participants from diverse walks of life, our project, *Entre nous Jean-Jacques*, won the grant.[1]

While the departmental guidelines stipulated involvement with the general population, it was the creation of interactive workshops held over a long stretch of time that allowed our project to succeed. This method is crucial, I believe, to avoid turning a philosopher's words into a fetish-like object and to keep them open to other people's ideas. Documentaries need that dynamism, the give-and-take with people, to allow new perspectives, ambiguities, and insights to emerge and engage the spectator. For me, this is also an ethical issue: unlike news reportage that is researched and staged ahead of time and edited after the fact, documentaries should be filmed and produced to resemble, as closely as possible, authentic and unadulterated experience. This means that we had to allow our participants to create their own words and images and that they had the final say on the finished product. *Entre nous Jean-Jacques* is their work as much as mine. Although I orchestrated the montage, each person's contribution remains intact. It is a little bit like how I imagine Denis Diderot and his collaborators working together to produce the famous eighteenth-century compendium *L'Encyclopédie*.

The four groups involved in *Entre nous Jean-Jacques* included schoolchildren in third or fourth grade (ten years old), high school students (age seventeen), members of a literacy class, and retirees living in a nursing home. We met for ten or twenty sessions of two to four hours each, with a goal of inspiring them to take on the role of author-directors of their own video letters to Rousseau. Out of this interaction we made thirty-two shorts which were then assembled into the fifty-six-minute documentary. One of the most motivating aspects of this experience for participants was the potential to see their personality on-screen, to raise issues that matter to them, and to reach a new audience. In this regard, I believe *Entre nous Jean-Jacques* made a particularly appropriate homage to Rousseau.

Like Rousseau's writings, in which autobiography and intellect are inextricably linked, documentary films are inevitably focused on the experience of real, living people. Rousseau drew his wisdom not from books but from his own life and feelings. He was not an "academic" philosopher; on the contrary, his writings were based in emotion and enriched by real-life personal encounters and experiences. I explicitly presented Rousseau this way to participants during our first workshops in order to create a sense of intimacy and closeness with his writing, and I believe that was an important strategy because so many of them had quite limited formal educations, due to their age or socioeconomic status. It was more important for me to inspire a sense of authentic connection with the man, rather than a scholarly mastery of his philosophy. In their effort to speak frankly to the camera and tell Jean-Jacques who they are and what they have to say, the apprentice philosophers of *Entre nous* brought an authenticity to the footage that recalls *The Confessions*. Theirs are the words of ordinary people; their thoughts may seem simple but they are often profound.

Rousseau is the consummate anti-hero: the Everyman. That was the way I conceived of him for our project, and it was a profile well suited for a creative documentary. Unlike trade fiction or blockbuster movies, creative documentaries do not aspire to highlight the lives of famous men and women but rather to highlight daily life and ordinary people, who often tell us more of real value. *Entre nous Jean-Jacques* was a very personal project, then, for all of us involved, and it brought us into close contact with autobiography as Rousseau conceived it. His philosophical works were important to us too. We debated his principles in our workshops, with special focus on the *Discourse on the Origins of Inequality*, and the ideas of inalienable rights, social contracts, and civic welfare from the *Social Contract*. But we also talked about the lyric Rousseau of the *Reveries* and his unremitting search for happiness. Philosophy should not be inaccessible. It is a natural search for meaning that everyone does without realizing it and that can be cultivated with a little help. That is how I sought to approach Rousseau's philosophy; not as an abstract discipline reserved for an elite but rather as a support, to help us when life's meaning seems elusive.

Documentary films are also meant to be shared and seen by others, and *Entre nous Jean-Jacques* is no exception to the rule. The use of images allowed us to anchor philosophical discourse in real, living voices; this is quite a change from most people's experience with such writing. For most of us, philosophy (to the extent that we think of it at all) is usually approached in the abstract and studied in solitude. The solitary character of his work and its inaccessibility to most readers were doubtless what made Rousseau's life as a writer so painful and what made him feel misunderstood (*incompris*). When I think about the future of *Entre nous Jean-Jacques*, how it will be screened in public, and how it will prompt new debate on his ideas, I cannot help but think that Rousseau would have been pleased.

For those who may be inspired to undertake similar public humanities projects, what follows are some concrete details on our organization. First, I organized debates around the big themes in Rousseau: nature, inequality, the social contract, happiness, and so forth, adapting each to the needs of individual groups. I invited philosophy teachers to join us on occasion. Our work was based on quotes taken from Rousseau's works, but it was supplemented by film screenings too.

To generate ideas, we watched and analyzed other video letters and first-person films by famous directors, such as *Lettre d'un cinéaste* by Alain Cavalier, *Lettre à Freddy Buache* by Jean-Luc Godard, and the works of Abbas Kiarostami and Víctor Erice.[2] The Cinésphère group, which I co-founded and which assisted with this project, had already worked extensively with the video-letter format and found it well suited to our goals.[3] Meanwhile, we had also been helping participants create images to be filmed or juxtaposed to their sequence—photos, drawings, collages, and abstract imagery—so they might enjoy the freedom of expression afforded by the medium.

Next, each participant (or group of two or three people) wrote a letter to Rousseau in which they echoed one of his three literary styles—discourse, reverie, or confession. They then read, declared, whispered, or improvised these letters out loud. For participants whose grasp of the French language was shaky—as in the literacy class—or whose vision was impaired—as in the nursing home—the improvisational method worked best. These performances were staged in front of the camera, in a setting of the participants' choice, or in a voice-over.

The epistolary form is interesting because it demands that the author reveal more of himself than is typical in filmmaking, and it also makes the spectator feel obliged to react, whether through praise and criticism, questions or accusations. The author has to have "something to say," and it is usually something personal, based on her identity or an urgent concern. The form is appealing because it supposes that the message will be communicated to the recipient of the letter (*destinataire*) and to future spectators. In our project there were two people involved from the beginning: the author and Rousseau. We played with this concept by putting Rousseau into the films in various ways: his face and body (through the use of masks, statues, and cardboard cut-outs; see fig. 59), his voice, and his ideas. Depending on the content of the short sequences, viewers identify with either the individual letter author or with Rousseau himself.

Although we tried to give participants a toolbox of cinematic techniques drawn from a variety of film screenings, and enough grounding in Rousseauian philosophy through our group discussions, the four filmmakers from the group Cinésphère were always on hand to help out and provide advice on the actual creative process. Our goal throughout was to follow the lead of the participants, whose suggestions were sometimes very surprising and provocative. Indeed we were more than once bowled over by their creative energies and reinvigorated by the process. I hope to return to some of them in the future, and to make a feature-length film that follows their daily lives through the shadow of Rousseau's influence.

DIGNITY AND THE EXPERIENCE OF *ENTRE NOUS JEAN-JACQUES*

In order to give a concrete example of our methods, here is the text we presented as an introduction to Rousseau for students in the literacy class:

> In the *Social Contract*, Rousseau tried to reconcile individual liberty and the well-being of society. In order to be just, society must be governed by all people, not just a few. Each person has to have some power. The social contract is supposed to express the general will of the group, as in a participatory democracy. But Rousseau's goals were not only political; he also sought to heal a divide he found within himself (and all mankind). He thought civilized society was too complex and unfair; it divided people and made them unhappy. He wanted to help people rediscover a simpler, happier, and more dignified way to live. Nature was the answer, according to him. In contemplating the natural world, he became more alert to simple pleasures of daily existence, more accepting of the cycles of life

and death, and more grateful for the essential freedoms we all enjoy on this earth. Man's dignity and happiness depend on realizing and asserting that last fact, Rousseau thought. Even if we must occasionally bow before forces more powerful than ourselves, we must never allow anyone the "right" to enslave or oppress us. As he wrote, "To renounce one's freedom is to renounce one's status as a man, the rights of humanity and even its duties. There is no possible compensation" (*SC*, CW, 4:135). Although he did not say as much, this statement suggests that all people are equal—men and women, children and adults, weak and strong—and that freedom is what makes us human. It is also what makes us moral creatures. Whether it is the relations between parents and children, workers and bosses, renters and landlords, or citizens and legislators, when we remember that each person is free, we realize what is right and wrong, acceptable or intolerable, and we act accordingly.

How did the creation of video letters allow participants to connect with the concept of dignity?[4]

By giving people of all ages the tools to talk about themes like injustice, happiness, community, and nature, and find a way to express themselves, *Entre nous Jean-Jacques* became a force for good. It enabled participants to achieve fulfillment for a while, despite their relative weaknesses, difficulties, and the other life issues that weigh people down. It allowed them to feel dignified. In the final analysis, dignity is about speaking up, creating, and being heard. Those are the values that sustained us in making *Entre nous Jean-Jacques*, and I am convinced that they will ignite a spark among the film's future viewers as well.

NOTES

1. My team included Oona Bijasson, Marie Famulicki, and Corinne Sullivan.

2. *Víctor Erice–Abbas Kiarostami: Correspondances*, Centre Pompidou, Paris, 2008. This exhibit focuses on two filmmakers, Abbas Kiarostami and Víctor Erice, who come from two very different cultures but who share a passion for representing childhood, memory, and the everyday life conflicts between individuals and society. It includes a filmed exchange of letters between the two men.

3. Our work includes *Dialogues de femmes,* where women speak to girls and girls speak to women, and *Les Âges de Saint-Ouen*, which stages an exchange of video letters between children and elderly people living in a poor suburb (*banlieue*) of Paris.

4. [Ed.: The second half of Delphine Moreau's contribution is reproduced below in part 4 of this volume, "Teach This!" where the director presents scenes from the film as produced by each contributor and comments on their relation to Rousseau.]

CHAPTER 3

Rousseau's Legacy and the Subjectivity of Photographic Meaning

GABRIELLE GOPINATH

Jean-Jacques Rousseau died in 1778, while photography was not invented until 1839. In retrospect, however, the emergence of photography can seem like a belated response to Rousseau's endorsement of subjective vision. Every photograph asserts an individual perspective peculiar to the person who "takes" that image at a given moment in time. So taking photographs seriously means taking other things seriously too, notably the value of individual identity and the validity of individual perception. Both concepts are central elements in Rousseau's thought.

Organized to mark the three-hundredth anniversary of Rousseau's birth, the DIGNITY exhibition of photography as it was displayed at Notre Dame made the case that contemporary forms of documentary photography embody the humanist values associated with Rousseau's legacy. Certainly, the photojournalists whose work was on display in this exhibition share an approach that accentuates subjects' individuality and their shared humanity. These photographers' pictures redefine what constitutes reportage. Capitalizing on the subjective dimension of photographic meaning, they redefine it as an asset rather than a liability. My essay enumerates the ways in which this approach actualizes aspects of Rousseau's thought. I approach these photographers' images from an art historical perspective, taking the hermeneutic operations peculiar to photography into account as well as considering the content and context of individual exhibition photos.

How should we begin to consider photographic meaning in relation to Rousseau's philosophy? The most obvious similitude is the fact that both describe the limits of reason. Rousseau criticized the hegemony of reason throughout his life. In the 1750 *Discourse on the Sciences and Arts,* his first major published work, he rejected the proposition that reason and progress had resulted in the improvement of society as a whole. This wholesale criticism of civilization and its fruits put Rousseau at odds with Enlightenment consensus. (Hostile caricatures of this position resulted in the lingering mischaracterization in which the philosopher posits primitive man as a "noble savage."[1]) However, Rousseau's relation to progress was not as straightforward as passages of this *Discourse* make it seem; his attitude toward the arts and sciences was radically conflicted as well. This becomes apparent when his first *Discourse* is considered in context.

In 1750 the young Rousseau was recognized—if at all—as an aspiring composer whose first opera, *Les Muses Galantes*, had provoked an embarrassingly public negative reaction at its premiere five years before.[2] So Rousseau's contemporaries were well aware that the vehement critique of the arts in the *Discourse* had been penned by a professional musician and composer. The ability to accept contradiction and the inclination to put it on public display continued to characterize Rousseau's life and thought from this point onwards. His philosophical project deployed the methodology of rational inquiry against reason, in order to delineate its limits.

Photographic meaning, of course, also exudes contradiction. It contains elements of objectivity and subjectivity all at once. In fact, the tension between photography's competing claims to the status of evidence and art has dominated photographic discourse since the medium's invention. The principle of paradox is the most significant point of comparison between the properties of the photographic image and the properties of Rousseau's thought.

Taken at face value, Rousseau's critique of scientific and artistic progress suggests that he would have found little to celebrate about photography (the scientific/artistic medium that exemplified nineteenth-century progress). But other aspects of Rousseau's thought imply potential affinity with the photographic medium—notably, his repeatedly expressed desire to overcome the gulf separating interior subjectivity from the external world of appearance. Every photograph actualizes this desire within a limited context, since every photograph externalizes a fragment of interior experience. Photographic reality is subjective because photographs offer an account of the world as it appeared from an individual vantage point, at a fractional moment of past time.

Rousseau's emphasis on the value of subjectively perceived inner truth is founded in his narrative of societal origins, which posits progress as the cause of moral corruption. In Rousseau's account primitive man enjoyed a state of uncompromised sincerity, having no inclination to externalize identity by staging it through the eyes of others. This resulted in social interactions that were characterized by spontaneity and transparency, which in turn fostered a harmonious relationship between the interior consciousness and its external, socially oriented manifestations. Rousseau understands this harmony as the cardinal component of virtue, but he believes it has become a casualty of progress. In his account the naturally unconflicted sense of self once possessed by primitive man has become self-conscious and divided. This corruption can be traced to the advent of civilized society, and specifically to the invention of private property.

For Rousseau, this loss is a secular analogue to the Fall of Man. It meant descent from a state of grace into a world where appearance and reality were reciprocally alienated. Crucially, no original sin is involved in this unorthodox account of the Fall: rather than playing the role of malefactor, Man is cast as an innocent victim. Rousseau altered the story of the Fall in order to invert its conclusion. The natural order was not a state of sin, but a state of grace.

In Rousseau's own estimation his lifelong preoccupation with man's Fall could be traced to a childhood incident in which he was falsely accused of breaking a comb (*Conf*, CW, 5:28–31). Appearances had been against the youthful suspect, as he ruefully recalled at a later date. The young Rousseau's protestations of innocence were not believed, and he was punished by being caned. Rousseau was profoundly affected by this first painful experience of the gulf that might open up between internal and external accounts of reality. As a result, the relatively insignificant story of the comb assumed great importance in the account of early development related in the philosopher's *Confessions*. Years later Rousseau remembered that after this first experience of injustice the world seemed lesser, diminished: "it seemed . . . depressing and empty, as if it had been covered by a veil that cloaked its beauties" (*Conf*, CW, 5:31). The happy childhood state of integrated selfhood, which recapitulated the early innocence of the human race, had been sundered. Though blameless, the young Rousseau had fallen from grace. Subsequent experience would be suffused by a sense of loss.

Rousseau's *Discourse on the Sciences and Arts* was inspired by a violent epiphany that brought home the connection between this experience of loss and the limits of reason. This experience struck him as it famously had Saint Paul—while he was on the road. Epiphany hit unexpectedly while Rousseau was walking the six miles from Paris to the fortress of Vincennes to visit Denis Diderot, who was imprisoned there at the time. Rousseau later described how, having stopped to rest, he opened the *Mercure de France* and noticed the announcement of an essay competition issued by the Academy of Dijon. The Academy posed the question: had the restoration of the arts and sciences tended to purify morals? Reading this challenge provoked an extraordinary reaction.

"The moment I read this I beheld another universe and became another man," Rousseau recalled (*Conf*, CW, 5:327). In a letter to his friend Malesherbes he elaborated, turning to the language of mysticism and even shifting into the present tense at one point to describe the sensations that ensued.

> If anything has ever resembled a sudden inspiration, it is the motion that was caused in me by that reading; suddenly I felt my mind dazzled by a thousand

lights; crowds of lively ideas presented themselves at the same time with a strength and a confusion that threw me into an inexpressible perturbation. . . . I feel my head seized by a dizziness similar to drunkenness.[3]

This vision unveiled the sublime existence of a higher truth made manifest in authentic perceptions rather than rational methods of deduction. Devaluation of this inner truth caused the degradation of experience, the corruption of the conscience, and a resultant sense of pervasive loss. After this revelation, Rousseau rejected Enlightenment empiricism. He dedicated his life to demonstrating the limits of reason and exploring the frontiers of subjective truth. "All the rest of my life and of my misfortunes followed inevitably as a result of that moment's madness" (*Conf*, CW, 5:328).

In the text he produced in response to the Academy's challenge Rousseau worked through the implications of his epiphany, considering the ways in which progress had accentuated the gap between appearance and reality. In his account the bourgeois desire for advancement is insincere because self-interested, driven in large part by the desire to win others' recognition and esteem. This impure ambition effects a growing divide between the way people really feel and the way they present themselves to others. The gap that has developed between appearance and reality blights civilized society; unfortunately, the pace of progress assures that this fissure will continue to grow. The arts and sciences thus exacerbate the corruption of man, who is born good but quickly falls from that state of grace. "Everything is good as it leaves the hands of the Author of things; everything degenerates in the hands of man" (*Emile*, CW, 13:37).

Rousseau's *Discourse on the Origin and Foundations of Inequality among Men*, written in 1754 for another essay competition, built upon the earlier work's conclusions. This second *Discourse* also responded to a question posed by the Dijon Academy: what is the origin of inequality among mankind, and does natural law decree inequality? Rousseau responded by issuing a blistering critique of social inequality, founded in an attack on the rational principles that justified such abuses. He argued that reason is "unnatural"—a poisonous apple of self-awareness, whose consumption exiles mankind from primitive Eden. "It is reason that engenders self-love, and reflection that strengthens it; it is reason that makes man shrink into himself; it is reason that makes him keep aloof from everything that can trouble or afflict him; it is philosophy that destroys his connections with other men" (*DOI*, CW, 3:107). The advent of reflection makes it possible for people to see themselves through others' eyes. As a result, appearance is confounded with reality. The potential for the revelation of inner truth is destroyed.

Is it not, perhaps, paradoxical to wage war on reason with the weapons of rational analysis? Rousseau anticipates and deflects this criticism by ventriloquizing his hypothetical interlocutors and exaggerating their concerns. ("What then? Must societies be abolished? Must *meum* and *tuum* be annihilated, and must man go back to living in forests with the bears?" [*DOI*, CW, 3:144]). However, he does not attempt to deny the substance of the paradox that animates his writing, because the paradoxical desire to illuminate and articulate what is invisible and unspeakable is at the heart of his philosophic project. One imagines Rousseau concurring with Walt Whitman, his nineteenth-century kindred contrarian: "Do I contradict myself? Very well, then, I contradict myself (I am large—I contain multitudes)."[4] Rousseau thinks that the corruption of enlightened modern man is irreversible, but that reason should nevertheless be subjected to critique. Ideally reason would be demoted from its status as the sole arbiter of truth and sincerity elevated in its place. In such a world, being true to one's own self (as the romantics would later put it) would count for more than factual evidence.

Rousseau's endorsement of sincerity brings us back to photography, initiating a point of comparison. After all, the photographic medium might be described as structurally sincere. The brevity of the moment elapsed while the shutter opens and closes means that photography, unlike all forms of non-photographic media, admits no temporal gap to separate the maker's intention from its material result. Despite the many forms of manipulation that may be brought to bear after the image is first taken, the photographic image remains one that is *taken* rather than *made*. It bears an indexical relationship to the real world.

Because of their extraordinary relationship to reality, photographs are often reflexively assumed to convey truth and accorded an importance that other kinds of images are not. This remains the case despite plentiful evidence that reveals the relationship between photographs and truth to be nowhere near straightforward. Even in the age of Photoshop the photographic image continues to be regarded as evidence, within the judiciary and elsewhere. People on the Internet tweet "pix or it didn't happen" millions of times a day. Should they know better? It is difficult to say. Photographs do, in fact, possess an indexical quality: it is what underwrites their structural sincerity. At the same time they often convey information that is very much at odds with observable reality. Their relationship to truth encompasses the undecidable.

Rousseau might have appreciated this dimension of paradox, despite the fact that he was—in theory at least—no friend to the arts. The theatre provoked his most sustained critique. In his 1758 *Letter to D'Alembert*, which addresses the hypothetical establishment of a theatre in Geneva, Rousseau condemns theatrical representation on the basis that it contaminates experience with artifice, distancing the viewer from the world. In Rousseau's opinion theatregoers contract a corrupt bargain, trading their authentic emotions and experiences for vicarious ones created by others (*D'Alembert*, CW, 10:300).

However, photography might be said to do the opposite. If the theatre contracts the sphere of individual perception, photography expands it. Photography makes it possible to grant others access to a private moment of one's interior perception. It permits others to access an otherwise inaccessible fragment of the photographer's optic experience. In fact photography actualizes Rousseau's otherwise impossible dream: it renders the invisible visible, reconciling external appearance with inner truth. Each photograph arrests and then externalizes a split second of subjective perception. Any photograph gives the viewer access to a past-tense fragment of another's interior experience. These fragments are genuine, despite the fact that they are miniscule in scope.

Today, the subjective dimension of photographic meaning attracts substantial amounts of critical attention. But it often goes unmentioned in early accounts of the medium's capacities. Early authors preferred to emphasize the photograph's startlingly objective appearance and its resultant capacity for documentation. In 1844 William Henry Fox Talbot referred to the calotype as the "pencil of nature," hoping to impress his readers with a sense of the medium's objectivity and its inaccessibility to authorial whim.[5] Fifteen years later Oliver Wendell Holmes was so sanguine regarding photographs' potential to usurp the significance of material objects that he imagined humanity would soon be happy to jettison the latter entirely.[6]

Talbot had used the camera to create inventories of objects in the 1840s. By the mid-nineteenth century, technological advances meant that photographers could begin to inventory human subjects instead. Photographic archives produced in pursuit of this goal exude an unquestioning confidence in the medium's objective powers that may appear naïve by contemporary standards. The nineteenth and early twentieth centuries saw no shortage of such projects. Colonial administrators and slaveholders arranged for the subaltern populations under their control to be photographically documented. The scientists Etienne-Jules Marey and Eadweard Muybridge independently produced photographic series that subdivided bodily motion into dozens of discrete, measurable moments, subjecting kinesthetic experience to rational analysis. Francis Galton took thousands of photographs of criminals en route to developing a composite image of a "criminal type," in the hope that this definitive information could then be used as a guide to eugenic measures. In a series of experiments designed to record the biological basis of expression, pioneering neurologist Jean-Martin Charcot photographed experimental subjects while their heads were poked with an electrode to stimulate a variety of facial expressions. These circumstances maximized the distance between appearance and inner truth; the resultant images present a grotesque parable of the hypocrisy that Rousseau abhorred.

For many decades photographic projects oriented toward objective documentation, like the ones described above, defined popular understanding of the medium's capacities. Yet the subjective dimension of photographic meaning has never been invisible, or inaccessible. (And despite photographers' best efforts, none of the photographic projects described above turned out to be flawlessly objective demonstrations of empirical reason.)[7] The history of photography is full of images that achieved notoriety precisely because it became obvious that they functioned poorly as evidence. In some cases this discrepancy was immediately obvious; in other cases it only became apparent over the passage of time. Especially during the period when the photograph was primarily conceived as a vessel of evidentiary truth, the recurrent emergence of such images confounded received ideas about photographic meaning. I will briefly consider three such famous images in the next pages: Hippolyte Bayard's *Drowned Man*, Robert Capa's *Falling Soldier*, and the "Hooded Man" photograph shot by an unknown photographer in 2004.

My first example dates from 1839, when a disappointed Hippolyte Bayard staged a photograph of his suicide by drowning. His image was created only months after the French Academy of Sciences announced the world's first photographic process, the daguerreotype, invented by Louis-Jacques-Mandé Daguerre. The two events were not unrelated. Bayard's *Drowned Man* was created in order to protest the Academy's patronage of Daguerre and its refusal to recognize the photographic process that he, Bayard, had invented independently. Bayard's process, which involved the creation of a unique photo positive on paper, predated the rival daguerreotype. However, Academy members had promoted Daguerre's process and facilitated the state's purchase of his patent rights in 1838.[8] Bayard mailed duplicate photographs of his "suicide" to several Academy members to protest this treatment. Each photograph carried a handwritten message on the verso that clarified the reasons for Bayard's chagrin, reinforcing the image's comitragic quality by allowing the author to seemingly speak from beyond the grave.

This is probably the first photograph that makes use of the medium's capacity to externalize subjective feeling. All photographic images contain a degree of subjectivity, as I have previously described: this image enhances and exaggerates that intrinsic quality. Bayard used his camera to record an inner truth, allegorizing subjective experience rather than confirming externally verifiable facts. Already, in the first year of photography's existence, the technology was being used for purposes that ranged far beyond the limits of empiricism.

The twentieth-century rise of photojournalism heightened expectations of photographic truth. When photographs are presented in a media context, it is understood that the meanings they produce should not demonstrably contradict external reality. Photographs belatedly demonstrated to fail this criterion may provoke embarrassment and chagrin—especially when, like Hungarian photojournalist Robert Capa's 1936 *Falling Soldier*, they have previously been accorded the status of icon.

Falling Soldier is the most frequently reprinted image of the Spanish Civil War. Despite the number of wars that have transpired since, Capa's image remains one of the most celebrated war photographs ever taken. It depicts a Republican soldier in the Spanish Civil War reeling backwards at the moment he is shot. When it was published in *Life* in 1937, the image bore the title *Loyalist Militiaman at the Moment of Death, Cerro Muriano, September 5, 1936*. It had been published in the French magazines *Vu* and *Regards* under similar titles the previous fall, but the exposure in *Life* made it internationally renowned. *Life* editors glossed Capa's photo with a caption that read: "Robert Capa's camera catches a Spanish soldier the instant he is dropped by a bullet through the head in front of Córdoba."[9]

For decades this information was taken as read. It was generally believed that the photograph had been taken in action at Cerro Muriano on the Córdoba front. However, doubts regarding the shot's supposed provenance have been voiced at least since the 1970s.[10] Recently, the scholar José Manuel Susperregui used sophisticated forms of topographic analysis to show that, in fact, the photograph was not taken on the battlefield at Córdoba. It was taken at the nearby town of Espejo, located approximately thirty-five miles away from the published location. Significantly, no fighting had been going on there at the time.[11]

If this evidence is accepted, the photograph cannot possibly mean what it has been supposed to mean all this while. But rather than solving the photograph's mystery, Susperregui's research raises still more questions. Does the image really depict a man being shot? To what degree, if at all, was it staged? To what end? It is impossible to answer these questions, especially since no negative or original documentation associated with the image is known to exist. The essence of the image is ambiguity. In the words of one of its skeptics, *Falling Soldier* "turns out to be not the clear and simple statement of fact that it at first sight appears."[12] But the photograph retains validity as an arrested moment of Capa's interior experience—what Rousseau might have called his inner truth—even while its claim to truth has been compromised.

What may now be perceived as the problematic nature of Capa's image *as evidence* stems not from the notion that the photograph's content is not real (whatever that would mean) but rather from the fact that its connotation deviates from its verifiable denotation. In my previous example, Bayard's *Drowned Man*, the same discrepancy is more obvious. Rather than being obscured, it is played for irony. In Bayard's photograph the image's status as an imaginative projection of inner truth is intended to be apparent—so much the better, to both satirize and commemorate the subject's pathos. In contrast, the popular misreading of *Falling Soldier's* significance was based on incorrect assumptions about the circumstances under which it was created. These assumptions appear to have been prompted by a less than straightforward blend of accident and design. What we see when we look at Capa's photograph and what we think we see are different things.

My third example of this principle involves a high-profile misidentification of the torture victim who appears in an iconic photograph taken in 2004 at the U.S. military prison at Abu Ghraib in Iraq. The photograph shows a hooded man in a black smock standing on top of a box, electrodes connected to his fingertips. The man's arms are outstretched in a pose that inescapably evokes images of the Crucifixion for many Western viewers. This notorious image of the so-called "Hooded Man" is the most frequently reproduced and, not coincidentally, the most formally striking of the photographs leaked from Abu Ghraib in 2004. Its publication prompted international outcry. Reproduced globally, it has become an emblem for the prisoner abuse and torture perpetrated by members of the American military at Abu Ghraib and elsewhere.

Filmmaker Errol Morris has described how this image became famous worldwide even though key elements of its meaning—such as, most obviously, the identity of the person it depicts—remain unknown. In his recent book on photography Morris recounts how the *New York Times* ran a front-page story in 2006 identifying one Ali Shalal Qaissi as the Hooded Man. The story was accompanied by a photograph of Qaissi holding a copy of the Hooded Man image.[13] The point of the article was that now, finally, it was possible to attach a face and identity to the horrific image of the hooded, so far anonymous victim. However, in reality the situation proved to be less straightforward. Qaissi had been an Abu Ghraib prisoner and torture victim; that much was undisputed. It would seem that he believed himself to be the subject of the photograph. He had even gone so far as to have printed business cards with his name and the Hooded Man's infamous silhouette. However, obvious reasons should have indicated that this identification was impossible. Abu Ghraib jailors had nicknamed Qaissi "Clawman" because of the shape of his left hand, which had been deformed by a congenital defect. This man could not possibly have been the man in the photograph, neither of whose hands is deformed. And yet not only did the *Times* publish a positive identification, Qaissi himself apparently believed it. Within a week the newspaper printed a retraction to the effect that Qaissi was not, in fact, the man in this particular famous photograph. The error remains mystifying, because evidence that should have been sufficient to refute the identification was openly legible upon the hand of the man in question.

It seems this mistake occurred because of the human willingness to believe what we *think* we see, regardless of the implications of available data. It is easy to confuse photographs with reality. Logically, it should have been obvious that Qaissi could not have been the man in the image. But evidence to that effect was simply not registered. Even the photograph of Qaissi that the *Times* ran on March 11 positioned its subject in such a way as to conceal the deformed hand that would have contradicted the story's identification. The subjective dimension of photographic meaning is enhanced by the fact that interpretation of photographs is heavily colored by preconceived ideas and expectations. This effect is never more powerful than when viewers are least aware of its operation. "Photographs allow us to think we know more than we really do," Morris observes. "In the pre-photographic era, images came directly from our eyes to our brains and were part of our experience of reality. With the advent of photography, images were torn free of the world, snatched from the fabric of reality, and enshrined as separate entities. They became more like dreams. It is no wonder that we really don't know how to deal with them."[14]

Now that the medium has existed for approximately 170 years, the slipperiness of photographic meaning is finally becoming more widely appreciated. The slow growth of popular skepticism regarding the medium's purported objectivity might be attributed, in part, to growing public awareness of situations like the ones described above. It has also, no doubt, been influenced by more diffuse aspects of late-twentieth-century poststructuralist thought. Concepts like the constructed nature of identity, the unknowable dimension of language, and the necessarily incomplete nature of knowledge itself accord poorly with the notion of the photographic image as indisputable empirical evidence.

Influential texts on photography produced since the 1970s tend to elaborate on this discrepancy. Roland Barthes's *Camera Lucida* delved deep into the medium's subjective dimensions, enshrining the aspects of photographic meaning that cannot be encompassed by rational analysis.[15] The critiques of photography's documentary function produced subsequently by Allan Sekula and Martha Rosler, among others, called attention to the malleability of photographic meaning by showing how the photograph lends itself to commodification and message drift.[16] Around the same time, artists working with media images, such as Cindy Sherman, Barbara Kruger, and Richard Prince, demonstrated that iconic photographs inevitably escape their makers' control. At large in the cultural slipstream, they continue to generate meanings that may eventually have little or nothing to do with the image's original subject.

This shift toward the subjective has inevitably been influenced by changes in the photographic hardware. One key factor was the emergence of digital photography in the 1990s and its rapid rise to near ubiquity. This changed the way people used the photographic image and conceived of its powers. Nonspecialist users in the digital era can subject their archives to professional levels of scrutiny, rejecting hundreds of images for every one that is ultimately preserved. Photoshop makes methods of photo manipulation once the province of the darkroom specialist easy for anyone with access to a digital camera and a computer. As a result of these technological changes, more people acquire hands-on experience with the way photographic appearance may deviate from observable reality. Consumers become increasingly aware of the massive amounts of retouching that often go into advertising and media images. In the twenty-first century, these changes are fostering increasing levels of immunity to the formerly automatic assumption that photographs reveal the truth.

As the previous examples have shown, photographs' connotations often diverge radically from empirical reality. Yet it is also true that a photograph's content bears an indexical relation to the content of the immaterial image that catalyzed the photographer's creative act. A photograph accurately replicates a momentary fragment of its maker's optic experience, regardless of its fidelity to reality (or lack thereof).[17] Every photograph valorizes personal identity and individual experience. It implies that these things are important. And so, as I suggested earlier, photography actualizes aspects of Rousseau's thought with strange precision. Because Rousseau was an important source of the subjectivity and relativism that saturate the postmodern world, we can understand photography as his spiritual heirloom. It did for the history of representation what his thought did for the history of ideas.

For Rousseau, truth-to-self was ultimately more significant than objective truth. Expressing one's inner truth as vividly and sincerely as possible was an ethical imperative.[18] Photography is uniquely equipped to externalize this inner truth. And more people appreciate this now than ever before because photographic meaning is increasingly being conceived, more accurately, as a complex derivation influenced by subjective as well as objective factors. This change has altered the perspective of people who make photographs, as well as those who consume them. As a result of these developments, many examples of contemporary photojournalism look radically different from earlier images produced within the same genre. The photographs in the DIGNITY exhibition exemplify this change.

DIGNITY brings together the works of five French and French-Swiss photojournalists working in different countries to document the lives of impoverished and exploited people. Images in the exhibition include: Guillaume Herbaut's photos from Guerrero, Mexico; Johann Rousselot's images from the state of Odisha in India; Philippe Brault's images from the Egyptian capital of Cairo; Michaël Zumstein's photographs of Lagos, Nigeria; and Jean-François Joly's images from Skopje, Macedonia. These photographers share a predilection for meticulously staged portraits and landscapes over the action shots traditionally associated with the photojournalist's profession. They eschew what have traditionally been defined as newsworthy events. Most of their photographs simply document the appearance of people who have suffered or are suffering. The exhibition text that accompanies these images describes their subjects' circumstances. In some cases, it describes the economic, social, and political systems that allow different species of injustice to be perpetuated. Some of the people in these photographs have endured horrific acts of violence, but in this exhibition trauma is restricted to the text. Most of those depicted here posed calmly for their formal portraits. The resultant images make it clear that the poverty, violence, and economic exploitation that structure aspects of these subjects' lives do not totally define them.

In the past, photojournalists have produced iconic images by adopting a spontaneous and unpremeditated approach to documenting news events. So much the better to capture what Henri Cartier-Bresson famously referred to as the "decisive moment": that split second of arrested time that seems to distill and summarize the meaning of a given event.[19] This approach defined the style of twentieth-century photographers like Robert Capa, who founded the photojournalists' cooperative Magnum Photos with Cartier-Bresson in 1947. As I previously observed in my discussion of Capa's *Falling Soldier*, the great photographs produced in this way create a powerful impression of truth. They look like incontrovertible evidence . . . of *something*. They transform quotidian experience into the stuff of icons. And yet the aura of veracity that such images exude is not underwritten by reason. One might even say that the more indelible the photograph, the greater the temptation to personalize its meaning—to believe that it means what we want it to. Despite what the ethos of the "decisive moment" suggests, the meaning of photographs is far from intrinsic. On the contrary, it is produced through images' interaction with myriad factors ranging from the external (captions, title, context) to the internal (viewers' expectations, preconceptions, and previous experiences).

Clearly, the photographers who took these images are motivated by humanist concerns. But none of them attempt to summarize a story of injustice by seizing a decisive photographic moment, as similarly motivated photojournalists from a previous generation might have done. Instead these photographers document inequity obliquely, focusing on individuals whose lives are implicated in large-scale stories. Their images assert that the simple fact of such individuals' existence possesses pictorial significance. A portrait by Johann Rousselot, for example, redefines what constitutes a decisive moment (fig. 21). Rousselot's subject, Trilachan Mohanta, appears shirtless from the waist up. His brown skin is bathed in even studio light; the contours of his body are sharply defined against a streaked blue-green wall. His posture is upright and poised. Leaning slightly forward, he confronts the viewer with an intense, unflinching gaze and an otherwise expressionless face. His extreme thinness is very apparent. But despite the fact that his emaciated arms and sunken chest are on display, the quality of his calm gaze leaves the most powerful impression. The clarity, detail, and sharp focus of this portrait derive in part from the photographic equipment used to create it. Like other photographers in this exhibition, Rousselot often eschews gear adapted for action such as long lenses and 35 millimeter film. Instead he often works with equipment like that used to create his portrait of Mohanta: elaborate studio-style lighting and medium format cameras that are unsuited to action but well suited to portraiture because of the high resolution and level of detail they provide.

The detailed quality of Rousselot's image is paralleled by the detail in the text that accompanies it, including the subject's name, age, and place of birth. The text provides more biographical details that would otherwise not be apparent. Readers learn that Mohanta has been infected with tuberculosis for a year and a half, has been unable to find work since the disease broke out, and belongs to a lower caste whose members are widely held in contempt in the Indian state of Odisha. Still, "he is fortunate to be in a doctor's care." This information underscores the fact of Mohanta's humanity. He appears as an individual rather than a face that represents a cause or a screen for the projection of viewers' generalized empathy. Mohanta's portrait is part of a portfolio Rousselot made to document the status of indigenous and low-caste people in Odisha. These people are being disenfranchised by multinational mining interests, which exploit the region for its mineral rights. Rather than seeking images that might seem to distill the essence of such corporations' malfeasance, Rousselot approaches the subject by registering the human lives that absorb the cost of such activities.

It may seem perverse for a documentarian to make the choice to reject action and incident in this way. A photojournalist's decision to document a situation by making posed portraits might seem like a contrary choice to show nothing rather than something. But the ethics of this choice become apparent upon reflection. The point of Rousselot's methodology is that it redefines the scope of what's important. This photographic approach reflects a shift in informed opinion regarding the camera's capacities. It manifests the conviction that photography proves unreliable at best when charged with the task of bearing evidence. On the other hand, the photograph's ability to sensitize us by calling attention to the fissure between the inner world of perception and the external world of appearance is second to none.

Seen from a strictly rational perspective, the impoverished and uneducated individuals who appear in these portraits are persons of no consequence. They exist outside of history, except perhaps insofar as they might function collectively to illustrate suffering or indict public policy. But by asking these people to pose for portraits as they wish to be seen, these photographers reject that narrative. Their images reveal megacity slum dwellers to be endowed with a degree of agency and possessed of consequential personal histories, just like their counterparts in the higher echelons of the world economic system. When they approach their subjects in this way, photographers assert that humanist perspectives are the ones that matter.

Respect for individual rights is also reflected in the way these photographers interact with the communities they document. All five of the photographers in this exhibition work by immersing themselves in a particular locality, often making repeated visits to the same neighborhood and becoming acquainted with the lives of the people they photograph. The trust that they are able to establish through these repeated visits makes it possible to photograph events that would otherwise remain inaccessible.

For instance, a portrait taken by Philippe Brault in the Ezbet Al-Haggana slum district of Cairo depicts a young bride, identified as Ihaab, on her wedding day (fig. 33). Ihaab smiles at the photographer, raising one hand lightly to her shoulder as she poses in front of a flowered curtain in her home. Studio lighting accentuates the details of her elaborate dress and glamorous makeup. The companion text relates details that attest to the photographer's proximity to the bride and her family: "That night, Ihaab's father used all of his savings to rent the garlands. The young men risked their lives to climb the massive pylons to light the party. The women filled the jerry-cans with water." Brault has stated that, without the trust and goodwill gained during previous visits, he would have been unable to arrange this shot.[20]

Getting to know subjects as individuals over a period of time humanizes the process of photography in another way as well. Subjects are empowered when photographers recognize their authority to dictate visual access. Approaching subjects in this respectful way may, to some extent, redress the imbalance of power that inevitably inheres when photographers from affluent Western countries visit indigent regions. In such a scenario the collusion of the photographic subject becomes necessary, rather than being viewed as an undesirable threat to the image's objectivity.

One of the images in this exhibition documents its subject's willingness to collaborate with a photographer to an unusual, notable degree. The image in question documents a simulated event. Its subject is cast in a fictional role, representing an event that really happened in his prior life. Guillaume Herbaut shot this photograph as part of a series documenting the population of indigenous Me'phaa people in the La Montaña district of Guerrero, Mexico. The text states that this remote region is disputed by a number of different armed factions, including drug traffickers, guerrillas, paramilitary organizations, and the Mexican army. According to the text, the lives of the indigenous people who live there are wracked by violence. Kidnapping, torture, and murder are commonplace events.

Herbaut's photograph depicts a shirtless man kneeling with his hands behind his head (fig. 9). The subject is viewed laterally from the torso up, so that his right elbow points toward the camera and his face is seen in profile. A golden light burnishes the man's skin and illuminates the perimeter of the stained, windowless concrete cell visible beyond him. The caption reads: "Raúl Lucas Lucía shows the position he was forced to hold when soldiers beat him in November 2003." Lucía collaborated with Herbaut to orchestrate this reenactment of his personal history, reprising the role of the torture victim he had actually been five years earlier. In the companion testimonial Lucía, an activist for indigenous people in La Montaña, tells how he was abducted and tortured by Mexican soldiers who suspected him of being a guerrilla fighter.

The image is a strange one: a theatrical representation of a real, traumatic historical moment that remains undocumented outside the subject's memory. It is a compelling simulation. It looks so convincing, in fact, that it might conceivably have passed as factual evidence if Herbaut had chosen to present it that way. Lucía's photograph confounds its viewers, conveying a powerful reminder of the difficulties that inhere when one relies on photographs to ascertain the difference between fact and fiction. It satirizes the notion that viewers are inherently well equipped to differentiate "true" images, which document empirically verifiable reality, from "staged" images, which document something more subjective. It confuses the categories of appearance and reality.

In 2009, the meaning of the image acquired yet another dimension when Lucía was murdered. An addendum to the exhibition text states that his death appears to have been ordered by the same military forces that had been responsible for his prior kidnapping and torture. As a result of this horrible turn of events, Herbaut's simulated document now reflexively illuminates not one, but two undocumented moments of genuine violence.

Herbaut appears to take it for granted that photographic truth always contains a subjective dimension because it mirrors the photographer's perceived reality at a moment in time. He does not strive for objectivity because he accepts the medium's complicated relationship to truth as given. His photograph of Lucía affirms the value of a humanist ethics vested not in rational documentation but in the righteousness of the authentic, individual conscience.

The image of Lucía calls attention to photography's potential for deception, obliging its viewers to contemplate the ways in which photographic images can make unreliable witnesses. Another photograph from Herbaut's La Montaña portfolio calls attention to the medium's unique positive attributes instead, foregrounding the peculiar powers that derive from the subjective dimension of its meaning. Of all the images in the exhibition, these two comment most directly on photography's limitations and capacities. They merit comparison as companion pieces.

This second photograph shows the upper body of a girl standing (fig. 5). The warm tones of her red dress are framed by darkness; her bowed head appears in foreshortened perspective. It is nighttime, but a small lamp illuminates her from below. The girl's face is doubled in the photograph's midsection by the life-size reproduction of a black-and-white photographic portrait depicting the face of a dark-skinned man. The text states: "Maria's father was assassinated in El Charco on June 7, 1998, in a military massacre in the village school during a coordination meeting attended by various local indigenous communities." The information allows viewers to surmise that the photograph is probably a portrait of the girl's murdered father. From the photographer's vantage point Maria's bowed head appears to adjoin her dead father's likeness, repeating its outline in the vertical register.

The scene is charged with an intensity that imputes an almost magical dimension to the photographic image. Here the photograph literally holds the place of an absent subject. Functioning as proxy *and* memorial, it carries the force of an individual identity beyond the grave. Herbaut's photograph speaks of brutality and resilience, but it also comments knowingly on the ways all photographs reference the grave. Every photograph commemorates a small loss, simply because the events it depicts happened in the past. This image provokes the realization that all such minute losses gesture metonymically to the larger loss of death.

Maria's image confronts viewers with one of photographs' most unique attributes: their weird ability to stand in for lost loves. Any photograph of a decedent brings survivors face-to-face with a frozen moment excised from the past life of that person, who is gone. This potential to evoke the uncanny may be one of the medium's most intrinsic qualities. As Roland Barthes wrote, describing a photograph of his dead mother: "The photograph is literally an emanation of the referent. From a real body, which was there, proceed radiations which ultimately touch me, who am here; the duration of the transmission is insignificant; the photograph of the missing being . . . will touch me like the delayed rays of a star."[21]

In addition to its other dimensions of meaning and mourning, the image of Maria with the photograph of her dead father endorses a position on photographic meaning. It advocates for photography, not as the vehicle of objective evidence but as the receptacle of memory and magic. Disregarding the expectations associated with the evidentiary role, this image proposes that photography's true power lies in the subjective dimension of its meaning. Despite the medium's convincing appearance of objectivity, it functions most compellingly in a role Rousseau might have championed: the conduit of inner truth.

NOTES

1. The phrase "noble savage" never appeared in Rousseau's writings, nor does it accurately reflect his account of primitive man. For more on the widespread tendency to misattribute this concept to Rousseau, see Ter Ellingson, *The Myth of the Noble Savage* (Berkeley: University of California Press, 2001).

2. For the story of the 1745 premiere at the Paris mansion of tax farmer Alexandre Jean-Joseph le Riche de la Pouplinière and the critique that Rousseau was subjected to there by the eminent composer Jean-Philippe Rameau, see Robert Zaretsky and John T. Scott, *The Philosophers' Quarrel: Rousseau, Hume, and the Limits of Human Understanding* (New Haven, CT: Yale University Press, 2009), 17–18.

3. Rousseau to Guillaume-Chrétien de Lamoignon de Malesherbes, January 12, 1762, in Rousseau, CW, 5:575. Cited in Zaretsky and Scott, *Philosophers' Quarrel*, 22.

4. Walt Whitman, *Leaves of Grass* (Philadelphia: David McKay, 1900), 92.

5. See William Henry Fox Talbot, *The Pencil of Nature*, ed. Beaumont Newhall (New York: Da Capo Press, 1969).

6. "Form is henceforth divorced from matter. . . . Give us a few negatives of a thing worth seeing, taken from different points of view, and that is all we want of it." Oliver Wendell Holmes, "The Stereoscope and the Stereograph," *The Atlantic Magazine* 3, issue 20 (June 1859): 738–48.

7. See Josh Ellenbogen, *Reasoned and Unreasoned Images: The Photography of Bertillon, Galton, and Marey* (University Park: Pennsylvania State University Press, 2012); Georges Didi-Huberman, *The Invention of Hysteria: Charcot and the Photographic Iconography of the Salpetrière*, trans. Alisa Hartz (Cambridge, MA: MIT Press, 2004); Anne Maxwell, *Picture Imperfect: Photography and Eugenics, 1870–1940* (Eastbourne: Sussex Academic Press, 2008); and Carol Armstrong, *Scenes in a Library: Reading the Photograph in the Book, 1843–1875* (Cambridge, MA: MIT Press, 1998).

8. For a detailed account of the unusual circumstances surrounding this photograph's creation and circulation, see Geoffrey Batchen, *Burning with Desire: The Conception of Photography* (Cambridge, MA: MIT Press, 1997), 157–73.

9. *Life* 3, no. 2 (July 12, 1937): 19.

10. For a comprehensive overview of the reasons for skepticism, see Phillip Knightley, *The First Casualty: From the Crimea to Vietnam; The War Correspondent as Hero, Propagandist, and Myth Maker* (New York: Harcourt Brace Jovanovitch, 1975), 209–12.

11. See José Manuel Susperregui, *Sombras de la fotografía: Los enigmas desvelados de Nicolasa Ugartemendia, Muerte de un miliciano, La aldea española y El Lute* (Bilbao: Universidad del País Vasco, 2009).

12. Knightley, *The First Casualty*, 212.

13. Hassan M. Fattah, "Symbol of Abu Ghraib Seeks to Spare Others His Nightmare," *New York Times*, March 11, 2006, section 1, page 1.

14. Errol Morris, *Believing Is Seeing: Observations on the Mysteries of Photography* (New York: Penguin Press, 2011), 92.

15. Roland Barthes, *Camera Lucida: Reflections on Photography*, trans. Richard Howard (New York: Hill and Wang, 1981).

16. See Allan Sekula, "The Body and the Archive," in *The Contest of Meaning: Critical Histories of Photography*, ed. Richard Bolton, 343–89 (Cambridge, MA: MIT Press, 1992), and Martha Rosler, "Post-Documentary, Post-Photography?" in *Decoys and Disruptions: Selected Essays, 1975–2001*, 207–44 (Cambridge, MA: MIT Press, 2004).

17. Rosalind Krauss opined that the photograph was the only image that was genuinely surreal—in the sense that the momentary fragment of reality it represents is truly unmediated, and so escapes the reach of its maker's retrospective intention. See Krauss, "The Photographic Conditions of Surrealism," *October* 19 (Winter 1981): 3–34.

18. See Arthur M. Melzer, "Rousseau and the Modern Cult of Sincerity," in *The Legacy of Rousseau*, ed. Clifford Orwin and Nathan Tarcov, 274–95 (Chicago: University of Chicago Press, 1997).

19. The influential concept of the "decisive moment," associated today with Cartier-Bresson, appeared in the preface to Henri Cartier-Bresson's 1952 book *Images à la sauvette*. The book was published later the same year in the United States as *The Decisive Moment* (New York: Simon & Schuster, 1952). The phrase, "There is nothing in this world that does not have a decisive moment" ("Il n'y a rien dans ce monde qui n'ait un moment decisif"), appeared as an epigraph taken from the seventeenth-century *Memoirs* of Jean François Paul de Gondi, cardinal de Retz.

20. Personal communication from Philippe Brault, South Bend, Indiana, March 6, 2012.

21. Barthes, *Camera Lucida*, 80–81.

Part Two

ROUSSEAU IN THE TWENTY-FIRST CENTURY:
WHAT IS HIS RELEVANCE FOR TODAY?

CHAPTER 4

Human Dignity, Rousseau, and the Catholic Church

DANIEL PHILPOTT

That a Catholic university would host the DIGNITY project was fitting. The dignity of the human person, which the *Catechism of the Catholic Church* makes clear is "rooted in his creation in the image and likeness of God," is central to the church's teachings about justice, virtue, and happiness.[1] Human dignity, the church teaches further, shines particularly brightly in the poor. The Gospel of Matthew even teaches in chapter 25 that in the poor we find Jesus Christ. The church's solidarity with the poor can be seen in the witness of the early church fathers, who exhorted their followers to befriend the poor directly; in the Spanish scholastics of the sixteenth century, who defended the human rights of native people in the New World; in the "personalism" of the contemporary Catholic Worker movement, which practices direct friendship with the poor; and in the inimitable public gestures of Pope Francis. The church's love for the poor resonates with the beautiful, poignant, and provocative pictures featured in the DIGNITY project.

Less obviously fitting at a Catholic university was the exhibit's emphasis on Rousseau. The church and Rousseau have never gotten along very well. Rousseau, who converted to Catholicism under somewhat pressured circumstances at age fifteen and converted to Calvinism at age forty-two, most likely in order to regain citizenship in Geneva, viewed the Catholic Church's hierarchy and dogmas as the sources of intolerance, corruption, civic disunity, and violence. For their part, the church and its defenders have viewed Rousseau as the originator of an ideology that would have the church exterminated. Is a rapprochement possible? While there are some insurmountable limits to harmony between the two, progress can be made, I believe.

It is precisely with respect to the exhibit's theme—human dignity—that a dialogue between the church and Rousseau can bear fruit. One of the most salient respects in which Rousseau and the church looked differently upon the question of human dignity was religious freedom. Rousseau considered the church intolerant not only for its views of salvation but also for its view that the Catholic faith ought to be upheld by the state, including through the suppression of dissenting views. Conversely, Catholics have held that Rousseau's thought and the event that it helped to spawn, the French Revolution, denied the church its freedom to practice its faith.

The church, though, evolved in its thinking on religious freedom, culminating in the declaration of the Second Vatican Council whose very title is *Dignitatis Humanae*. That this evolution can be seen as the fruit of a dialogue was suggested by Pope Benedict XVI in his Christmas Address of 2005. There, he credited the Enlightenment with provoking a historical dialogue with the church that ultimately led to the church's embrace of religious freedom as a civic right. He insisted, though, that the church grounded religious freedom in a very different philosophical and theological view than did Enlightenment thinkers, among whom he could easily have included Rousseau. Such was the mutuality of the dialogue, in which the church came to accept a political innovation but supplied it with its own foundation. One would hope that, had Rousseau been involved in this dialogue of decades, he would have evolved in his own views of religious freedom, widening them and deepening them.

Let us take a closer look at this possibility of rapprochement over dignity—first at why the church and Rousseau have been so far apart, and then how common ground might be found.

ROUSSEAU ON THE CATHOLIC CHURCH

Rousseau remonstrated most strongly against the Catholic Church at the close of his most famous work on politics, *The Social Contract*, in a section on civil religion. In previous writings, Rousseau had described a state of nature where solitary noble humans lived happily and harmoniously through their instinct. It was the development of society, particularly private property and the envy and rivalry that it generated, that brought corruption, struggle, and violence. Humanity, then, is "born free and everywhere in chains," as Rousseau famously begins *The Social Contract*. His solution? The sovereignty of the people, ruling through an indestructible "general will," through which freedom and equality would be recovered.

To be unified and stable, Rousseau thought, a state, even one ruled by the general will, needs religion. "[A] State has never been founded without Religion serving as its base," he avers (*SC*, CW, 4:219). Shortly thereafter, he continues, "It matters greatly to the State that each Citizen have a Religion that causes him to love his duties" (*SC*, CW, 4:222). The kind of religion that serves the state is one that the state can control rather than one that becomes the state's rival. Ideal was the ancient world, where each state had its own gods. "The departments of the Gods were, so to speak, fixed by the boundaries of Nations. The God of one people had no right over other peoples," Rousseau explained (*SC*, CW, 4:216). In this way, religion neither challenged the state nor pitted states against one another. "Far from men fighting for the Gods, it was—as in Homer—the Gods who fought for the men. Each man asked his own God for Victory and paid for it with new altars" (*SC*, CW, 4:217). Religion unifies by promoting values—or what he calls positive dogmas—that hold the state together and by discouraging values that divide the state, or negative dogmas. The dogmas friendly to the civic order are: "The existence of a powerful, intelligent, beneficent, foresighted, and providential Divinity; the afterlife; the happiness of the just; the punishment of the wicked; the sanctity of the social Contract and the Laws" (*SC*, CW, 4:223). In other words, religion has value insofar as it serves the state and can be controlled by the state. In arguing this, Rousseau borrows directly from his predecessor, Thomas Hobbes (*SC*, CW, 4:218–19).

Catholicism was manifestly not the civil religion that Rousseau had in mind. When Christianity entered world history, Rousseau argues, it demanded otherworldly loyalties and separated theological from political systems, thereby creating perpetual jurisdictional conflict. The worst offender is "Roman Christianity," a system that is "so manifestly bad that it is a waste of time to amuse oneself by proving it" (*SC*, CW, 4:219). The Catholic Church's theological intolerance in claiming that "there is no Salvation outside of the Church" necessarily leads to civic intolerance, for "[i]t is impossible to live in peace with people whom one believes are damned" (*SC*, CW, 4:223). Civic intolerance, in turn, will mean that "the Sovereign is no longer Sovereign, even over temporal matters. From then on, Priests are the true masters; Kings are merely their officers" (*SC*, CW, 4:227). Catholicism, then, cannot serve as a unifying national religion.

Rousseau also considers the possibility of a Christianity expressed as "the pure and simple religion of the Gospel," that is, a set of moral duties without "temples, altars or rites" (*SC*, CW, 4:219). Echoing Machiavelli, though, he rejects Christian morals as enfeebling. Again, the problem is otherworldliness, which leads people to accept tyrants and to fail to fight war (*SC*, CW, 4:220–21). In the end, the problem is the same: such a religion does not serve the interests of the state.

Filling out Rousseau's views of religion is a memorably drawn portion of his great work, *Emile*, entitled "The Savoyard Vicar." Here, Rousseau depicts a humble and kindly, if naïve and hapless, priest whose views of religion serve to educate the young Emile. The story of the priest is told to Emile by a narrator who, we learn, has been alienated by priests and dogma, having been pressured to convert as a youth while living at a hostel and having seen much corruption among priests—echoing Rousseau's biography. He then comes under the influence of the Savoyard Vicar, who convinces him that priests, rites, and hierarchy are of little value and that the big theological questions are unanswerable, unsettlable, and damaging when churches present them as absolute truths. Religion, however, still has great value insofar as it expresses universal moral truths like love your neighbor, gives people a feeling of happiness through worship, and offers the people of a country an object of devotion. If a religion does these things, says the Savoyard Vicar, then it does not matter what dogmas it propounds. So people ought to hold on to the religion of their homeland, live the virtues embodied in its pure, simple core, and be tolerant of other faiths, he counsels.

What view of religious freedom emerges from Rousseau's analysis? Religious freedom is the civil right of persons and religious associations not to be coerced in the expression and practice of their faith. In his espousal of tolerance in *Emile* and in several passages in *The Social Contract*, Rousseau seems to support religious freedom. For instance, he says in *The Social Contract* that the state should not concern itself with dogma and leave individuals to decide such matters for themselves. States ought to take an interest in religious teachings only to the degree to which these teachings impinge on civic order. The latter clause, however, turns out to be rather significant—and troubling for religious freedom. If Rousseau judges problematic those religions whose claims on people's loyalties compete with those of the state, then, by his own analysis, all of Christianity, and especially Catholicism, is subject to heavy restriction if not prohibition. Rousseau calls rather for "a purely civil profession of faith, the articles of which are for the Sovereign to establish, not exactly as Religious dogmas, but as sentiments of sociability without which it is impossible to be a good Citizen or a faithful subject" (*SC*, CW, 4:222). Then he turns harsh:

> Without being able to obligate anyone to believe [these articles of civil faith], the sovereign can banish from the State anyone who does not believe them. The sovereign can banish him not for being impious, but for being unsociable; for being incapable of sincerely loving the laws, justice, and of giving his life, if need be, for his duty. If someone who has publicly acknowledged these same dogmas behaves as though he does not believe them, he should be punished with death. He has committed the greatest of crimes; he lied before the laws. (*SC*, CW, 4:222–23)

Given that the vast majority of French were Catholics, Rousseau's proposals were a prescription for no small amount of strife.

Arguably his proposals were a prescription for the French Revolution. Rousseau died before the revolution began in 1789, and so we can never know if he would have supported the Reign of Terror. We do know that his ideas were influential on Jacobin thought and that several features of the revolutionaries' program bore an uncanny resemblance to Rousseau's ideas. Freedom, equality, and rule by the will of the people all resounded Rousseau. The Cult of Reason and the Cult of the Supreme Being were bald attempts to create a religion, fitted out with rites and obligations, that would replace Christianity and serve the state. Following the script of *The Social Contract* further, the revolutionary government mandated that priests be elected and not chosen by bishops, and severed the connection between bishops and the pope in Rome—a direct effort to nullify that part of the church's authority that competed most with the state. Though the government gave religious freedom to Jews and Protestants as individuals—which they had lacked under the Catholic monarchy—it created a state body to manage the authority of these communities. Meanwhile the government's war against rebellious peasants in the Vendée expanded into a veritable genocide against Catholics, including civilians. All of this reflected a condition where religious freedom was limited sharply by the authority and purposes of the new state.

THE CATHOLIC CHURCH ON ROUSSEAU

After the dust of the French Revolution settled, over the course of the nineteenth century and well into the twentieth century, the church continued to condemn the revolution and everything associated with its legacy. Remembering the revolution's violence against Catholics and its direct attack on the authority of the church, associating the revolution's philosophy with "latitudinarianism" and "indifferentism" that amounted to relativism and skepticism, the church rejected the entire program of liberal republicanism, including its calls for civil and political rights that have since become standard features of liberal democracies. Nineteenth-century popes were memorably stentorian in their condemnation of liberalism. Pope Gregory XVI called it "perverse," "absurd," and "evil" in his encyclical of 1832, *Mirari Vos*. Pope Pius IX condemned "progress, liberalism, and modern civilization" in his *Syllabus of Errors* of 1864, which attracted wide notice across Europe.

In the writings of Catholic thinkers who sympathized with the popes, Rousseau receives prominent mention. Even those of the nineteenth and early twentieth centuries who looked more favorably upon liberal rights and democratic institutions were keen to distinguish what they thought were valid grounds for these institutions—drawn from classic Christian thought—from the mistakes that they associated with Enlightenment thinkers, prominent among whom was Rousseau. Examples of this pattern can be found in the writings of England's John Henry Newman, America's Orestes Brownson, and France's (and later America's) Jacques Maritain.

Indeed, the theological and philosophical differences between the thought of the Catholic Church and Rousseau are great. Most obviously, in the matter of religion, the church held that it was established by God through his incarnation as Jesus Christ and was not something that could be reinvented or reformed according to the purposes of the state. Rather than the validity of gods being dependent on states, the validity of any state was dependent on God. Catholic thinkers like Brownson disputed Rousseau's claim that Christianity's historical influence on politics was to create civic disunity and to drain loyalty from the state. Much to the contrary, by introducing into history a community and an authority competing with that of the state as well as a transcendent set of loyalties, Christianity made possible limited government and the division between powers that are characteristic of liberal democracy.

Numerous philosophical differences have divided the church from Rousseau's thought as well. Differing from Rousseau's view of the nature of the human person as he depicted it prior to the corruption of society, Catholic thought regards the person as ruled by reason and free will, not by instinct, but also corrupted by sin, which begets conflict and strife even apart from social institutions. In contrast to Rousseau, who thought society corrupting, Catholic thought holds that humans are naturally social and find fulfillment of their natural ends commonly in association. Human freedom is essential to the Catholic view of the person, as it is for Rousseau, but it is a freedom to pursue the good as specified by natural law and the teaching of Christ, not a good otherwise defined. Catholic thought is also typically chary towards the sovereignty of the collective people, worrying that it will override the dignity of individual persons.

As for religious freedom, Rousseau was not altogether wrong about the church. During his time, and indeed right up through the 1950s, the magisterium of the Catholic Church held that the ideal state was one that established and actively supported the church and that could in principle exercise coercion against the public expression of dissent from its teachings. In the church's view, state and church each lived under the lordship of Christ and were called to play separate but complementary roles in forming a society in which the truth that the church taught would be proclaimed and lived. Religious freedom is indeed quite important as a dividing issue between Rousseau and the church. The church's intolerance, he thought, was the key reason it was a threat to the political order. Rousseau's intolerance towards the church, played out in the French Revolution, the church believed, was the most significant problem in his thought.

TOWARDS A RAPPROCHEMENT

Can the distance between Rousseau and the Catholic Church be bridged? It has been bridged substantially already. At the close of the Second Vatican Council in 1965, the council promulgated *Dignitatis Humanae*, which declared religious freedom to be a natural, universal human right. Again, prior to this point the church had held for centuries that a state could permissibly exercise coercion against the public expression of beliefs contrary to the Catholic faith. Its turn towards this doctrine of politics began at least as far back as Augustine, who reluctantly concluded that Roman authorities ought to exercise force to quell the activities of the Donatists, whose doctrines the church had condemned. By the High Middle Ages, a period when the papacy had been strengthened and a Christian civilization had developed, the church exercised coercion against heretics through the Inquisition. As Thomas Aquinas argued, heretics endangered other souls through their public witness, which he compared to counterfeit money. As late as the nineteenth century, popes condemned the right of religious freedom in the same statements, mentioned above, in which they condemned other liberal rights. They did so in part because of their adherence to a medieval model of relations between the church and temporal authorities that envisioned them working together to uphold a Christian civilization, but also because they associated religious freedom with Enlightenment philosophy and attacks upon the church.

Dignitatis Humanae, then, was a signal change. In my view, the change was not a contradiction of previous dogmatic teaching, for the church had never rejected religious freedom with its full authority. Prior to Augustine, figures like Lactantius and Tertullian had taught religious freedom. Even during the Middle Ages, Aquinas's teachings on the importance of conscience were radical in all of human thought and formed a seed of the later teaching of *Dignitatis Humanae*. Still, as an authoritative teaching, *Dignitatis Humanae* was new. It was what Newman had called a doctrinal development, argued the church. Clearly, too, it broke from a centuries-old political doctrine.

What is most important for the essay at hand—and in light of the DIGNITY exhibit at Notre Dame—is the basis that the church offered for religious freedom: the dignity of the human person. The council fathers held that to coerce a person on the basis of his or her beliefs is to interfere with the authentic search for truth that is endemic to human dignity. Even if a person is in error, he or she still has a civil right to believe, speak, and act according to conscience.

A long essay could be written about the historical factors that led to the church's new thinking. The role of Catholic intellectuals like John Courtney Murray and Jacques Maritain; the decline of hostility to the church in Western liberal democracies; the vindication of freedom in the Second World War; and the rise of new threats to the religious freedom of the church like communism were all important. All of these factors and the church's response to them constitute the grand historical dialogue depicted by Pope Benedict XVI, a dialogue in which the church gradually came around to one of the central ideas proposed by its former enemies of the Enlightenment.

The legatees of Rousseau and the French Revolution have also required some evolution in their thinking in order to arrive at the respect for the dignity of the person of which *Dignitatis Humanae* spoke. Their challenge was to respect Catholics in their associational life—that is, in their practice of their faith within a visible hierarchy, educational institutions, monasteries, and religious orders. This respect, too, has been long in coming and even to this day is attended by controversy. Religious freedom is a two-way street. When each side comes to respect this freedom, though, it is a victory for human dignity.

NOTES

1. *The Cathechism of the Catholic Church*, para. 1700.

CHAPTER 5

Reinventing Dignity

FAYÇAL FALAKY

In *Climate of Fear: The Quest for Dignity in a Dehumanized World*, Nigerian Nobel laureate and human rights activist Wole Soyinka ponders over the importance of dignity for sentient human beings, and why such a concept has been given prominence across so many cultures, civilizations, and political upheavals, including, as he puts it, "in the charter that resulted from one of the bloodiest revolutions in human history—the French."[1] The problem with such an assertion, of course, is that in its fundamental moral sense as a natural and even sacred prerogative, dignity was never included in the 1789 Declaration of the Rights of Man and Citizen; and it is only in 1948, with the Universal Declaration of Human Rights, that it becomes elevated to the rank of inalienable human right. Yet we may consider Soyinka's lapse as benign because before its legal consecration in the twentieth century, dignity, as we know it today, had already been since the eighteenth century a matter of philosophical, intellectual, and political debate. Although the term was never mentioned in the Declaration of the Rights of Man and Citizen, the concept of equality as conceived by the constituents of the National Assembly implied that every man was entitled to dignity, respect, and equal treatment in the eyes of the law. As François d'Escherny puts it in his *Tableau historique de la Révolution*, it is not only liberty that is pursued but also "the ideas of equality, of noble pride, and of the dignity of man."[2] In the philosophical terrain, the concept of an intrinsic human dignity can be found most prominently in the works of Immanuel Kant. As was the case for the French revolutionaries, dignity for Kant was not a matter of aristocratic exclusion but a quality that resided in the autonomous will and the self-respect inspired by our rational duty to follow an intrinsic moral law.[3] In one of the finest passages of the *Observations on the Feeling of the Beautiful and Sublime*, Kant writes:

[T]rue virtue can be grafted only upon principles such that the more general they are, the more sublime and noble it becomes. These principles are not speculative rules, but the consciousness of a feeling that lives in every human breast and extends itself much further than over the particular grounds of compassion and complaisance. I believe that I sum it all up when I say that it is the *feeling of the beauty and the dignity of human nature*. The first is a ground of universal affection, the second of universal esteem; and if this feeling had the greatest perfection in some one human heart, this man would of course love and prize even himself, but only so far as he is one of all those over whom his broadened and noble feeling is spread.[4]

In a disquisition on this passage, Russian-born French sociologist and jurist Georges Gurvitch notes that "these words are a faithful reproduction of Rousseau's thoughts in the *Profession of Faith of the Savoyard Vicar*."[5] That Rousseau may have influenced Kant's thoughts on the notion of dignity is very plausible. After all, it is in a well-known note penciled into his copy of the *Observations* that Kant declared his admiration for the Genevan philosopher. After declaring that there was a time when he felt contempt for the masses, he wrote, "Rousseau has set me straight. This delusory presumption vanishes. I learn to honor men and I would find myself more useless than the common laborer if I did not believe that this consideration could extend to all others a worth capable of establishing the rights of mankind."[6] What Kant means by this homage is that self-esteem or dignity can no longer be reserved to the few and privileged but that it should be extended to every man. It also goes without saying that Rousseau's influence had colored the way in which the French revolutionaries thought about dignity. To give but an example, we may cite a proposal at the National Assembly to erect a monument in honor of the apostle of liberty and equality in which we learn that among Rousseau's contributions to the French nation is that he has unveiled "the dignity of man in the best of lights and has acquainted the people with their true rights."[7]

As we shall see, Rousseau's influence in defining as well as universalizing the concept of dignity is not without merit. Following Kant, we may say that Rousseau is the "Newton of the moral world," one of the first to have justified man's self-esteem on natural rather than social and exclusive grounds. Yet, for the most part, when Rousseau speaks of dignity throughout his works, he does so in a quite negative manner. This is less a contradiction than the reflection of a semantic shift in which Rousseau plays a crucial part. More than anyone else, Rousseau took a term associated with privilege and inequality and refounded it on the basis of a natural feeling common to all. In a sense, this act of reclamation is also the story told by the many faces portrayed in the DIGNITY exhibit. Irrespective of wealth or status, or the misery and hardships in which one lives, dignity, these faces say, is a fundamental human right.

Arguably the most famous censure of dignity in Rousseau's works is in a passage from his *Letter to D'Alembert on the Theater*. Recalling the open-air spectacle of a military dance that had struck his imagination as a boy, Rousseau asks, "Ah! Dignity, daughter of pride and mother of boredom, have your melancholy Slaves ever had a similar moment in their lives?" (*D'Alembert*, CW, 10:351). Thus posed, the question serves to contrast the natural gaiety and *désinvolture* of the public festivals he envisioned for the Genevan republic—"all heads were spinning with a drunkenness sweeter than that of wine"—with the insufferable boredom and uptightness that characterizes French theater etiquette. The meaning given to the term here suggests that dignity is more of a burden, a constraining and even enslaving force imposed by social conventions and expectations, rather than a virtue to be lauded. It is for this reason that whenever Rousseau had guests over, he made it a principle to treat them without ceremony, setting up dinners in a ground-floor room that served as both dining-room and kitchen, and sometimes, as Boswell learned from experience, inviting them to help with the cooking.[8] Thus, after a visit paid to the Hermitage by Sophie d'Houdetot, one that Rousseau describes as having "somehow the air of the beginning of a novel," he urges his partner Thérèse Levasseur to "forget dignity to make a rustic collation" (*Conf*, CW, 5:363). It was also in this manner that he wanted to treat the sickly grandson of Monsieur de Luxembourg. Believed to be gravely ill, the child was placed entirely under the care of Doctor Bordeu who prescribed him a diet that was poor on food and heavy on drugs. Rousseau, however, did not want to have any part of that. Not only did he believe the doctor a quack but he also took pity on the starved boy, feeding him when the occasion arose:

> How glad this poor child was when he could obtain permission to come to Mont-Louis with Mme de Boufflers to ask Therese for a snack, and put some food in his famished stomach! How much did I deplore within myself the miseries of greatness, when I saw this sole heir of such great property, of such a great name, of so many titles and dignities devour a poor little piece of bread with the eagerness of a beggar. In sum, I might well speak and act, the Doctor triumphed, and the child died of hunger. (*Conf*, CW, 5:460)

Whether it be the magnificence of a noble and wealthy family or the pompous braggadocio of the all-knowing doctor, dignity comes off as a ridiculous masquerade. Not only does it disguise a miserable reality but it also sets its victims into a rigid and unbending decorum susceptible of causing death. As Jean-François de La Harpe puts it, "Dignity often masks a deficiency."[9]

That one of Rousseau's more famous critiques of dignity appears in the midst of his views on theater is not surprising. For Rousseau, as for contemporaries like La Harpe, for example, the term dignity connoted the kind of affected or histrionic posturing characteristic of aristocratic *bienséance* or decorum. To understand the history behind such a perception, an etymological analysis is imperative. The term dignity comes from the Indo-European root *dek*, which is also the root for terms such as orthodox, doctor, disciple, discipline, doctrine, dogma. From one of the stems of the root, *deknos*, was eventually derived the Latin *decet*, an impersonal verb that can be translated as "it is decent, suitable, or proper." This verb has given rise to a number of derivatives, including *decus*, which means honor, distinction, decency, and propriety, and *decor*, which is used to describe anything that is seemly or becoming, especially a physical beauty that is matched by a moral poise. *Decus* also gave birth to the adjective *dignus*, whose modern English equivalent would be "worthy of" or "fitting," and which we can render in French as "digne de." It is from this adjective that the term *dignitas* is derived, and it is not surprising then that in its first meaning, the notion was inseparable from the honorific offices of the state and the aesthetic majesty (*décor*) that such distinctions were supposed to confer. In *De inventione*, Cicero remarks that "Dignity is the honorable authority of a person, combined with attention and honor and worthy respect paid to him" (*Dignitas est alicujus honesta et cultu et honore et verecundia digna auctoritas*).[10] In this view, we may argue that the original use of the term was to represent and emphasize social hierarchy as well as exceptionality. In fact, in Cicero's Rome, dignity was a privilege accorded solely to the Roman citizen, and foreigners as well as slaves and women were, by their very condition, theoretically excluded from such virtue.[11] This sort of social inequality was also behind the concept and usage of dignity during France's old regime. In fact, the first legal definition of the three estates—nobility, clergy, and commoner—appeared in a text written in 1610 by Charles Loyseau and aptly titled *Traité des ordres et simples dignités*. In it, we read the following:

> We cannot live in a society where everyone is equal; it is necessary thus that some command and others obey. Those who command are of different ranks: sovereign lords command all those in their state, addressing their commandment to the great, the great to the intermediate, the intermediate to the minor, and the minor to the people. And the people, who obey all of these, are again divided in different orders and ranks. . . . Some are devoted to the service of God, some to bear arms and protect the state, and others to nourish it and maintain it by the exercises of peace. These are our three Orders or estates-general of France: the clergy, the nobility, and the third estate.[12]

After defining an estate as "Dignity with aptitude for public power,"[13] Loyseau recommends distinguishing between them through the use of titles, ranks, and, following the examples of the Romans, "external ornaments."[14]

It goes without saying that for the author of the *Discourse on Inequality*, this kind of dignity went against everything he stood for. Not only did it represent the kind of political injustice and social inequality he wrote against; at a more philosophical level, it also exemplified one of the recurrent preoccupations of his thinking—the gap between being and appearance. Instead of being an inner quality, dignity as he saw it carried all the marks of a superficial imposture. Through arbitrary titles, garbs, accents, affectations, and mannerisms, dignity becomes nothing more than an accessory in everyday social role play. It is symptomatic of the vanity of social man who, "always outside himself, knows to live only in the opinion of others" (*DOI*, CW, 3:66). Not only did it perpetuate social comparisons and inequality but also, as Christopher Kelly notes in this volume when speaking of Rousseau's reproof of distracting entertainments, dignity oriented "ourselves away from ourselves." Dignity, in other words, was yet another fixture of the superficial and theatrical mask worn by man in society.

In *Julie*, Rousseau portrays the relationship between dignity and the modern man's histrionism in the clearest of terms. To criticize the upper-class practice of taking seats on the theater's stage, a custom that disappeared only in 1759, Rousseau notes through Saint-Preux's pen that:

> They appear both as represented in the middle of the stage and representing on the two sides; they are characters on the stage and comedians on the benches. And so it is that the Sphere of the world and of authors is shrinking; so it is that the modern stage never sheds its boring dignity. They know only how to show people in gilt clothing. You would think France were inhabited only by Counts and Chevaliers, and the more the populace is miserable and beggarly the more its tableau on stage is brilliant and magnificent. As a result, by depicting the ridiculousness of the estates that set the example for the others, they spread it rather than stifling it, and the populace, forever ape and imitator of the rich, goes to the theater less to laugh at their follies than to study them, and becomes even more crazy than them by imitating them. (*Julie*, CW, 6:207)

What links the stage of theater and the stage of the world is a shallow dignity embodied by the marquis who dared to break the fourth wall. Rousseau himself experienced the theatricality of social life firsthand. Describing his inability to find happiness anywhere else other than in the countryside, he writes in the *Confessions* that while in Paris he was in the "whirlwind of high society, in the sensuality of suppers, in the brilliance of spectacles, in the fumes of vainglory," and in Venice, in the course of public affairs, he was "in the dignity of a position as a sort of representative" (*Conf*, CW, 6:337). Whether it be on the grand stage that is Paris or through the privilege of acting a political role, representation inhibits the individual determination of the self. It is for this reason that during these moments, Rousseau finds himself longing for a less artificial setting, "my groves, my streams, my solitary walks." Whether real or imaginary, nature becomes a space where one can finally escape social constraints and be reunited with the inner self. This is also Rousseau's lesson in *Emile*.

First he inveighs against the pedagogues and the little minds (*petits esprits*) who take upon themselves a magisterial dignity (*d'affecter toujours la dignité magistrale*). Then he attacks the conceited moral hypocrites of his century, telling them: "Be forever without naturalness, without vitals. Temper and harden your iron hearts in your vile propriety. Make yourselves contemptible by dint of dignity." Finally, he enjoins his readers to follow a different path: "love nature, despise opinion, and know man" (*Emile*, CW, 13:396).

Yet, despite all of this, Rousseau does not cease to claim dignity for himself or for those who, like him, chose to turn their back to the shallow pomp of *l'ennuyeuse dignité*. In these cases, the term loses its historical connotations of privilege and honor and denotes rather an autonomous and self-driven sensibility. Just as the sentiment of justice appears in the face of injustice, we may say that true dignity for Rousseau was a natural sentiment that defied the social indignities he saw around him. We may also say in this regard that dignity follows the path of terms such as modesty (*pudeur*) or justice, which often take conflicting meanings in Rousseau's works. In a seemingly contradictory passage from *Emile*, Rousseau states that "although modesty is natural to the human species, naturally children have none" (*Emile*, CW, 13:368). The ambivalence of this sentence reflects Rousseau's thoroughgoing desire in *Emile* to distinguish between the natural, moral order and its societal ersatz. What separates the first modesty from the second is essentially the relational self-consciousness that separates the child and the adult, the natural and the institutional. Although "modesty" was but another word of the "metaphysical jargon," a word by which adults hoped to frighten their children into submission but which awakened them instead to an evil of which they initially had no idea, this prelapsarian ignorance did not presume that children lacked any kind of moral preserve. On the contrary, Rousseau believed that children—before their social corruption in any case—were modest despite lacking any notions of modesty. This is what Rousseau means when he adds: "Children do not have the same desires as men; but since they are just as subject to uncleanness offensive to the senses, they can from that very subjection get the same lessons in propriety. Follow the spirit of nature which, by putting in the same place the organs of the secret pleasures and those of the disgusting needs, inspires in us the same cares at different ages, now due to one idea, then due to another; in the man due to modesty, in the child due to cleanliness" (*Emile*, CW, 13:368).

No longer associated with the sinful but with the outright disgusting, modesty goes from being a moral and arbitrary quality invented by men to an intrinsic virtue. It is no longer a chimerical notion derived from a desire for divine grace or fear of eternal damnation but rather, as the terms "property" and "uncleanness" suggest, a natural disposition towards hygienic self-preservation. Rousseau treats the terms "justice" and "goodness" in a similarly ambivalent fashion. Although factitious notions when considered from a moral point of view, these virtues, he says, are derived nonetheless from the primitive instincts that nature had implanted in man: "*justice* and *goodness*," he writes, "are not merely abstract words—pure moral beings formed by the understanding—but are true affections of the soul enlightened by reason, [and] are hence only an ordered development of our primitive affections."[15]

When Georges Gurvitch links Kant's conception of dignity to Rousseau, the passage he has in mind is precisely this one. Gurvitch's point, of course, is to show how the inner sentiment or the divine instinct in Rousseau's work plays the same practical, precritical role as Kant's autonomous morality. What is also implied in this comparison is that the notion of dignity as conceived by Kant is derived from Rousseau's conception of conscience as an inborn and universal moral instinct. "According to Kant," says Gurvitch, "the doctrine of human dignity is the central pillar of Rousseau's system."[16] Given Rousseau's censure of dignity, this declaration may seem surprising, but the reality is that here we are dealing with an entirely different concept. Although a social attribute at first, dignity, with Rousseau, takes on a more existential definition. *Dignitas* becomes a universal value rather than a luxury. In a sense, we may say that Rousseau pries dignity from the grips of social vanity and reinscribes it into the natural sentiment of self-preservation (*amour de soi*). This, at least, was the understanding of many a reader who deemed Rousseau's primitive man a "noble savage." Although Rousseau never used the phrase, it came to connote a natural dignity that is common to all and that precedes the social and aristocratic need for recognition. For Louis-Sebastien Mercier, this dignity was not just a right restituted to man but also a rightful attack against the so-called "dignities" of the old regime's nobility. In *De J. J. Rousseau, considéré comme l'un des premiers auteurs de la Révolution*, Mercier notes, "What is most shocking to the slaves of the court, these decorated mongers, is this *equality of rights*, this solemn restitution made to man; this is their torment and their hell; as if it was aberrant to have a perfect equality of rights in all of human societies or to think that there exists a common and primitive dignity which is that of being a man."[17]

For Mercier, this restitution of rights was the work of one man. Rousseau, writes Mercier, "paints man in his nakedness; and man has always more grace and more dignity thus than when he is covered in clothing. . . . Rousseau seems to be the enduring enemy, not of natural laws and lawful authority, but of all the haughty and irksome laws that man has imagined."[18] No longer dependent on rank or the external ornament, the grace of this new dignity is that it is inherent to all human beings, even to those who, under the old system, had usurped it for their own ends. The nobles, writes Mercier, will be "dispensed from fawning at the court, trying to find favor with assistants; if collars and ribbons no longer distinguish them from the multitude, at least, slaves freed from courtly vanity, they can give themselves over to the wisdom of our constitution, learn to cherish it and admire the fact that it lifts up the dignity of man without humiliating anyone."[19]

Bereft of any marks of distinction, man rediscovers a dignity that has more to do with *decus* than *décor*. This dignity is no longer that of the alienated, social man who draws his sense of self from other peoples' judgments but worthy of the self-sufficient and autonomous savage of the *Discourse on Inequality* who "lives within himself" (*DOI*, CW, 3:66).

Although, as we have seen, Rousseau often considers the term in a quite negative sense, there are a few instances where dignity takes on its modern meaning under his pen as an ethical value rooted in human nature. The duke of Orleans is described, for example, as "simple like the rest of us, renouncing the pomp consecrated to his rank without renouncing his dignity" (*Or*, CW, 12:260). The Savoyard Vicar is a "worthy master" (*mon digne maître*). He possesses "virtue without hypocrisy, humanity without weakness, speech that was always straight and simple, and conduct always in conformity with this speech" (*Emile*, CW, 13:423). In each of these two cases, dignity is not a social mark of distinction but an inherent, natural right that exists beyond and despite conventional views on wealth, power, or greatness. In fact, most of the times Rousseau portrays true dignity, whether the subject depicted is person or scene, what stands out is the intentional disdain for all that is ostentatious. A perfect example of this starkness is the depiction of Monsieur de Wolmar and Julie's wedding. Julie arrives at the church, described as a "simple and august place," and draws the reader's attention to the "dim light in the building, the profound silence of the Spectators, their modest and meditative demeanor. . . . The purity, the dignity, the holiness of marriage" (*Julie*, CW, 6:291). Yet, what strikes the reader the most is mainly what is not there. There is no music, no ornaments, not even flowers. The ceremony, however, is brimming over with an abundance of feelings.

For Rousseau, this specific contrast was also the mark of a true dignified style. When criticizing the French theater in *Julie*, Saint-Preux remarks that "there is a certain affected dignity in gesture and diction, which never allows passion to speak exactly its language, nor the author to enter his character and transport himself to the scene of action, but keeps him ever in chains on the stage and under the eyes of Spectators" (*Julie*, CW, 6:208). This depiction of the pretentious and unnatural style of Parisian theater stands at opposite ends of what Rousseau says about his own writing, full of passion and indifferent to literary *bienséances* or classifications: "In these transports, in the midst of such lofty images, will love evoke them in pedestrian terms? Will it bring itself to lower, to sully its ideas with vulgar phrases? Will it not elevate its style? Give it nobility, dignity? How can you speak of Letters, of epistolary style? When writing to one's beloved, who cares about that! It is no longer Letters one writes, but Hymns" (*Julie*, CW, 6:10–11).

The fact that Rousseau uses the term dignity in both these passages is a testament to its changing signification. By reclaiming dignity, Rousseau does not only dissociate it from the external sign, the exclusive *décor* of privilege and inequality, but he inscribes it in a realm that is common to all: the realm of feeling. From the dignities of Rome or the old regime, we move gradually to a dignity that is proper to the essence of every man, that is the same for all and that does not distinguish between the elite and the masses. This is what Kant meant when he said that Rousseau set him straight, and this is also the poignant message of the DIGNITY exhibit. Beyond the magisterial decorum that may gild the vanity of the rich and powerful, dignity as redefined by Rousseau is indifferent to wealth and class distinctions and resilient even in the face of poverty and injustice.

NOTES

1. Wole Soyinka, *Climate of Fear: The Quest for Dignity in a Dehumanized World* (New York: Random House, 2005), 90–91.

2. François d'Escherny, "Les idées d'égalité, de noble fierté, de dignité de l'homme," in *Tableau historique de la Révolution jusqu'à la fin de l'Assemblée Constituante*, vol. 2 (Paris: Treuttel et Wurtz, 1815), 291.

3. See Michael Rosen, *Dignity: Its History and Meaning* (Cambridge, MA: Harvard University Press, 2012).

4. Immanuel Kant, *Observations on the Feeling of the Beautiful and Sublime*, trans. John T. Goldthwait (Berkeley: University of California Press, 1960), 60.

5. "[C]es paroles reproduisent précisément les développements de Rousseau dans la *Profession de foi du vicaire savoyard*." Georges Gurvitch, *Ecrits allemands: Fichte* (Paris: Éditions L'Harmattan, 2006), 24.

6. Cited in John H. Zammito, "The Pursuit of Science as Decadence," in *Kant's Observations and Remarks: A Critical Guide*, ed. Susan Meld Shell and Richard Velkley (Cambridge: Cambridge University Press, 2012), 236.

7. "[L]a dignité de l'homme dans son plus beau jour, et fit connaître aux peuples leurs véritables droits." Article in *Le Moniteur*, January 7, 1794, reprinted in *Réimpression de l'ancien Moniteur*, vol. 19 (Paris: Plon, 1841), 143.

8. "In a remarkable scene described by Boswell," writes Casey Blanton, "he and Rousseau eat simply in Rousseau's kitchen and discuss another one of Boswell's intense interests: politics, specifically despotism vs. freedom in society. The scene is a remarkable one as a piece of travel literature because it is so intimate and so universal at the same time—the things Boswell does best. Boswell helps Thérèse Le Vasseur cook. He describes exactly what they eat: soup, vegetables, cold pork, stoned pears and chestnuts, and wine. It is a scene of domestic ease, yet as Boswell is certainly aware, he is sitting in the kitchen of the greatest writer of Europe asking him deep philosophical questions." In *Travel Writing: The Self and the World* (New York: Routledge, 2002), 38.

9. "L'étiquette est l'esprit de ceux qui n'en ont pas. La dignité souvent masque l'insuffisance." These lines appear in a poem written in 1773 titled "Réponse d'Horace à Voltaire." See *Œuvres choisies et posthumes de M. de La Harpe*, vol. 3 (Paris: Chez Migneret, 1806).

10. In *The Orations of Marcus Tullius Cicero*, vol. 4 (London: H. G. Bohn, 1856), 376.

11. I owe most of this etymological survey to Michel Pauliat. See his "De la *Dignitas* à la dignité," in *Justice, éthique et dignité*, ed. Stéphane Gaboriau and Hélène Pauliat, 29–36 (Limoges: Presse Universitaire de Limoges, 2006).

12. "[N]ous ne pourrions pas vivre en égalité de condition; ainsi il faut par nécessité que les uns commandent et que les autres obéissent. Ceux qui commandent ont plusieurs degrés : les souverains Seigneurs commandent à tous ceux de leur État, adressant leur commandement aux grands, les grands aux médiocres, les médiocres aux petits, et les petits au peuple. Et le peuple qui obéit à tous ceux-là est encore séparé en plusieurs Ordres et rangs [....] Les uns sont dédiés particulièrement au service de Dieu; les autres à conserver l'État par les armes, les autres à le nourrir et maintenir par les exercices de la paix. Ce sont nos trois Ordres ou États généraux de France, le clergé, la noblesse et les tiers Etat." In Charles Loyseau, *Traité des ordres et simples dignités* (Paris: Abel Langellier, 1610), 1–2.

13. "Dignité avec aptitude à la puissance publique." Ibid., 4.

14. "L'ornement externe." Ibid., 7. After writing about estates in a general manner in chapter one, chapter two is entitled "Des Ordres Romains."

15. *Emile*, CW, 13:389. These examples reflect a larger paradox inherent in Rousseau's pedagogical enterprise. Since his goal is to give Emile "only natural and purely physical knowledge" (358) alone, Rousseau's approach to education is no different from the methodology enjoined by the materialists. He treats moral issues with an equal amount of distrust and considers them instead from a physical point of view alone. Yet, by attributing to instinct such notions as modesty, justice, or goodness, Rousseau's materialist methodology transposes within nature's physical realm the same theo-metaphysical concepts that he did not hesitate to qualify as either factitious or chimerical.

16. "D'après Kant, la doctrine sur la dignité de l'homme est le pilier central du système de Rousseau." Gurvitch, *Ecrits allemands*, 23.

17. "[C]e qui choque le plus les esclaves des cours, les mangeurs décorés, c'est cette *égalité de droits*, cette restitution solennelle faite à l'homme; voilà leur tourment et leur enfer; comme s'il ne devait pas exister dans toutes *sociétés humaines* une égalité parfaite de droits, en ce qu'il existe parmi les hommes une dignité commune et primitive qui est celle d'être homme." Louis-Sébastien Mercier, *De J. J. Rousseau, considéré comme l'un des premiers auteurs de la Révolution*, vol. 1 (Paris: Chez Buisson, 1791), 152.

18. "Rousseau peint l'homme nu; et l'homme a toujours plus de grâce et de dignité lorsqu'il est peint ainsi, que lorsqu'il est couvert d'habillements. . . . Rousseau paraît être l'ennemi constant, non des lois naturelles ni de l'autorité légitime, mais de toutes les lois hautaines et tracassières que l'homme a imaginées." Mercier, *De J. J. Rousseau*, 12.

19. "[D]ispensés de valeter dans les cours, et de plaire à des commis; si des *colliers*, des *rubans* ne les distinguent plus de la multitude, du moins . . . ils peuvent se livrer à la sagesse de notre constitution, apprendre à la chérir et à l'admirer en ce qu'elle relève toute la dignité de l'homme, sans en humilier aucun." Mercier, *De J. J. Rousseau*, 187–88.

CHAPTER 6

Cultivating the Seeds of Humanity
Republicanism, Nationalism, and the Cosmopolitan Tradition in Rousseau

ANDREW BILLING

ROUSSEAU AND COSMOPOLITANISM TODAY

The cosmopolitan tradition and the figures of the "global" or "world citizen" that are the contemporary glosses on the classical Greek *kosmou politês* have inspired numerous recent attempts to rethink the political in a period characterized by an array of diverse and often incommensurable challenges to the autonomy of the nation-state and the principle of state sovereignty.[1] Critics have argued that the cosmopolitan ideal of allegiance to a universal community of human beings is a "thin" abstraction unable to command the loyalty of more concrete local identities, or that it is compromised by its parochial roots in stoic and Enlightenment universalism.[2] Nonetheless, in the context of a questioning of the nation-state, its essence, and its boundaries, the philosophical heritage of cosmopolitanism has seemed to many to offer an alternative to discredited "particularisms" as a means of conceptualizing rights and duties in a globalized post-national age. For both advocates and critics of the new cosmopolitanisms, the principal historical point of reference has been the Enlightenment version developed in two short essays by Immanuel Kant, and characterized by Pheng Cheah as the "single most important philosophical source for contemporary normative theories of international relations."[3] Although the importance and influence of these texts is undeniable, Jean-Jacques Rousseau's earlier writings on cosmopolitanism have often been neglected in the contemporary reevaluation of the cosmopolitan heritage. Moreover, despite Kant's recognition of a debt owed to Rousseau in the elaboration of his moral and political philosophy, Kant and Rousseau have often been opposed as advocates of cosmopolitanism and nationalism respectively.[4] Rousseau has been viewed as the proponent of a republican patriotism or, in the terms of Bonnie Honig, as the "great theorist of democracy as a national form."[5]

It is true that on occasion Rousseau explicitly denounces the cosmopolitan, while his major political works often suggest that republican democracy requires a firm anchoring in a national community and calls for the inculcation of patriotic sentiment as the affective bond of the nation figured as a political family. Nonetheless, consideration of the full range of Rousseau's political writings reveals a more nuanced picture. Rousseau is actually one of the first writers in French to pose the question of the relation between the national community and the *cosmopolite*, and his conception of nationalism is both sensitive to the possibility of nationalist excesses and leaves room for larger or overlapping loyalties.[6] Moreover, in the years after the publication of the *Discourse on the Origin and Foundations of Inequality among Men* (1755), in a period in which he is engaged with the political writings of the Abbé de Saint-Pierre, Rousseau pursues a reflection on the compatibility of republican government with an international order organized on cosmopolitan lines. This period produces several texts that make a significant contribution to the development of cosmopolitan theory and are the key influence for Kant's own theory of cosmopolitical right. However, it also marks a crisis in Rousseau's political thought, the consequences of which determine in profound ways the contours of the subsequent major works, from the *Social Contract* to *Emile*.

In his writings on international relations and war and peace, Rousseau recognizes the merits of a normative cosmopolitan model as a means to contain the conflicts between states that he comes to view as a structural feature of international relations independent of their internal constitutions. An association of states organized in terms of cosmopolitan principles promises to end the anarchy and violence characteristic of the international system. However, Rousseau identifies an impasse in the irresolvable conflict between the objective of lasting peace and the means required to establish the cosmopolitan association. Rousseau's reflection on cosmopolitanism, then, while sincere, situates him as a sympathetic internal critic within the cosmopolitan tradition. Furthermore, the inability to resolve this impasse uncovers a constitutive instability of republican government on the national level, insofar as even well-founded states prove to be permanently and precariously exposed to the threat of anarchic violence in their external relations. In this essay, I will argue that this dilemma of international relations accounts for the increasingly idealistic and conjectural tone that Rousseau's republicanism adopts after this period, as well as in part for the move from political theory to fiction and pedagogy. Rousseau's *Emile* can be interpreted as an avowal of the impracticality of republican government, even as it also marks the culmination of the cosmopolitan strand in Rousseau's thought, albeit in the weaker form of the moral universalism that underpins Emile's education in the pedagogical treatise. It is this moral cosmopolitanism, centered on respect for the dignity of the human person as expressed in humanitarian sympathy, relief, and assistance in the development of self-sufficiency, that therefore stands as Rousseau's final cosmopolitan legacy.

PATRIE, PEUPLE, NATION

Rousseau's political concepts are notorious for the diverging interpretations they have produced and for the accusations of self-contradiction that critics have frequently leveled against him. Rousseau's conceptions of the nation and of cosmopolitanism are typical in this respect. On one view, Rousseau is a theorist of democracy as a national form of government,[7] a nationalist who conceives the nation as an exclusive object of attachment,[8] or even a "xenophobic theorist of self-identity"[9] whose conceptions of democracy, nationalism, and patriotism are incompatible with the larger loyalties required by a cosmopolitan scheme. Georg Cavallar has recently asserted an opposing view that Rousseau is not a nationalist at all but a republican: "Rousseau's patriotism in turn closely follows the republican tradition, and is similar to Montesquieu's. *La patrie* is a political, not an ethnic, concept, and forms a close alliance with 'laws' and 'liberty.' Rousseau's reputation as a precursor of nationalism is predominantly the result of a gross misinterpretation."[10] For Cavallar, Rousseau's republicanism, like that of Montesquieu, is compatible with at least a mild "moral" form of cosmopolitanism, of which Rousseau himself provides a model in *Emile*.[11] Cavallar is certainly right to place Rousseau in the republican tradition, and while Rousseau's conception of patriotism is presented occasionally in exclusionary terms,[12] elsewhere in the political writings he suggests that patriotism is compatible with broader cosmopolitan loyalties. The charge that he endorses a xenophobic nationalism is clearly overstated. Nonetheless, Cavallar's claim that it is a "gross misinterpretation" to link Rousseau to nationalism simplifies his complex relation to this nascent tradition and passes over some crucial tensions in his political doctrines. Although Rousseau's political theory, like Kant's, emerges prior to the spread of nationalism as a political ideology in Europe, his political texts frequently employ the term *nation* to describe the political community, albeit less often than the term *peuple* with which it is nonetheless usually interchangeable.[13] For Rousseau, the nation is a recognized unit of political association and solidarity, although its relation to his republicanism remains enigmatic, if not conflictual.

Of Rousseau's principal political writings, the text that best supports Cavallar's interpretation is the *Discourse on Political Economy* (1755), which presents an explicit defense of patriotism and patriotic virtue within a republican frame, and also suggests that patriotism is partly derived from a broader humanitarian sentiment. The topic arises during a discussion of the means to ensure that individuals obey the law. According to Rousseau, the purpose of political society is to guarantee "the goods, life, and freedom of each member by the protection of all" (*PE*, CW, 3:145). A well-ordered society is consequently advantageous to individual *amour-propre* or self-interest in absolute terms,[14] but there is nonetheless the risk of conflicts between individual interests and the law in particular cases, where individuals might perceive their advantage to lie in an evasion of their duties. For this reason, true respect for the law can only be produced when citizens are firmly encouraged to identify private interests with those of the collective. This identification is most easily established through the inculcation of *amour de la patrie* in public education,[15] which produces patriotic citizens by encouraging them "to feel themselves to be members of the fatherland; to love it with that delicate feeling that any isolated man feels only for himself" (*PE*, CW, 3:155). The patriot's conversion of *amour-propre* into a general *amour de la patrie* requires an expansive identification with the collective as a second self. However, *amour de la patrie* also requires a restrictive modification of another sentiment, pity or "commiseration":

> It seems that the sentiment of humanity evaporates and weakens as it is extended over the whole world, and that we can't be moved by calamities in Tartary or Japan as we are by those of a European people. Interest and commiseration must in some way be confined and compressed to be made active. Now since this inclination in us can only be useful to those with whom we have to live, it is good that the sentiment of humanity, concentrated among fellow citizens, gains fresh force through the habit of seeing one another and through the common interest that unites them. It is certain that the greatest miracles of virtue have been produced by love of fatherland. By combining the force of amour-propre with all the beauty of virtue, this sweet and ardent sentiment gains an energy which, without disfiguring it, makes it the most heroic of all the passions. (*PE*, CW, 3:151, translation slightly modified)

In addition to its manipulation of *amour-propre*, then, patriotism entails the concentration of commiseration "among fellow citizens," the productive activation and conversion of an otherwise vague sentiment into a bond of allegiance entailing concrete obligations. Here, Rousseau's paradoxical claim that the "sentiment of humanity" invariably weakens as it extends to include the universal community of human beings resembles criticisms of the cosmopolitan ideal as an insubstantial abstraction. In suggesting that patriotism is partly derived from humanitarian sentiment, however, Rousseau suggests that a universal capacity to relate to and identify with the other retains a primacy, even if it is vitiated by facts such as the effects of distance or the organization of humanity into rival political communities. Moreover Rousseau's example of "our" response to the calamities of the Tartars or the Japanese not only points to a wider sympathy between European peoples beyond the limits of the nation, but even as it links sympathy to proximity does not assume indifference to the sufferings of those more remote.

The compatibility between republican patriotism and larger loyalties that remains largely implicit in *Political Economy* is indicated more clearly in the subsequent "Geneva Manuscript" of the *Social Contract* (1760) in the chapter entitled "On the General Society of the Human Race." Here, Rousseau claims that we "conceive of the general society on the basis of our particular societies; the establishment of small Republics makes us think about the large one, and we do not really begin to become men until after we have been Citizens" (*GM*, CW, 4:81). Republican citizenship itself provides an experience in collective association that may subsequently be universalized; according to Grace Roosevelt, only "by participating in a legitimate political community governed by a will for the common good, in other words, can people form ideas of justice that could be applied to a more general society of the human race."[16] It is true that the emphasis on the sentimental bonds of association and the notion that patriotism itself is partly a derivation from a humanitarian sentiment are missing here. However, Rousseau's argument is directed against the natural law notions of a natural sociability and an originary "general society," and his claim that "the development of society stifles humanity in men's hearts by awakening personal interest" remains in line with his earlier analysis of pity in the *Discourse on Inequality*.[17] In this context, the institution of legitimate republics is a means to revive and enrich a sense of common humanity lost in the passage from nature to society.[18]

Political Economy and the *Geneva Manuscript* suggest that republican citizenship and patriotism derived from a general humanitarian sentiment point intrinsically towards a broader cosmopolitan perspective. Yet these texts present a relatively uncomplicated picture of citizenship that includes little reference to the form of community that binds citizens. Rousseau's *On the Social Contract* (1762) provides a more complete account, but at the same time it introduces tensions challenging for the view that his concept of republican community is a purely political one. At the outset, Rousseau attributes a conventional origin to the political community. The original contract does not institute legitimate political authority or government but society itself—it is "the true basis of society" (*le vrai fondement de la société*) or "the act by which a people becomes a people."[19] Unlike the simple "multitude" produced by the coercive will of a despot and in which "scattered men" are "successively enslaved by one individual," Rousseau's people produces itself freely, through an act that is the first expression of its general will (*SC*, CW, 4:137). However, this contractualist representation is complicated in book 2 in the discussion of the function of the legislator. Although he is initially called to institute the law or discover "the best rules of society suited to Nations," later his task is to "undertake the founding of a people" through the transformation of "each individual, who by himself is a perfect and solitary whole, into a part of a larger whole from which this individual receives, in a sense, his life and his being."[20] Here, the initial distinction between the people or nation and the multitude becomes blurred. The institution of the people is no longer a free act of self-constitution but instead is realized by an exterior agent who moreover acts with a certain violence. Yet a crucial continuity subsists insofar as it remains assumed that society does not precede the formation of the political community but must itself be instituted. A more serious tension appears in the subsequent chapter entitled "On the People." Here, Rousseau uses organic figures to imply both that the existence of the people precedes the intervention of the legislator and that it derives its unity from some form of particularized internal principle. The people now has a unique character to which the law must be suited, similar to the "soil" on which an architect constructs a building, or a life-cycle like that of organisms in which its degree of "maturity" determines its capacity to benefit from instituted legislation.[21]

Although some commentators have suggested they are "simple comparisons," Rousseau's use of organic figures to represent the people or nation as a naturalized community that preexists and whose characteristics determine the action of the legislator resonates with ideas contained in writings as early as the *Discourse on Inequality*.[22] There, he claims that rudimentary forms of social organization gradually differentiate in each country into "a particular Nation, unified by morals [*mœurs*] and character, not by Regulations and Laws but by the same kind of life and foods and by the common influence of Climate" (*DOI*, CW, 3:47). A conception of the nation as a social reality that preexists and conditions the formation of political society thus has its own genealogy in Rousseau's political thought, even if the relation between this idea and his commitment to contractualist political models is not clearly worked through.[23] Moreover, it arguably bears witness to a moment of historical transition in the concept of society towards nineteenth-century organic conceptions of national personality, and at the least signals a recognition of the historical facticity of nations as well as the extent to which historical national identities might function as a constraint on political action, including the formation of a republican polity.

In the *Social Contract*, the concept of a people's maturity suggests a potential conflict between the nation and the action of the legislator, but the problem of conflict *between* nations is not foregrounded. In the *Discourse on Inequality*, however, although the period of primitive nations is characterized as "the least subject to revolutions, the best for man," Rousseau explicitly thematizes the prospect of international conflict based on national differences (*DOI*, CW, 3:48). Speculating on the formation of the first properly political societies, Rousseau claims that their relations are marked from the beginning by a logic of competition:

> It is easily seen how the establishment of a single Society made that of all the others indispensable, and how, to stand up to the united forces, it was necessary to unite in turn. . . . The Bodies Politic, thus remaining in the state of Nature with relation to each other, soon experienced the inconveniences that had forced

individuals to leave it; and among these great Bodies that state became even more fatal than it had previously been among the individuals of whom they were composed. Hence arose the National Wars, Battles, murders, and reprisals which make Nature tremble and shock reason. (*DOI*, CW, 3:55)

Characteristically for Rousseau's unfocused treatment of nationalism, it is not clear whether these newly constituted political societies are continuous with the primitive nations characterized earlier by their harmony. Nonetheless, inherent competition between political societies effectively politicizes national identities, which in turn intensify political rivalries and cause warfare. National rivalries originate in the first instance in the structure of relations between states, which, following Hobbes, Rousseau characterizes as an international state of nature analogous to that between individuals.[24] Within this context, in an inverted representation of his later treatment of patriotism in *Political Economy*, the "horrible prejudices" of national preference give rise to the ironic virtues of bloodshed and "National Wars." Similarly, whereas in *Political Economy* the constriction of the sentiment of humanity necessary to establish republican community left open the possibility of broader sympathies, here in another inversion patriotic attachment is incompatible with cosmopolitan identification that becomes the privilege of an elite: "commiseration . . . losing between one Society and another nearly all the force it had between one man and another, no longer dwells in any but a few great Cosmopolitan Souls, who surmount the imaginary barriers that separate Peoples" (*DOI*, CW, 3:54).

Rousseau's descriptions of the politicization of national identities and the dangers of national identification contradict the more positive representation of patriotism in *Political Economy* and by implication in the *Social Contract*, as well as the notion of a compatibility between patriotism and cosmopolitanism, and raise the controversial problem of the relationship between the *Discourse* and the *Social Contract*.[25] One solution is to contrast the critical, historical perspective of the *Discourse on Inequality* with the constructive and normative perspective of the *Contract*; in this case, it could be supposed that Rousseau holds that the prejudices denounced in the *Discourse* can be moderated or avoided within a legitimate, contractualist republican state, in which a form of patriotism can be inculcated that is not intrinsically aggressive, and in which the "establishment of small Republics makes us think about the large one."[26] However, the tension between contractual and national models of community *within* the *Social Contract* itself undermines any straightforward distinction between the perspectives of "fact" and those of "right" in Rousseau with respect to the national question. Rousseau simply does not clarify the relation between contract, nation, and history, or adequately differentiate legitimate from destructive forms of national attachment. Furthermore, the passages in the *Discourse on Inequality* on international relations establish a problematic that is not opposed to but which situates and contextualizes his republicanism. Whatever the historical existence of nations, the passage from the *Discourse on Inequality* suggests that the international state of nature politicizes national attachments and extrinsically encourages conflict, and there is no reason to believe republics are immune to this process.

ROUSSEAU'S WRITINGS ON WAR AND PEACE

Despite the contrast between Rousseau's denunciation of the excesses of nationalistic violence in the *Discourse on Inequality* and his exaltation of republican patriotism in *Political Economy*, the later work also contains warnings concerning the potential injustices of particularistic identifications within the state and on the international level, even if these are not explicitly linked to nationality. Just as he emphasizes the importance of promoting respect for the law through the inculcation of *amour de la patrie*, Rousseau claims in his discussion of popular sovereignty in this work, anticipating the *Social Contract*, that public deliberations must eschew the false seductions of "private interests" (*intérêts particuliers*) and strive to conform to the "general will" that is the criterion of justice and legislative legitimacy within the republic (*PE*, CW, 3:144). However, in the context of international relations this same general will becomes particularized, as the "private and individual will" of a state in its relations with others. Consequently there is no necessary correlation between internal and external justice; for example, "it is not impossible for a well-governed republic to wage an unjust war" (*PE*, CW, 3:143, 144). In short, republican government itself is not sufficient to ensure peaceful international relations. Granted, this understanding of generality and particularity remains compatible in theory with a cosmopolitan conception of relations between states. Just as individual citizens within the republic subordinate their particular interests to those of the general will, individual states ideally consult the law of nature as a norm to govern their interactions, so that "the large town of the world becomes the body politic, of which the law of nature is always the general will and the various states and peoples are merely individual members" (*PE*, CW, 3:143). Yet unlike the individual state that can compel citizens who refuse to obey,[27] there is no coercive agency that can force states in the "large town of the world" to forgo short-term advantages when these run counter to natural law, even if respect of natural law principles is in their long-term best interest.[28]

These problems of conflict between the interests of states and peoples and the means by which peaceful solutions can be enforced become the focus of Rousseau's writings in the years following *Political Economy* and during his work on the political ideas of the Abbé de Saint-Pierre, culminating in his 1761 *Abstract of Monsieur the Abbé de Saint-Pierre's Plan for Perpetual Peace*. The *Abstract* is ostensibly the précis of the Abbé's solution to the problem of post-Westphalian interstate rivalries, in which "the relative state of the Powers of Europe is properly speaking a state of war."[29] For the Abbé, although an informal "system of Europe" comprised of political, religious, moral, economic, and cultural relations dating to the period of the Roman Empire binds the peoples of Europe in "a social relation, imperfect, but closer than the general and loose knots of humanity," the same system perpetuates structural rivalries between the great powers (*Abstract*, CW, 11:33, 36). In Rousseau's revised formulation, however, this European state of war with its local particularities and parochial jealousies is reframed as a case of a general theoretical problem of international politics.

Combining arguments from *Political Economy* and the *Discourse on Inequality*, Rousseau claims that the origin of international conflict is both largely independent of the internal constitutions of states and inscribed in the structure of international relations: "since each of us is in the civil state with his fellow citizens and in the state of nature with all the rest of the world, we have forestalled private wars only to ignite general ones, which are a thousand times more terrible" (*Abstract*, CW, 11:28). The figure of a conflictual international state of nature recalls the *Discourse*'s image of a Hobbesian condition of anarchic violence intensified by the prejudices of particularistic self-preference rather than the idealistic image of the "large town of the world" in *Political Economy*. That this picture of international conflict is taking form as Rousseau's definitive view is confirmed in a fragment probably composed at the same time as the *Abstract of the Plan for Perpetual Peace*, entitled *The State of War*.[30] Here, Rousseau identifies the same contradiction in international relations as the source of endemic war: "From man to man, we live in the civil state and subject to laws; from people to people, each enjoys natural freedom: which at bottom renders our situation worse than if these distinctions were unknown." The cause of this condition of war lies above all in the rivalrous intimacy that characterizes relations between states. The "imperfect social relation" of European states is again confirmed as a universal characteristic of relations between states, who are defined in purely relative terms.[31] Moreover, Rousseau now definitively rejects the notion that international relations can be regulated consensually through an appeal to "the right of nations" since "it is certain that, for lack of a sanction, its laws are only illusions" (*SOW*, CW, 11:62, 66–67).

In the *Abstract*, Rousseau describes the Abbé's solution to the European state of war as a "form of confederative government" or "European Republic," a contractual union with legislative, judicial, and coercive authority that permits institutional regulation and in which state sovereignty is bound to the confederation in the name of a peace based on the respect of existing constitutions and boundaries (*Abstract*, CW, 11:28, 38). Rousseau's universalization of European political conflicts implies that a similar model contains the solution to the conflicts inherent in all international relations. In *The State of War*, Rousseau seems to endorse such a confederal solution, writing, "In the mixed condition in which we find ourselves . . . by doing either too much or too little, we have not done anything, and we are put into the worst state in which we could find ourselves" (*SOW*, CW, 11:62). Given the lack of guarantees for international law, the claim that "too much or too little" has been done in the establishment of political societies implies that barring a utopian return to the state of nature, a solution to the problem of warfare between states lies in confederal juridical order. Yet Rousseau clearly comes to reject this confederal model. Although circumspect in the *Abstract* with respect to the failure of the Abbé's plan to win general endorsement,[32] Rousseau presents more substantive criticisms in the supplementary *Judgment of the Plan for Perpetual Peace*, unpublished in his lifetime, where the key difficulty turns on the problem of implementation.

Although the Abbé's plan proposes a confederation intended to preserve the existing post-Westphalian balance of power, Rousseau claims in the *Judgment* that the plan also entails consequences for the internal relations of states: "one feels very well that the government of each State is no less settled by the European Diet than its boundaries are, that one cannot guarantee Princes against the revolt of subjects without guaranteeing the subjects against the Tyranny of the Princes at the same time and that otherwise the institution could not continue to exist" (*Judgment*, CW, 11:54). It is not clear whether safeguarding of the universal rights of individuals within member states of the confederation is logically bound to its objective of ending conflict or whether this is intended as a moral injunction by Rousseau, but its effect is to enrich the Abbé's internationalist scheme with a more radical cosmopolitan dimension. In requiring a more stringent internal standard, however, Rousseau also recognizes that the likelihood of a consensual adoption of the scheme is low: "Now I ask whether there is in the world a single sovereign who, limited in this way forever in his dearest plans, would without indignation put up with the mere idea of seeing himself forced to be just, not only with Foreigners, but even with his own subjects" (*Judgment*, CW, 11:54). Implementation of the confederal scheme encounters a problem analogous to the problem of particularity identified in *Political Economy*: "what is useful to the public hardly finds its way in except by force, considering that private interests [*intérêts particuliers*] are almost always opposed to it" (*Judgment*, CW, 11:60). Given the need to use force to compel sovereigns to act in the interest of their peoples, the implementation of the confederation is caught in a vicious circle in which the solution to the problem of violence between states itself depends upon violence, and thus not only its practical efficacy but its legitimacy are in question.[33]

Rousseau is still writing primarily in the *Judgment* with respect to the European context, in which most of the states are monarchies whose rulers are taken to be firmly opposed to any limitation of their prerogatives. For this reason, the question remains open with respect to legitimate republics, who might see their interest as being tied to such a confederation and thus consent to join it. A number of critics have argued that Rousseau's confederalism is limited only to such an association.[34] Rousseau alludes to the concept of a confederation of republics in the *Social Contract* in a passage in which he claims that "I shall show later how it is possible to combine the external power of a great People with the ease of regulation and good order of a small State" (*SC*, CW, 4:194). In a note to this claim he writes that this is what "I had thought of doing in the sequel to this work, when in dealing with foreign relations, I would have discussed confederations. This subject is altogether new, and its principles have yet to be established."[35] A similar allusion appears in the final chapter, where Rousseau concludes: "After setting forth the true principles of political right and trying to found the State on this basis, what remains to be done is to buttress the State by its foreign relations. . . . But all that constitutes a new object, too vast for my limited purview [*ma courte vue*]" (*SC*, CW, 4:224). The passages suggest that while Rousseau remains committed to a confederal solution to the contradictions of international relations, the lack of a theory of confederations in his work derives simply from the labor involved rather than any particular theoretical difficulties.

Nonetheless, Rousseau also provides substantive reasons to be pessimistic regarding the likelihood that even republican states will consent to a confederalist solution. Given his argument in *Political Economy* in which the general will of the republic becomes a particular will in the international context, his concerns with implementation can be generalized, based on his claim in the *Judgment* that "what is useful to the public hardly finds its way in except by force, considering that private interests [*intérêts particuliers*] are almost always opposed to it" (*Judgment*, CW, 11:60). Within the theoretical framework he has consistently adopted, the particularity of opposing interests is a general problem of international relations rather than one specific to monarchical despotism, and it is not clear how republics could be reliably induced to recognize their interests as aligned with those of a confederacy or to join it except by force. It is true that an analogous problem occurs for individuals in the state of nature, but in the *Discourse on Inequality* the problem is solved by subterfuge and swindle, while the solution in the *Social Contract* is the recourse to the legislator, for whom there is no obvious equivalent on the international level.[36] Moreover, comparison of the state of nature for individuals and for nations reveals a fundamental disanalogy. Republics have particularized identities like individuals, but these identities are collective and, as the *Discourse on Inequality* suggests, colored by a form of nationalism that the very structure of the international order has politicized and exacerbated.

In summary, although the topic of international relations preoccupies Rousseau as his political thought matures, the hesitations suggest that he retreats from the logic to which it leads. This is not to deny Rousseau's attraction to holistic and at times totalizing solutions to problems of political theory. However, his claims in the *Social Contract* are probably largely disingenuous and the evidence is that by the time he wrote that text, Rousseau had effectively abandoned the search for a resolution to the problem of international relations in his political writings. Rousseau's ideas on international relations and cosmopolitanism remain provocative, suggestive, and consequential, and the link between his writings on war and peace and Immanuel Kant's conception of a perpetual peace based on cosmopolitical right is clear. Nonetheless, from a strictly logical point of view Rousseau's theory of international society reaches an impasse, and the problems of particularity and force in international relations prove insoluble within the republican framework. Moreover, this impasse has dramatic consequences for the viability of republican government itself, perpetually menaced by violence from the outside or forced to seek refuge in forms of isolation and autarky.[37] Yet the *Social Contract* does not represent Rousseau's last word on cosmopolitanism. The "moral" cosmopolitanism that he advocates in *Emile* may be read as an attempt to resolve the impasses of cosmopolitanism encountered in the political writings on another level, in the form of literature and fiction.[38]

COSMOPOLITAN CULTURE AND THE "SEEDS OF HUMANITY" IN *EMILE*

The cosmopolitan logic that underlies Rousseau's confederalism in his writings on the Abbé de Saint-Pierre and the *Social Contract* appears far removed from the preoccupations of his pedagogical treatise *Emile, or, On Education* (1762), which is usually read as a plan for a private education, a "domestic education or the education of nature" rather than a "public education."[39] Rousseau's framing of the difference between domestic and public education is couched in terms familiar from the writings on war and peace. In a passage that recalls the analysis of patriotism in *Political Economy,* Rousseau claims that the purpose of true public, political education is to "denature" the individual in order to get him to identify with the state as a second self and subsume his particularity in the generality of the community: "Good social institutions are those that best know how to denature man, to take his absolute existence from him in order to give him a relative one and transport the *I* into the common unity, with the result that each individual believes himself no longer one but a part of the unity and no longer feels except within the whole" (*Emile*, CW, 13:164). However, Rousseau now laments public education as the hallmark of a lost classical age of republican government: "Public instruction no longer exists and can no longer exist, because where there is no longer fatherland, there can no longer be citizens" (*Emile*, CW, 13:165). The turn to domestic education, then, reflects a pessimism similar to the one that informed Rousseau's negative judgments on the prospects for confederations in the *Judgment*, but now turned more radically to the republican project itself. Moreover, the spiritually impoverished systems of public education enforced by the despotic political structures of contemporary Europe are denounced as installing "contradictions" between nature and society that resemble those embodied in the anarchy of the international system: "He who in the civil order wants to preserve the primacy of the sentiments of nature does not know what he wants. Always in contradiction with himself, always floating between his inclinations and his duties, he will never be either man or citizen" (*Emile*, CW, 13:164). Since the reform of public education is contingent on an improbable reform of the absolutist political structures of Europe, the only alternative to these contradictions seemingly lies in the private sphere, in a domestic plan for a private individual that is also figured as a return to nature.[40]

The most perplexing interpretative question posed by *Emile* concerns Rousseau's concept of a natural education. Passages at the beginning of the work suggest that it is premised on something like a return to the state of nature, yet as Rousseau later puts it, "although I want to form the man of nature, the object is not, for all that, to make him a savage."[41] However, if education is represented as a form of cultivation and its condition of possibility is a malleability or lack in nature in which "[e]verything we do not have at our birth and which we need when we are grown is given us by education," the concept of a natural education risks theoretical incoherence (*Emile*, CW, 13:162). It is true that Rousseau often associates domesticity and nature in his representations of the private sphere, where the concept of the natural serves to delineate an order whose primary task is the regulation of gender roles and sexuality (e.g., the *Lettre à d'Alembert* and *Julie, ou la nouvelle Héloïse*). This broader conception of naturally determined gender roles is employed in book 5 of *Emile* in Rousseau's discussion of the education suited to prepare Emile's bride Sophie for marriage, but does not account for the crucial passages in book 4 that treat Emile's socialization and preparation for a public life beyond the domestic realm.[42] A more promising solution is to suggest that the tension between nature and education or culture and society can be minimized once it is understood that Emile's education presupposes a sociability that is not given immediately in nature but is a natural potentiality that can be cultivated.[43] Yet it remains unclear whether this elegant interpretation can account for Rousseau's insistence that Emile's education diverges from the socialization of the mixed system that leaves its pupil "always in contradiction with himself."

In fact, comparison of *Emile* with the political writings provides an answer to this question, revealing that Rousseau's account of Emile's alternative socialization invokes a logic based on a cosmopolitan version of the more limited model of public, political education. At the core of this process is the cultivation of the humanitarian sentiments in a manner analogous to the inculcation of patriotism in political education in *Political Economy*. In *Emile* these sentiments, including "goodness, humanity, commiseration, beneficence," have their origin in pity, the "first relative sentiment which touches the human heart according to the order of nature" (*Emile*, CW, 13:375, 374). The reference to pity implies that these sentiments are natural, but Rousseau insists that they must be deliberately cultivated by the educator: "The first sentiment of which a carefully raised young man is capable is not love; it is friendship. The first act of his nascent imagination is to teach him that he has fellows [*semblables*]; and the species affects him before the female sex. Here is another advantage of prolonged innocence—that of profiting from nascent sensibility to sow in the young adolescent's heart the first seeds of humanity" (*Emile*, CW, 13:371–72). The imagination awakens spontaneously in adolescence, permitting the recognition of the other as a *semblable* with whom one can identify and through whom one can attain an awareness of a common humanity. However, as in *Political Economy*, the full development of this nascent sensibility requires the active intervention of the teacher, through his careful sowing of its first seeds in the young adolescent's heart.

As in *Political Economy*, the successful cultivation of the seeds of humanity is also premised upon a process of identification in which the individual substitutes for a particular identity an identity as part of a collective totality. In the earlier text Rousseau claimed that public education must help individuals "to identify themselves in some way with this larger whole; to feel themselves to be members of the fatherland" (*PE*, CW, 3:155), and at the beginning of *Emile* Rousseau writes that unlike natural man who is a "numerical unity, the absolute whole," civil man "is only a fractional unity dependent on the denominator; his value is determined by his relation to the whole, which is the social body" (*Emile*, CW, 13:164). The same idea underlies Emile's own education, except that for the social body Rousseau substitutes the universal community of human beings: "So long as his sensibility remains limited to his own individuality, there is nothing moral in his actions. It is only when it begins to extend outside of himself that it takes on, first, the sentiments and, then, the notions of good and evil which truly constitute him as a man and an integral part of his species" (*Emile*, CW, 13:371). Rather than the preservation of a natural "numerical unity" or "absolute whole" Rousseau implies that Emile's education for humanity presupposes, like the education of a citizen, the relation to a "denominator." Emile's sensibility must extend beyond the limits of the individual if he is to become an "integral part of his species." Moreover, Rousseau reiterates the need for the active participation of the educator who must direct his pupil's imagination for the purpose of "ordering his affections"; in accordance with the principle of the natural education, this process initially seems intended to maintain the pupil within the limits of nature: "to set forth the proper means for keeping him in the order of nature is to say enough about how he can depart from it" (*Emile*, CW, 13:371). Yet this apparent warning to the instructor proves equivocal given Rousseau's insistence that Emile's sensibility must "extend outside of himself." The very possibility of leaving one's place, the transportation of the self outside itself by means of the direction of the imagination, proves to be the condition of becoming human. In the education of the man of nature, man himself is produced through a departure from nature, a denaturalization that once again recalls the objective of political education to "transport the *I* into the common unity." However, the difference here, both with respect to political education and its debased contemporary variant, lies in Rousseau's sense that this departure remains in harmony with natural principles, with the potential inherent in the seeds of humanity dormant in each individual.

The fact that *Emile* follows a cosmopolitan logic at odds with the ostensible focus on private education has been noted by some critics, including Ernst Cassirer who claims that Emile's education is intended to "found a new and truly universal humanity."[44] However, Cassirer's framework remains Rousseau's writings on republicanism and the *Social Contract*, and this universal humanity is referred to the context of a future state.[45] More recently, Grace Roosevelt has insisted on the work's cosmopolitan aspect and argues like Cassirer that "Emile's education does not deny him citizenship, but his is a citizenship that will be humanitarian rather than patriotic."[46] Roosevelt puts *Emile* in the context of the writings on war and peace rather than the *Social Contract*, and claims this education is compatible with the theory of confederations elaborated in the *Abstract*.[47] Yet although Emile's education clearly invokes the principal figures of the political texts, the logic of the particular and the general that underpins both Rousseau's conceptions of political education and of international relations culminates in his pedagogical treatise in a cosmopolitan universalism that is moral rather than political, as the author indicates in the passage above in the claim that as long as his "sensibility remains limited to his own individuality, there is nothing moral in his actions." Moreover, in light of the *Judgment* and Rousseau's failure to resolve the impasses of international relations, this moral cosmopolitanism must be read as essentially consolatory, as the work's disillusioned final pages confirm when Rousseau claims that Emile's subordination of his particular interest to the universal community of humanity obeys a higher law radically opposed to those of all existing governments.[48]

In the opening pages of *Emile*, following his claim that "every patriot is harsh to foreigners. They are only men. They are nothing in his eyes," Rousseau warns his reader against "those cosmopolitans who go to great length in their books to discover duties they do not deign to fulfill around them" (*Emile*, CW, 13:164). In light of the potential compatibility of patriotic allegiance with larger loyalties in *Political Economy*, this view of patriotism as radically incompatible with humanitarian feeling seems jaundiced, while the suggestion that cosmopolitanism entails the substitution of a bookish relation to humanity for fulfillment of duties to one's fellow citizens disavows the cosmopolitan logic that subsequently underpins Emile's own education. Rousseau's educator finally exhorts Emile to fulfill his humanitarian commitments locally and through the "love of neighbor," in the bucolic context of "the patriarchal and rustic life, man's first life," where from his "simple retreat" he and Sophie might "vivify the country and reanimate the extinguished zeal of the unfortunate village folk" (*Emile*, CW, 13:668). This suggestion that a real and authentic cosmopolitanism requires practical action on the local level through the relief of suffering and the promotion of individual dignity through pastoral independence and self-sufficiency[49] remains indissociable, however, from what amounts to a withdrawal from politics—the "large town of the world" has here become the village. Furthermore, the increasing fictionalization of *Emile* itself, the movement from the first predominantly theoretical sections to the concluding romance of Emile and Sophie, invites the charge that the work's "solution" to the impasses of international relations is itself no more than a literary and imaginary compensation.[50] Nonetheless, *Emile* reveals more clearly than the previous writings in its conception of the seeds of humanity the extent to which, for Rousseau, the imagination and its capacity for identification are themselves formative of community.[51] Moreover, it suggests that even if Rousseau is right that conflict between states is structural and endemic and that there is no essential correlation between justice and good government in national as opposed to international affairs—in other words, that the cosmopolitan ideal of perpetual peace is but a dream—it does not follow that we are relieved of an obligation to pursue cosmopolitan goals understood in moral terms, particularly when our domestic political institutions also appear broken and unreformable.

Finally, Emile's teacher's injunction to act locally aims only to preclude empty talk in lieu of deeds and does not impede effective humanitarian action on the national and international level. Instead, Rousseau's *Emile* affirms that humanitarianism, rather than a narrow nationalism, must become the principle underpinning our moral, educational, and social commitments. It is here that we find Rousseau's final cosmopolitan legacy—in an ideal whose principles are also recognizable as those of the DIGNITY project—and of this book.

NOTES

1. Among the most influential remain Jürgen Habermas, "Kant's Idea of Perpetual Peace: At Two Hundred Years' Historical Remove," in *The Inclusion of the Other*, ed. Ciaran Cronin and Pablo De Greiff (Cambridge, MA: MIT Press, 1998); Seyla Benhabib, *Another Cosmopolitanism* (Oxford: Oxford University Press, 2006); Jacques Derrida, *Cosmopolites de tous les pays, encore un effort!* (Paris: Galilée, 1997); Bonnie Honig, *Democracy and the Foreigner* (Princeton: Princeton University Press, 2001); Julia Kristeva, *Etrangers à nous-mêmes* (Paris: Fayard, 1988); and Martha Nussbaum, "Patriotism and Cosmopolitanism," in *For Love of Country: Debating the Limits of Patriotism*, ed. Joshua Cohen, 3–17 (Boston: Beacon Press, 1996).

2. On the distinction between thick and thin moral concepts, see Michael Walzer, *Thick and Thin: Moral Argument at Home and Abroad* (Notre Dame, IN: University of Notre Dame Press, 1994). See Costas Douzinas's critique of "military humanitarianism" in *Human Rights and Empire: The Political Philosophy of Cosmopolitanism* (New York: Routledge-Cavendish, 2007), and Paul Gilroy's indictment of "armored cosmopolitanism" in *Postcolonial Melancholia* (New York: Columbia University Press, 2005), esp. chap. 2, "Cosmopolitanism Contested." For a recent defense of nationalism, see Benedict Anderson, "Nationalism, Identity, and the World-in-Motion: On the Logics of Seriality," in *Cosmopolitics: Thinking and Feeling beyond the Nation*, ed. Pheng Cheah and Bruce Robbins, 117–33 (Minneapolis: University of Minnesota Press, 1998).

3. Pheng Cheah, "The Cosmopolitical—Today," in Cheah and Robbins, *Cosmopolitics,* 23. For Kant's writings on cosmopolitanism, see "Idea for a Universal History with a Cosmopolitan Purpose," 41–53, and "Perpetual Peace: A Philosophical Sketch," 93–130, in *Kant: Political Writings,* ed. Hans Reiss, trans. H. B. Nisbet (Cambridge: Cambridge University Press, 1991).

4. For Kant's acknowledgment of Rousseau's influence on his ideal of a global order regulated by cosmopolitan right, see "Idea for a Universal History with a Cosmopolitan Purpose," 47.

5. Honig, *Democracy and the Foreigner,* 13.

6. According to Rousseau's Pléiade editors, "Rousseau est, semble-t-il, le premier de nos écrivains du XVIIIe siècle à avoir employé le mot *cosmopolite* dans le sens d'ami du genre humain et de citoyen de l'univers." J.-J. Rousseau, *Œuvres completes,* vol. 3, ed. Bernard Gagnebin and Marcel Raymond (Paris: Gallimard, 1959–95), 1414.

7. See Honig, *Democracy and the Foreigner,* and also Kenneth N. Waltz, *Man, the State, and War: A Theoretical Analysis* (New York: Columbia University Press, 1959), 176–77.

8. "Rousseau was the apostle not only of the small state but of modern nationalism." F. H. Hinsley, *Power and the Pursuit of Peace: Theory and Practice in the History of Relations Between States* (Cambridge: Cambridge University Press, 1963), 55.

9. Honig, *Democracy and the Foreigner,* 30.

10. Georg Cavallar, "'La société générale du genre humain': Rousseau on Cosmopolitanism, International Relations, and Republican Patriotism," in *From Republican Polity to National Community: Reconsiderations of Enlightenment Political Thought,* ed. Paschalis M. Kitromildis, 89–109, Studies on Voltaire and the Eighteenth Century 9 (2003): 90.

11. See Cavallar, "La société générale," 90. For a similar view, see Grace Roosevelt, *Reading Rousseau in the Nuclear Age* (Philadelphia: Temple University Press, 1990), 87–89.

12. Honig's interpretation is supported by the notorious line from *Emile*: "Every patriot is harsh to foreigners. They are only men. They are nothing in his eyes" (*Emile,* CW, 13:163).

13. On the spread of nationalist ideology in Europe, see Pheng Cheah, *Inhuman Conditions: On Cosmopolitanism and Human Rights* (Cambridge, MA: Harvard University Press, 2006), 23–24. On *peuple* and *nation,* see book 2, chapters 7–8, of the *Social Contract,* in which Rousseau uses the terms interchangeably, e.g., "For nations as for men there is a time of youth, or maturity if you prefer, that must be awaited before subjecting them to laws. But the maturity of a people is not always easy to recognize" (*SC,* CW, 4:158).

14. In *Political Economy,* "interest" and "commiseration" are analogues for the sentiments of *amour-propre* and "pity" that Rousseau first theorizes in the *Discourse on Inequality* (*DOI,* CW, 3:15, 36–38). Rousseau also uses the term *amour-propre* as a synonym for interest in *Political Economy,* and in the *Discourse on Inequality* he explains that *amour-propre* is the debased social form of *amour de soi,* defined as the natural sentiment that "interests us ardently in our well-being and our self-preservation" (*DOI,* CW, 3:15); *amour de soi* is translated as "love of oneself" in the CW, while *amour-propre* is left untranslated; see the editor's note (3:181). Rousseau is thus consistent when he claims later in the *Social Contract* that political societies are instituted when the capacity of individuals to satisfy their needs independently in the state of nature is outmatched by "obstacles to their self-preservation" (*SC,*

CW, 4:138). However, this origin of the state in *amour de soi* or *amour-propre* also motivates Rousseau's insistence that it is not sufficient to respect individual liberty or formal equality before the law or for the state "to have citizens and protect them; it is also necessary to think about their subsistence" (*PE*, CW, 3:157). Insofar as it functions as a *political* concept, Rousseau's conception of *amour de soi* entails not just a right to life but a right to what is needed to sustain oneself in life free of personal dependency, and thus has redistributive implications so that "with regard to wealth, no citizen should be so opulent that he can buy another, and none so poor that he is constrained to sell himself" (*SC*, CW, 4:162). For this reason, it can also be viewed as introducing a basic conception of the dignity of the human person—understood as the right to an economic minimum—into his political theory.

15. As Rousseau wrote, "every man is virtuous when his private will conforms on all matters with the general will, and we willingly want what is wanted by the people we love" (*PE*, CW, 3:151).

16. Roosevelt, *Reading Rousseau in the Nuclear Age*, 89.

17. *GM*, CW, 4:78. As Roosevelt notes, the chapter critiques both the jurisnaturalist tradition identified with Grotius and Pufendorf and the article "Natural Right" written by Diderot in the *Encyclopédie* in 1755. Roosevelt, *Reading Rousseau in the Nuclear Age*, 77.

18. The "violent interlocutor" who prefers his private interest to the common good is enjoined to observe "the loveable harmony of justice and happiness in a better constituted order of things . . . that reason which led him astray will bring him back to humanity" (*GM*, CW, 4:82).

19. *SC*, CW, 4:137. See also book 3, chapter 1: "Thus those who claim that the act by which a people subjects itself to leaders is not a contract are entirely right" (*SC*, CW, 4:166–67).

20. *SC*, CW, 4:154, 155. This conception of the legislator's function draws on the earlier discussion of political education in *Political Economy*.

21. *SC*, CW, 4:157–58. A similar figure appears in *Political Economy*: "The body politic, taken individually, can be considered to be like a body that is organized, living, and similar to that of a man" (*PE*, CW, 3:142).

22. See for example Robert Derathé in his foreword to the Pléiade edition of the political writings, Rousseau, *Œuvres complètes*, 3:lxxxiv.

23. For F. H. Hinsley the tension between contract and history in the *Social Contract* reflects Rousseau's confusion of state and society "from his disposition to argue that some times that society was the result of a contract, of the willful use of art and contrivance, and at others that it was the product of long historical growth." Hinsley, *Power and the Pursuit of Peace*, 56.

24. Rousseau argues against Hobbes, however, that unlike the international state of nature, the state of nature for individuals is "le plus propre à la Paix, et le plus convenable au Genre-humain" (*DOI*, CW, 3:153).

25. The best general discussion of this problem remains Jean Starobinski, *Rousseau: La transparence et l'obstacle* (Paris: Gallimard, 1971), 36–48.

26. The position adopted in Roosevelt, *Reading Rousseau in the Nuclear Age*, 87–89.

27. In the *Social Contract*, Rousseau writes that this condition "alone gives legitimacy to civil engagements which without it would be absurd, tyrannical, and subject to the most enormous abuses" (*SC*, CW, 4:141).

28. This problem of competition versus cooperation in pursuit of a common interest is encapsulated in Rousseau's account of the "stag hunt" often studied as a prototype of the social contract, whether national or international, by game and international relations theorists (*DOI*, CW, 3:45). Most common interpretations emphasize the obstacles to cooperation in Rousseau's parable of the hunt, obstacles that Rousseau's own analysis of the problems of international political society nonetheless explores in a more sustained and nuanced fashion. See Brian Skyrms, *The Stag Hunt and the Evolution of Social Structure* (Cambridge: Cambridge University Press, 2004), and Ken Binmore, *Game Theory and the Social Contract*, vol. 1, *Playing Fair* (Cambridge, MA: MIT Press, 1994), 121–24.

29. *Abstract*, CW, 11:32. The Pléiade editors note that in accepting the commission to write abstracts of the Abbé's works Rousseau reserved the right to comment and to some extent introduce his own ideas. Rousseau, *Œuvres complètes*, 3:cxxvii.

30. See Rousseau, *Œuvres complètes*, 3:cxlvi, for a discussion of the history of the fragment.

31. As Rousseau writes, "since the size of the body politic is purely relative, it is forced constantly to compare itself in order to know itself; it depends on everything that surrounds it, and must take an interest in everything that happens there" (*SOW*, CW, 11:67).

32. "Thus, if, in spite of all this, this Plan remains unexecuted, it is not because it is chimerical; it is because men are insane, and because it is a sort of folly to be wise in the midst of fools" (*Abstract*, CW, 11:49).

33. "One does not see federative Leagues established by any way other than by revolutions, and on this principle who among us would dare to state whether this European League is to be desired or to be feared. Perhaps it would cause more harm all at once than it would prevent for centuries" (*Judgment*, CW, 11:60).

34. See Waltz, *Man, the State, and War*, 185, who views Rousseau as a strong advocate of federalism. See also Joseph-Lucien Windenberger, *Essai sur le système de politique étrangère de J.-J. Rousseau: La République confédérative des petits états* (Geneva: Slatkine, 1982), who claims that "le Contrat social postulait le Contrat international" (49) in the form not of a federal state but of a confederation of nationalities; also, C. E. Vaughan, who follows Windenberger with some misgivings: *The Political Writings of Jean-Jacques Rousseau* (New York: John Wiley and Sons, 1962).

35. *SC*, CW, 4:194. According to the *Confessions*, the *Social Contract* is the excerpt of a larger unfinished work called the *Institutions politiques* and which Rousseau supposedly burnt (*Conf*, CW, 5:432). Rousseau's theory of confederations can be taken to represent a part of this unfinished work, along with the fragment on the *The State of War*. See the note by the Pléiade editors, Rousseau, *Œuvres complètes*, 3:cxlvi.

36. "All ran to meet their chains believing they ensured their freedom" (*DOI*, CW, 3:54). "Since the Legislator is therefore unable to use either force or reasoning, he must necessarily have recourse to another order of authority, which can win over without violence and persuade without convincing" (*SC*, CW, 4:156).

37. See the *Plan for a Constitution for Corsica* (1765) and the *Considerations on the Government of Poland* (1771); it is doubtful whether Rousseau imagined these plans could be implemented.

38. Louis Althusser suggests such a relation between the political and fictional texts in his Marxian analysis of the *décalages* in the *Social Contract*: "il reste pourtant un re-

cours . . . le transfert de l'impossible solution théorique dans l'autre de la théorie, la littérature." Louis Althusser, "Sur le *Contrat Social*," in *Solitude de Machiavel*, ed. Yves Sintomer (Paris: Presses Universitaires de France, 1998), 93.

39. *Emile*, CW, 13:165. On this point, see Laurence Mall, *Emile ou les figures de la fiction* (Oxford: Voltaire Foundation, 2002), 39, and Pierre Burgelin, *La Philosophie de l'existence de J.J. Rousseau* (Paris: Presses Universitaires de France, 1952), 497.

40. "Forced to combat nature or the social institutions, one must choose between making a man or a citizen, for one cannot make both at the same time" (*Emile*, CW, 13:163).

41. *Emile*, CW, 13:412. "Natural man is entirely for himself. He is numerical unity, the absolute whole which is relative only to itself or its kind" (*Emile*, CW, 13:164).

42. "[E]ach, in fulfilling nature's ends according to its own particular purpose" (*Emile*, CW, 13:532).

43. Thus, although in the *Discourse* Rousseau writes that nature little "prepared [men's] Sociability," he also claims that from pity "flow all the social virtues" (*DOI*, CW, 3:33, 37). For a reading along these lines see Yves Vargas, *Introduction à l'Emile de Rousseau* (Paris: Presses Universitaires de France, 1995) and *Rousseau: L'énigme du sexe* (Paris: Presses Universitaires de France, 1997).

44. Cassirer, *The Question of Jean-Jacques Rousseau*, trans. Peter Gay (Bloomington: Indiana University Press, 1963), 124.

45. As Cassirer writes, "Rousseau's plan of education by no means rules out Emile's education to citizenship, but it educates him exclusively to be a 'citizen among those who are to be.'" Cassirer, *The Question of Jean-Jacques Rousseau*, 123.

46. Roosevelt, *Reading Rousseau in the Nuclear Age*, 165.

47. "[T]he pedagogy of *Emile* provides an apt preparation for the interdependent world of the *Project for Perpetual Peace*." Roosevelt, *Reading Rousseau in the Nuclear Age*, 9.

48. "Laws! Where are there laws, and where are they respected? Everywhere you have seen only individual interest and men's passions reigning under this name. But the eternal laws of nature and order do exist. For the wise man, they take the place of positive law. They are written in the depth of his heart by conscience and reason" (*Emile*, CW, 13:666–67). Compare also Rousseau's analogous distinction between the "religion of man" and the "religion of the citizen" in the *Social Contract* (*SC*, CW, 4:216–24).

49. Just as in the legitimate state respect for individual dignity involves the provision of an economic minimum necessary to prevent personal dependency, the conclusion of *Emile* makes clear that for Rousseau the duties flowing from humanitarian sentiment include not only a sympathetic response to suffering but also practical assistance intended to strengthen the *amour de soi* of the recipient through economic independence.

50. On this topic see Peter Jimack, *La Genèse et la rédaction de l'Émile de J.-J. Rousseau* (Geneva: Institut et Musée Voltaire, 1960).

51. Compare with the *Discourse on Inequality*, and the "few great Cosmopolitan Souls, who surmount the imaginary barriers that separate Peoples and who, following the example of the sovereign Being who created them, include the whole human Race in their benevolence" (*DOI*, CW, 3:54).

CHAPTER 7

The Madness of the Double
Rousseau Judge of Jean-Jacques

Serge Margel
Translated by Alison Rice and Eva Yampolsky

> *Nothing is as unlike me as myself.*
> —Jean-Jacques Rousseau, *Le Persifleur*

From the *Confessions* to *Rousseau Judge of Jean-Jacques: Dialogues* to the *Reveries of the Solitary Walker*, Rousseau created a new fictional space in autobiography: a space of writing that is at once literary and political, and which underlines the link between autobiography and fiction. In order to speak of oneself, to write about one's life, a certain space is necessary. But this must be an *other space*, a space that is other than the place of language, one that always addresses someone and cannot help saying something to someone else. Rousseau speaks of this space while he invents, constructs, and produces it; he stages it as the one and only place, the last place where his voice could be heard, his speech expressed, or his soul seen in all of its truth. And who better than Rousseau to question the ambiguous status of truth and problematize the discourse of truth? Before the modern philosophers and authors such as Friedrich Nietzsche, Antonin Artaud, or Michel Foucault, there was no one who revealed the rhetorical operations beneath truth and lies, there was no one who brought them to light, and more pointedly, there was no one who denounced them better than Rousseau did. Under what conditions is a discourse of truth possible? To what extent can one *say* the truth, since every discourse is in principle already predetermined, interpreted, or falsified, always caught in the trap of denial, deceit, or lie? Isn't it precisely in order to tell the truth that fiction making becomes necessary? According to Rousseau, truth is not opposed to fiction, nor is there any truthful discourse that can exist without fiction. There can be no truth, then, without a fictional operation that permits one to invent or to fictionalize a space that does not exist. The space in question does not yet exist, nor does it exist anymore; it is another space, a space of "unworking" or *désoeuvrement*, as Rousseau says in the *Reveries*. It is a place out of context and out of view; it comes from another world at the limits of language. Yet it nonetheless provides discourse with the means to produce its own conditions of truth.

Rousseau constructed a space of unworking as he wrote each successive text, moving from the *Confessions* to the *Dialogues* to the *Reveries,* but more importantly, in each text he reinvests or reconsiders each of the others as a fictive staging of his own unworking. Indeed, the fiction of the *Confessions* is not that of the *Dialogues*, nor that of the *Reveries*. Nevertheless, fiction is reproduced from one text to the next, each one anticipates the next and intertwines or links itself to the others. The *Reveries* speak of the *Dialogues* as well as of the *Confessions*, while the *Confessions* already announce the *Reveries* and their *unworking*. Let us begin with the *Dialogues* because it is a key, pivotal, and controversial text. It is also a difficult text, which resists analysis, refuses categorization as a literary genre, defies criticism, and shrugs off the rules of classical autobiography. The dialogical form of the *Dialogues* is more monological than ever. In other words, it is the splitting of voices that "divides" speech— to use Rousseau's word—from within, and that divides the subject's life into two individuals: a man and an author. This radical divide is without return; it is a veritable trauma and allows for no repair, restoration, or reestablishment. Rousseau suffers from it because he puts himself in it, that is to say, he subjects himself to the fictional operation of autobiography. The *Dialogues* not only speak of this place, indicating it, evoking it, and describing it as a place of thought, salvation, and survival, but by their very form, by its genre, narration, and syntax, they elaborate it as a place of fiction.

When finishing the *Confessions*, between 1767 and 1770, Rousseau asked to be called Jean-Jacques Renou, a pseudonym or mask that he abandoned when writing *Rousseau Judge of Jean-Jacques: Dialogues*. Signing his texts once again in his name, his being was divided into two individuals, and the unified figure of Jean-Jacques Rousseau, his own identity, disappeared from the *Dialogues*. It split or faded away and became a ghost. Three new names, figures, or identities appear from this point on: first of all there is "Rousseau," who, beneath the features of an honest man, is reduced merely to the name of the author, the only thing the public knew of Rousseau in his lifetime. Second, there is "the Frenchman": the anonymous figure of the public. He is an actor in an imposturous plot who steals Rousseau's proper name, falsifies it, and accuses it of crimes. He reduces it to the imposters' understanding, or misunderstanding, of his work. Finally, there is the ghostlike, spectral character of "Jean-Jacques": a third party dispossessed of any social identity and deprived of a patronymic proper name. An ever-present, recurrent, dominant figure, Jean-Jacques alone represents the place of scission that splits the individual from within. There is the Jean-Jacques of Rousseau, who represents the author of the books, and the Jean-Jacques of the Frenchman, who is neither more nor less than the author of the crimes. As the Rousseau of the *Dialogues* declares, "I told you without mystery and I will repeat it for you without evasion. The strength of your proofs leaves me with no doubt whatever about the crimes they attest, and about that I think exactly as you do. But you combine things that I separate. The Author of the Books and of the crimes appears to you to be the same person. I believe I am correct to see them as two. This, Sir, is the key to the enigma" (*Dialogues*, CW, 1:13).

From the outset, the voice is split and thus creates a new space of fiction. It is precisely the fictional space that the *Dialogues* stage, between the two figures of a character, dispossessed and deprived of his proper name. This doubling of the individual—this divide between the author of the books and the author of the crimes, between he who wrote *The Social Contract* and *Emile* and he who was slandered, cursed, accused of all possible infamies—arises from a genealogy of alienation. In the *Dialogues*, Rousseau speaks of his alterity as a biographical event and as a fictionalized, psychological trauma. But the moment of alienation was real. It can be dated, situated, verified, and archived. In fact, it coincides with the moment when he was published, and thus with the advent of a public audience and with an authorial name. It also coincides with the first occurrence of a plot—in particular the quarrel with Hume—that led to the loss of his proper name. One could call this the trauma of name confusion; in the *Dialogues* it is described hence: "You must admit that this man's destiny has some striking peculiarities. *His life is divided into two parts* that seem to belong to two different individuals, with the period that separates them—meaning the time when he published books—marking the death of one and the birth of the other" (*Dialogues*, CW, 1:14, my emphasis).

The two parts of the torn individual separate here: one dies and the other is born. From here on, one becomes or is confused with the other, just as the Frenchman seeks to *combine* what Rousseau intends to *separate*. The *Dialogues* present a new system of alterity which is directly connected to the fictional operation of autobiography. In the opening lines of the *Confessions*, Rousseau evoked the figure of the other as the mark of singularity, a trait of irreducible difference, of the unique, the incomparable, that inscribes itself in the legendary chain of exemplarity: "I am forming an undertaking which has no precedent, and the execution of which will have no imitator whatsoever. I wish to show my fellows a man in all the truth of nature; and this man will be myself. Myself alone. I feel my heart and I know men. I am not made like any of the ones I have seen; I dare to believe that *I am not made like any that exist*. If I am worth no more, at least I am different. Whether nature has done well or ill in breaking the mold in which it cast me, is something which cannot be judged until I have been read" (*Conf*, CW, 5:5, my emphasis).

Here, alterity represents a figure of absolute difference that founds or legitimizes the value of a discourse of truth. Inasmuch as I am absolutely and irreducibly other, my alterity guarantees the value of my discourse. In the *Dialogues*, however, the figure of the other represents a genesis, a becoming-other, a transformation, a transfer, in which one dies in the other, thus creating a new discursive system. In order to speak of oneself, to create a self-portrait or to depict oneself truthfully, it no longer suffices to determine a discourse, to affirm, to defend, or to shield one's truth from a public, because the public wants nothing of it, despite what the *Confessions* had affirmed and hoped. It is no longer enough to move forward, naked in one's alterity, to tell the truth, "to count on winning back the public," or renewing its agreement, recognition, and love, as Rousseau writes in the *Reveries* (*Reveries*, CW, 8:6). Confronted with the anonymous ghost of the public who judges, sees, and speaks only in order to inflict hurt, the singularity of Rousseau—his thoughts, the confessions of his heart, and his voice—no longer suffice. The fictional space of discourse deepens from the *Confessions* to the *Dialogues*. In order to tell the truth, to speak of myself truthfully, I can no longer simply say that I am other or present myself in my alterity; from now on I must produce that alterity, invent it by taking the place of the other—by seeing myself as if I were an other. This is the very purpose of the *Dialogues*:

> A proud, disdainful silence is more appropriate in such a case, and would have been more to my taste. But it would not have fulfilled my purpose, and to do so, *it was necessary for me to say through which eye, if I were another, I would see a man such as I am.* I have tried to discharge such a difficult duty equitably and impartially—without insulting the incredible blindness of the public, without proudly boasting about these virtues it refuses to see in me, yet without accusing myself of vices I do not have, with which it [the public] takes pleasure in charging me— by explaining simply what I would deduce about a constitution like mine carefully studied in another man. (*Dialogues*, CW, 1:6, emphasis mine, translation slightly modified)

How is this sentence to be read, since it makes the "purpose" of the *Dialogues*— its objective, goal, and intention—into the very problem and the main question to be addressed? How are we to understand the following: "it was necessary for me to say through which eye, if I were another, I would see a man such as I am"? How is this statement to be interpreted, if the *Dialogues* were written only with the objective to "fulfill [this] purpose"? Finally, in all the ambiguity of its grammar, syntax, and rhetoric, in the uncertainty of its meaning as well, has this statement not already traced an invisible guiding thread, a fictional space, that continues from the *Confessions* to the *Reveries*? It is indeed this fictional space that allows one to read or to reread the *Confessions* through the *Reveries*, autobiography through unworking, truth through fiction. This statement speaks of the *Confessions*. By allusion, it evokes the desperate search for justice, the expectation from the public, the wish to find at least one man on earth capable of seeing Rousseau as he is, beyond all lies, deceit, and artifice. This project of justification, explanation, and excuses, the desire to confess, to "show all of oneself to the public," will never fulfill the purpose of the *Dialogues*. Once again, when confronted with the public's lies and the immortal plot of imposture, confessing or justifying oneself to another in the expectation that the other will see me in my truth, recognize me in my alterity, and acknowledge my alterity as a value of truth, is no longer enough in order to tell the truth of a "man such as I am."

The new purpose of the *Dialogues* also implies or supposes another language, another way of saying, addressing, or referring to something. The language of the *Dialogues* no longer speaks to anyone, for the speaking subject here is not trying to say something to someone else in order to convince them, to receive their reply, or to gain their acceptance. Quite to the contrary. The dialogical force here invents a new system of alterity, of address, and of the addressee. Not only is the other in the *Dialogues* no longer reduced to the figure of difference—mine or that of the other—but his very reality is invented like a work of fiction. The language of the *Dialogues* is spoken by a subject who is permeated by fiction, as is proper to his alterity. It is no longer the same person who speaks to the other, yet it will always be a subject who can only speak in the place of the other: "it was necessary for me to say through which eye, if I were another, I would see a man such as I am." Later, Rousseau would comment on this statement. Everything rests on the question of the *eye*, the eye of the other, and even more on the *discourse* that enunciates, names, and points it out. One must name this eye, situate its point of view, and indicate the scene or the space from which this eye—of the other—will see a man such as I am. Indeed, the eye of the other represents the fictional space of autobiography, thereby inventing another system of alterity.

To speak of this eye, according to Rousseau, one must explain "simply what I would deduce about a constitution like mine carefully studied in another man." Three discursive layers—an explanation, an inference, and study—sediment to express this eye. Like an ethnologist or an anthropologist who analyzes himself as the object of his fieldwork, I study "in another man" a "constitution like mine," then I deduce something that I proceed to explain. The fictional space of discourse that speaks of the eye of the other comes into play at this moment of deduction. The goal of such a hypothesis—and the purpose of the *Dialogues*—is not simply to study oneself in another man, nor to project oneself onto another, nor to imagine or to fantasize oneself in the place of the other. It is not a question of a paranoid discourse, in which one takes oneself for another, but rather of a discourse that hypothesizes the other, or more precisely that *deduces* from this hypothesis the conditions that allow me to see a man such as I am. There is an operation in progress here, one that is staged like a new space of fiction. The other does not exist before being hypothesized by a fictional discourse. In this sense, fiction could be reduced to the conclusion drawn from this hypothesis, in other words, to the *Dialogues* themselves, occuring as they do in the fictive space of the eye of the other.

If I could see myself through the eye of the other, not only would I see myself as I am, but, more importantly, I would no longer need the gaze of the other in order to see myself. I would no longer need to wait for the other to see me, to judge me, to love or condemn me, in order to know who I am. I would no longer need to show myself completely to the public, in my difference and alterity. This eye, the eye of a fictive other, is not the eye of a hypothetical other, but the hypothetical eye of another. What interests Rousseau most has to do with the *eye* of the other, rather than with the singular difference or the individuality of the other. What is at stake is the point of view or the position of the onlooker's eye, the gaze. The objective is not to understand what I would be if I were another, nor to know how I would see myself, but rather to *say* what the position of this eye consists of. Thus the author's need to invent another discourse or language, a space or a *place from which* I could see myself as I am. This new language within language would exist within the natural language of signs, of meaning and reference, of intentions, of lies and truth. It would allow the fiction of another language to say and enounce its own conditions of truth. Such is the language of the *Dialogues*, imbued from the beginning with a plurality of voices that always speaks from within the place and instead of the other.

The language of the *Dialogues* represents the traumatic moment of a cut that divides the subject into two individuals, as we have seen. But it also constitutes the fictional space of a point of view that situates the subject in the place of the other and uses a new language to name the subject and invent it as the traumatic place of fiction. To understand language as the purpose of the *Dialogues*, I believe that it is important to consider these two statements together: "it was necessary for me to say through which eye, if I were another, I would see a man such as I am," and, "You must admit that this man's destiny has some striking peculiarities. His life is divided into two parts that seem to belong to two different individuals." By determining the eye, one ultimately affirms that all discourse will need to be spoken in its relation to the divided, split, and traumatized subject. While the language of the *Confessions* implies the ideal of a subject who speaks in his own name and in the name of his alterity or his difference in order to name a truth falsified by the judgment of the other, the language of the *Dialogues* speaks from within the place of the traumatized and divided subject, a subject who is always already in the place of the other. Thus, the position of the split subject is no longer simply observed, spied upon, judged by the eye of the other, rather, that subject can speak, express, or observe himself but only from the place of the other. Whether it is invented or produced in the language that enunciates it, this fictional substitutive operation represents the purpose of the *Dialogues*. Nonetheless, this purpose is by definition unattainable, for no discourse could ever conceptualize it.

According to the first *Reverie*, the purpose of the *Dialogues* was not fulfilled. This text of over three hundred pages that meant to say "the eye of the other" failed to enunciate it, name it, situate it, or describe it; it did not even manage to identify it. According to the *Reveries*, "I was mistaken" in the *Dialogues*. Not mistaken about the "purpose" or the necessity to speak of this eye, its place, and its alterity, but rather about my hope, my expectation to see or to imagine that one day, in another generation, there might be another history or another memory in which I would finally be seen as I am:

> But I still counted on the future; and I hoped that a better generation, examining more fairly both the judgments made about me by this one and its conduct toward me, would easily unravel the cunning of those who direct it and would finally see me as I am. This is the hope which made me write my *Dialogues* and prompted me to a thousand foolish attempts to pass them on to posterity. This hope, though remote, held my soul in the same agitation as when I was still looking for a just heart in this century; and the hope that I cast in vain into the future also rendered me the plaything of the men of today. I stated in my *Dialogues* what I founded this expectation on. I was mistaken. (*Reveries*, CW, 8:5)

The fatal error of a life is the failure to see the demonic immortality of collective bodies. The error of the *Dialogues* was the failure to discern *in* the eye of the other, in the traumatic cut where I always see myself in the place of the other, the evil eternal return of the public. This return always proceeds by erasure, denial, disavowal, or repression. Therefore, the return of the public represents here, in the *Reveries*, the metaphor of erasure. One could now begin to read or to reread the *Reveries* as a focus on the failure of the *Dialogues*, and of the *Confessions* too, for which the *Reveries* serve as an "appendix" (*Reveries*, CW, 8:7). *The Reveries of the Solitary Walker*, as the appendix to the failure of the public's return, would be Rousseau's last book.

Finally, I would like to propose here a general hypothesis: the public's return always stems from a logic of erasure. As we have seen, the *Dialogues* attempt to efface the traumatic cut that splits the subject into two individuals. The book tries to eliminate the difference between the man and the author, but only by an act of falsification: it *equates* the author of the books with the author of the crimes. In the *Reveries*, the erasure is even more radical. It is no longer a question of simply denying or undermining what the living subject says nor of falsifying Rousseau's own thought, but of effacing his very memory or the traces that "my memory after my death" might leave.

With this denial of erasure and the desire to nullify one's own survival, one must reconsider the eye of the other. Not only is it necessary to give up the desire to be accepted, but one must also leave behind all expectations for the future. The eye of the other must be considered in different terms of alterity and temporality from those of the public and of history. Faced with this logic of erasure, a *force of unworking* must be developed. As Rousseau wrote in the *Reveries*: "I wrote my first *Confessions* and my *Dialogues* in constant anxiety about ways to keep them from the rapacious hands of my persecutors in order to transmit them, if it were possible, to other generations. With this work, the same worry no longer torments me; I know it would be useless. And now that the desire to be better understood by men has been extinguished in my heart, only profound indifference remains about the fate of my true writings and of the testimonies to my innocence—which have perhaps already all been forever reduced to nothing" (*Reveries*, CW, 8:8).

The *Reveries* continue the *Confessions*, following in the footsteps of the *Dialogues*, but by other means. It is no longer a question of *resisting* the logic of erasure, but of *resigning* oneself to developing this new position of unworking, the only gesture still possible to allow the divided, torn, traumatized subject to speak or to say "through which eye, if I were another, I would see a man such as I am." With this gesture of unworking, the subject of the discourse speaks from the place of his death, as Rousseau writes in the First Promenade: "despite the desuetude of my body, my soul is still active; it still produces feelings and thoughts; and its internal and moral life seems to have grown even more with the death of every earthly and temporal interest. My body is no longer anything to me but an encumbrance, an obstacle, and I disengage myself from it beforehand as much as I can" (*Reveries*, CW, 8:7).

Here we see how the force of unworking not only liberates the author, allowing the enemy no further hold on him, but above all how it allows him to invent a space, to produce a place beyond all identity and alterity. This unworking represents what the author calls "the death of every earthly and temporal interest." It already represents, here and now, in his lifetime, the place of his death and his survival, a phantom place where he is "buried alive in a coffin," as Rousseau says in the *Dialogues* (*Dialogues*, CW, 1:129). According to the *Reveries*, the self intends to stay here in a state of unworking. What's more, he intends to consider this unworking as the eye of the other, from which he would see a man such as he is. For whatever objective, goal, hope, or expectation one may have for an oeuvre, it is no longer "I" who unworks "myself," not even for a return that is always already falsified by the public. Instead, I am nothing but that which is seen through the eye of another who is himself unworked. The force of unworking is the *unworking of the other*, the collapse or exhaustion of all logic of erasure. Speaking from the place of one's own death, as the last position of the other's unworking, implies speaking from the place where no one could take my place, whether to speak or to die in my place. As Rousseau wrote in the Sixth Promenade: "As for me, let them see me if they can; so much the better.

But that is impossible for them. They will never see *in my place* anyone but the Jean-Jacques they have made for themselves and made to their heart's desire to hate at their ease. I would therefore be wrong to be affected by the way they see me. I ought to take no genuine interest in it, for it is not I whom they see in this way" (*Reveries*, CW, 8:56, my emphasis). By the force of unworking, I construct the space of the other as one where no other could take *my place*. I thus invent the fictional space of a discourse that determines the distribution of places, the conjugation of subjects, and the discernment of roles. Above all I stage a death, or a space from which I can see myself as if I were already dead.

From the *Confessions* to the *Dialogues* to the *Reveries*, Rousseau created a new space of discourse: fictional, political, and literary. It no longer simply directs the speaking subject to address the other, or his alterity. Rather it attributes the subject's place to the place of his death. It is the final place, at once possible and impossible, livable and unlivable. It is a space where no one may die in my place, or see me as if I were already dead. Most importantly, it is a place where no one may *say* in my place "through which eye, if I were another, I would see a man such as I am."

CHAPTER 8

Rousseau and the Sense of Dignity

P H I L I P S T E W A R T

Dignity and integrity are central notions in much of Rousseau's work, both morally (concerning individuals) and socially (with respect to citizens). They are closely allied, especially in the earlier work, to the sort of primitive wholeness (*mâle vertu*) that ultimately degrades with the advent of refinement and its associated effeminateness. In other words, they are inherently ambiguous notions with both intrinsic ("spiritual") and extrinsic (social) aspects, which is perhaps why it is the obligation of a political system to allow for reinforcement of the individual's sense of value, however that is to be achieved. The *Social Contract* explains how this personal dignity is retained within a system where the individual must nevertheless often be subordinate to the collectivity. The worldly Parisians described by St. Preux in part 2 of *Julie* have become so alienated from a sense of self that they mistake foppishness for worth and stature.

But one work, known as *Rousseau Judge of Jean-Jacques*, is entirely devoted to recovering a public sense of dignity that he claims has been stolen from him by his enemies. It immediately addresses that loss, which is summarized in a statement about men's behavior towards each other: "I have often said that if someone had fed me the notions about another man which my contemporaries have been fed about me, I would not have behaved toward him as they do toward me" (CW, 1:3).[1] He therefore adopts in this work the rather odd rhetorical strategy of trying to represent himself as seen from outside, as if he were precisely this "other man," in order to ask whether the way he, Jean-Jacques Rousseau, is being treated could be justified.[2]

In a way, however, self-defense is intrinsically humiliating, not to mention distasteful (CW, 1:5), even when approached with the inside-out posture of the work (where *I* is transposed to a *he*). Rousseau of course immediately comes up with reasons why he "has to" do it anyway; in any event, he has no hope that anyone else will do it for him. There are further rhetorical questions that must be confronted, but still it all comes down to the question of dignity, often expressed in one or more of several synonyms: "But what tone will that person adopt who feels worthy of honor and esteem, yet whom the public freely disfigures and defames, in order to do himself the justice he is due?" (6). The opposition is demoralizing, but it is the injustice that humiliates. By discouraging any unsympathetic reader, he adds a little further on, he at least may "avoid the ultimate indignity of seeing the picture of the miseries of my life [used as] anyone's object of amusement" (7). Far from reestablishing his dignity, the sole purpose even if it is not merely *for his own sake*, he could be precipitating the "ultimate indignity" that makes his enterprise worse than worthless.

ESTRANGEMENT

The analysis delivered by "Rousseau" (that is, the character who happens to bear that name) in the second dialogue of *Rousseau Judge of Jean-Jacques*[3] portrays as his subject (called J.-J.) an individual who, left to himself, is simple and unassuming, frugal, shy but at bottom sociable, and above all absolutely genuine: "Of all the men I have known," he reports, "the one whose character derives most thoroughly from his temperament alone is J.-J. He is what nature made him" (CW, 1:101–5, 107). But that man is perceived by few and indeed is all but impossible to observe directly because he must protect himself to the point of refusing to open his door to most of those who request an interview and whose motives are generally, in any case, anything but charitable.

Thus the man most people see, or think they see, is on the contrary "cruel, fierce, and harsh to the point of depravity . . . , intractable, inflexible, . . . a ferocious misanthrope" (CW, 1:106). He inundates the world of books with malicious, antisocial propaganda and musical works, which he must necessarily have stolen from others because he is innocent of any knowledge of music. He has taken to collecting plants and studying chemistry so he can concoct poisons in his home (134–35), all the while hoarding his wealth while feigning penury. Reduced in reality to bare subsistence, he is called arrogant for refusing alms as one "who plays the beggar though he is rich" (47). He is in a word "the cleverest hypocrite and the most devious scoundrel who could exist" (155), one who does evil for the love of evil.

The disparity between that outside perception and the reality is explained by the fact that the real Rousseau is the original victim of identity theft: his very self, as it were, of which the original person gets but occasional glimpses, has been all but usurped by outside forces[4] in order to lend him a factitious character, just as they have commandeered his likeness to persuade people that he is some kind of ogre.[5] This action they view (or rationalize) as a kind of civic duty: "Can you see a serpent slither into the public square without shouting to everyone to beware of the serpent?" (CW, 1:39). They make him the laughingstock of the rabble and drown him in mire—the metaphors go on and on—heaping on him the contradictory accusations that there is no crime he has not committed and that, had he "not committed any, he would be no less capable of them all"; the least plausible accusations are indeed assumed to be the most telling (65, 62).

This is the tribulation to which he earlier alluded in the *Confessions*: "Here begins the work of darkness in which I have found myself enveloped for the past eight years, unable, however I might try, to pierce its terrifying obscurity. Submerged in an abyss of woes, I feel the impact of the blows directed at me, I perceive their immediate instrument, but I cannot see either the hand that directs it or the means it deploys. Opprobrium and misfortune befall me as if unaided and for no apparent cause" (*Conf*, CW, 5:493). This work of darkness begins with surveillance but, as this passage suggests, one so discreet as to be imperceptible. As stealthy as the enemies are, they are diabolically thorough and have everything under control. Again *Rousseau Judge of Jean-Jacques* emphasizes the threat, noting: "As soon as he settles somewhere [says the 'Frenchman'], which we always know in advance, the walls, the floors, the locks, everything is organized around him for the purpose we intend, and we do not neglect to provide him with appropriate neighbors, which is to say venomous spies, clever imposters, obliging women whom we have well trained" (CW, 1:41).

They take "infinite care" and go to "huge expense" in order "to surround him with so many traps, to deliver him into so many hands, to ensnare him in so many ways that in the midst of this feigned freedom he can neither say a word, nor take a step, nor move a finger unless they know it and want him to" (CW, 1:39–40). This is a terribly frightening scenario, because it suggests that even acts of his free will are not free because they are willed by someone other than him. These invisible handlers also take the reins of activity about him so that everyone he comes in contact with already has some (seriously flawed but negative) information about him: "If he enters some public place he is viewed and treated as if he had the plague: everyone surrounds him and stares at him, but keeping their distance and not talking to him, simply to present a barrier to him. . . . He has been pointed out, tagged, targeted everywhere to messengers, clerks, guards, spies, chimney-sweeps, in all the theaters, cafés, to the barbers, the merchants, the peddlers, the booksellers" (42).

In this local situation the public domain becomes, instead of the kind of general cauldron (à la Habermas) where ideas mix, just another controlled environment, manipulated at will by mysterious others. For Rousseau has been surrounded with a virtual reality in which he receives no information that is not false or unreliable: "If he inquires about something no one knows anything; if he asks about someone no one knows him; if he asked a bit eagerly about the weather, no one would tell him" (CW, 1:45–46). Indeed, "never since the world began"—a typical hyperbole to express the extremity of his situation—"has a mortal lived in such degradation."

At the same time, his sensitivity to these details is further evidence of his inner dignity: "Infamy is hurtful only in proportion to the honor a man has in his heart. . . . Scorn has little effect on someone who knows he deserves it: it is a judgment to which his own heart has already quite accustomed him" (44, 65).

Any reader of *Rousseau Judge of Jean-Jacques* will note the insistence of certain types of vocabulary that of course are constitutive of themes but more than that are, despite the variety of their formulations, repetitive to the point of obsession. They all point to a helplessly beleaguered man. To begin with, in the 257 pages of the text there are twenty-three occurrences of "persecutors" plus two of "persecutions"; forty-nine occurrences of "enemy", singular and plural, plus two of *adversaires*; and fifty-two mentions of the hostile plot (*complot*). The seventeen occurrences of *ténèbres* (darkness) show up in haunting metaphors of isolation—"triple walls of darkness," "triple enclosure of darkness," the "immense edifice of shadows they have built around him" (CW, 1:71, 196, 225). Another recurrent analogy is that "they have buried him alive among the living"; still another is, unsurprisingly, the trap (*piège*) in which he is snared (91–94). Sometimes he seems like an insect caught in some sort of infernal spiderweb.

His tormentors expropriate his writings, taking over the texts so they can produce corrupt editions of them and attribute to him whatever else they see fit (CW, 1:177). As they control public perceptions, so do they control the public sentiment toward him, their ultimate aim being to drive him to suicide so they will bear no blame. But he is a tough customer and it is to no avail:

> By dint of terrible but tacit abuse, by dint of being mobbed, of whispers, sneers, cruel and hostile or insulting and mocking stares, they were able to drive him out of every assembly, every theatre, out of cafes and public promenades; their purpose is to . . . make his life so unbearable that he can no longer endure it. In short, by . . . leaving him only one way out, it is clear they wanted to force him to take it. But they took into account, no doubt, everything except the resources of innocence and resignation. Despite age and adversity his health has improved and remains good: his inner calm seems to rejuvenate him; and although he has no hope left among men, he was never farther from despair. (CW, 1:197)

Here it is useful to remember that despair (or despondency), especially if it led to suicide, was a mortal sin according to Christian traditions, so these are weighty terms, even if the persons involved do not take their theological terms literally. While they "drink in slowly the sweet spectacle of his misery," Jean-Jacques, who does not "think of true dignity the way they do,"[6] can "find a very pleasant enjoyment in the alternation of work and recreation" (CW, 1:129, 138).

The consummate indignity, which sums them all up and gives, if not shape, at least theme to the whole of *Rousseau Judge of Jean-Jacques*, is his inability to confront his accusers in public so as to establish his innocence (CW, 1:44), an outrage not just to the individual but to universal human dignity. But even if he could arrange for the formal hearing he has been demanding, what would keep it from going all awry, given the degree of outside control that he cannot hope to parry? "Where would he find judges who were not in on the plot, witnesses who were not suborned, faithful consultants who would not lead him astray? Alone against a whole conspiring generation, from whom would he demand the truth without a lie answering him instead? What protection, what support would he find to stand up to this general conspiracy?" (221). Thus the obliteration of his public honor, cynically engineered, is so thorough that it also precludes any attempt, even imaginary, to reverse the process.

SERENITY

At the same time, the lamentable Jean-Jacques thus circumscribed and humiliated insists on his perfect serenity, as if nothing had occurred: "I see that despite all the measures they have taken, he continues on as before, not the least troubled by the observers he sees on every side" (CW, 1:49). This antithetical discourse often surfaces, insisting defiantly that despite the efforts of his indefatigable enemies, Jean-Jacques manages to live a quite bearable life. In this context he often, despite all the adversity, evokes his private joys: "this man could pride himself despite his hardships on thus spending a life as full of happiness and enjoyment as any other mortal on earth"; "he doesn't lose a moment of enjoyment, and as soon as he is alone, he is happy" (119, 121).

To his forced isolation, this sort of internal banishment, the victim has responded, relates "Rousseau," with a voluntary exile of his own: "weary of these mocking and deceitful displays, and indignant at being thus the plaything of his supposed friends, he ceased to see them, withdrew without disguising his disdain, and after long seeking a true human without success,[7] put out his lamp and shut himself completely within himself." This quasi-fetal position is just a counter-measure, a form of self-protection and self-insolation. "He flees men not because he hates them, but because he is afraid of them," which helps explain his having taken up the botanical pastime that characterizes his last years; "I would gladly leave the society of plants, he told me, for that of men, at the first hope of I could ever again find some" (CW, 1:102, 98).

One way to read *Rousseau Judge of Jean-Jacques* is as a long and insistent cry for the autonomy of his person, an attempt to claw back possession of his own being. While presenting his version of a true portrait of himself, he is simultaneously shouting: Leave me alone! For the effect of his enemies' activities is that everything about him has been falsified, and the means is that they have invaded and appropriated his life so thoroughly that what they say is more credited than what he can say for himself. Many passages develop the theme of isolation as a way of closing out the world, which is after all experienced as a hostile and punishing environment, to allow a place where that incessant harassment is no longer relevant.[8] It may exist in the recesses of conscience, but it is not actively perceived: "He does not have the merit of forgiving offenses, because he forgets them; he does not love his enemies, but he doesn't think about them." It is this willful passivity—as when you concentrate in order to relax a muscle—that allows him to avoid conflict and retreat into himself: "Now he seems to desire nothing more. Indifferent to the rest of his career, he takes pleasure in seeing its end approaching, but without hastening it even in his wishes. I doubt whether another mortal has ever better and more sincerely said to God, *Thy will be done*; and that is doubtless not very praiseworthy resignation for someone who sees nothing more on this earth that can appeal to his heart" (CW, 1:154, 152). This posture confers on him a state of ruddy health as well as a sense of well-being. He has lost the sallowness of his days of writing because "his soul is at peace"; "[e]ver since he has gone back to the pleasant leisure of his youth, he has recovered its serenity: he keeps his body busy and rests his head; this agrees with him in every way" (159). He is not describing *productive* time, since paradoxically—despite the manuscript obviously in the process of being written—he has abandoned being a "writer" also.

All these benefits emerge because the self alone is true when all the rest and all the others are false. He contemplates at great length and with fond complacency the intricacies of his own temperamental and psychological makeup (e.g., CW, 1:109, 112–15, 121). "Rousseau" remarks of him: "I was especially struck to find his spirits were never so gay and serene as when he had been left alone and undisturbed, or when he returned from his solitary walk" (118). He must still be on guard against those who seem most sympathetic to him, those very ones who try to befriend him, because they are plants, and this defensive reaction is also turned against him by the conspirators who propagate and sustain the notion that he is savage and uncouth.

He thus turns, by inclination, to meditation. In this there is no despair: "If he were as they represent him to us, the prosperity of his enemies, the opprobrium they heap on him, his powerlessness to avenge would already have killed him with rage. In the solitude he seeks he would have found nothing but despair and death. What he finds there is peace of mind, tranquillity of soul, health, life" (CW, 1:150). At times he is said by "Rousseau" to soar into a quasi-mystical realm that conveys a happiness beyond mere security: "In the midst of all their successes he escapes them, and taking refuge in the ethereal regions, lives happily there in spite of them; even with all their machines, they will never pursue him that far" (119–20). He is freed from constraints of the real in these moments that he attributes—so as to avoid any religious implications—to the play of the imagination: "He is beyond their reach; he does not require their suffrage to be wise or their favor to be happy. In short, such is the power and such the influence of the imagination over us that from it springs not only virtues and vices, but all the joys or sufferings of human life, and it is principally the manner in which we yield to it that makes men good or bad, happy or unhappy on this earth" (120).

Alone, and *rediscovering himself*, he is consoled and reinforced because of re-affirmation of the self but also of (what should be) its perception from the outside:

> The source of all his consolations is in his self-esteem. He would be the most virtuous of men if his strength responded to his will. But with all his weakness he cannot be a vile man, because there is no ignoble inclination in his soul to which it would be shameful to yield. The only one that could have led him to evil is false shame,[9] against which he has struggled all his life with efforts as great as they were futile, because it comes from his timid disposition which presents an invincible obstacle to the ardent desires of his heart, and forces him to turn them aside in a thousand often blameworthy ways. (CW, 1:184)

Yet to this image corresponds a counter-image promulgated by the conspirators, which deftly makes of each aspect of his withdrawal and consequent happiness a further symptom of his rebarbative nature: "This man who seems so gentle and sociable to you flees everyone without exception, disdains every caress, rejects all overtures, and lives alone like a werewolf. He feeds on visions, you say, and entrances himself with chimeras; but if he scorns and repels humans, if his heart is closed to their company, what difference does it make to them if he consorts with imaginary beings as you suggest?" (CW, 1:168). The description of this exalted though not ecstatic experience runs close to the kind of reverie that Rousseau described at various other points in his life,[10] and was to give its title to his very last work.

And so it is that one track of *Rousseau Judge of Jean-Jacques* (that is, leaving aside the project set up by "the Frenchman" and "Rousseau" at the very end) ultimately merges with the (rhetorically, as least) new orientation set forth early in the *Reveries of the Solitary Walker*:

> I struggled along for a long time as violently as vainly. Wanting skill, craft, dissimulation, and prudence, candid, open, impatient, exasperated, I only entangled myself more by struggling and gave them ever new purchases which they have made sure not to neglect. Finally, feeling how useless were all my efforts, and tormenting myself to no avail, I took the only course I could, which was to submit to my fate and cease to rail at necessity. In this resignation I have found compensation for all my woes through the tranquility I gain thereby, one which could not go together with the continual effort of a resistance as demanding as it was fruitless. (*Reveries*, CW, 8:4)

Thus ends, according to one scenario, Rousseau's quest for dignity: one that succeeds, but which he alone can appreciate, invisible to the rest of the world.

THE ENEMY WITHIN

And yet . . . there is a second discourse woven into the pages of *Rousseau Judge of Jean-Jacques* that relates all the above, and it greatly complicates the picture, for the apparently appeased victim of a vast plot, ostensibly led by Diderot and two or three of his closest allies, ultimately fails to rid his mind of them:

> The illustrious Diderot, who does not dirty his hands with mercenary work and disdains petty, usurious profits, is in the eyes of all Europe a sage as virtuous as he is disinterested, while the copyist J.-J. earning ten sols a page working to help make his living is a Jew universally scorned for his greed. But Fortune, despite its harshness, seems in this instance to have put everything back in order, and I do not see that the Jew J.-J.'s usuries have made him very rich nor that the disinterestedness of the philosophe Diderot has made him poor. (CW, 1:142)

This little passage contains in its way both versions, both visions or representations, of the characters in play. Diderot's lies rob Jean-Jacques of his dignity but fail because the latter secretly maintains his sense of self, and neither the natural nor the human order of things seems to be affected. These two worlds are separate and ultimately have no effect on each other: "He loves himself and they hate him: both sides have the same occupation; he is everything to himself, he is also everything to them: for they are nothing either to him or to themselves, and as long as J.-J. is miserable, that is all the happiness they require" (155).

The careful and extensive analysis of the enemy's activities that follows, however, essentially gives the lie to the blissful autonomy thus posited. What better proof of his inability to detach himself than to dwell so unremittingly on their insidious devices? "Great imitators of the Jesuits' ways, they were their most ardent enemies, no doubt out of professional jealousy, and now, governing minds with the same control, with the same dexterity as those others governed consciences, shrewder than they in that they hide themselves better as they act, and gradually replacing religious intolerance with their own, they are becoming without attracting attention more dangerous than their predecessors" (CW, 1:178). This ironic reversal of intolerance would be a significant charge if it did not reveal more about Rousseau, who sees the world as revolving about himself, than about the philosophes. Historians of course do not see in their movement or project, despite its real achievements, either such central control or such triumphant power; but that is not the point. What matters for us here is the way this perception shapes Rousseau's notion of the process by which he has been shackled.

Why discourse so lengthily on *them*, indeed, if *they* have been once and for all put out of mind? This is, of course, a paradox that has always been patent in *Rousseau Judge of Jean-Jacques*. But there is more: it also affects the representation of the self in the same pages. While there is much complacent, even narcissistic, lingering on the purely domestic and humble self, the discussion still reverts frequently to the victim in his confrontations with the outside world, which cannot simply be bracketed as if they did not occur at all:

> Picture the unfortunate J.-J. on the street or on his walks surrounded by people who, less from curiosity than derision, since most have already seen him a hundred times, turn about and stop to stare at him with a gaze that surely owes nothing to French urbanity: you will always find that the most insulting, the most mocking, the most assiduous of them are young people who in an ironically polite manner amuse themselves by giving him all the signs of insult and hatred that can afflict him without compromising themselves. (CW, 1:178–79)

"Rousseau" in the dialogues concedes that the "patience with which he bears" his woes "in no way lightened the impression they made on him" (191). Repetitions of illustrative instances of Jean-Jacques's almost terrified constraint of action in the world fill many pages of the work. The continual suffering that is denied on one level is insistently re-affirmed on another. As "Rousseau" concedes, "our true *self* is not entirely within us" ("notre vrai *moi* n'est pas tout entier en nous": 118, emphasis in original).

A ROLE FOR HEAVEN

Although the machinations so extensively described are almost never flagged with underworldly attributions,[11] it will not have escaped any reader that they incorporate all the infinite cunning of a satanic design; for the conspirators have taken care to erase not only the "vestiges of truth" but also their own footprints, so that no evidence of any kind remains: "Can you believe that, in so carefully avoiding any kind of explanation, the originators and leaders of this plot neglect to destroy and denature everything that might one day serve to confound them, and in the more than fifteen years it has been in full execution, haven't they had all the time they needed to succeed in that? The further they move into the future, the easier it is for them to obliterate the past or give it the turn most convenient to them" (CW, 1:220–21).

This, as "the Frenchman" is pointing out, has implications not just for the present but also the future possibility of truth, for the conditions have been fundamentally altered. Public opinion, the progressive gelling of consensus in the public sphere, has become a policy decided centrally and promulgated by a sort of shadow government; indeed even real government authorities largely seem to take orders from this mafia. On another level that also risks mortgaging the future, it has established temporal power beyond anything previously imagined: "Ever since the philosophical sect has come together in a body under leaders, those leaders through the art of intrigue to which they have applied themselves having become the arbiters of public opinion, are through it also the arbiters of the reputation and even the destiny of individuals and through them of that of the state" (CW, 1:236–37). Their ability to rewrite his life and even his work means that he will likely be denied posthumous dignity as well (231–32). The final round will be control of his status beyond his own lifetime, the conspiracy being able to define his posterity in advance.

Thus his struggle for a future dignity was for something that might eventually replace the one that has been stomped out in the present. For want of any immediate satisfaction—"I no longer hope and I have very little desire to see in my lifetime the revolution that will disabuse the public with respect to me" (227)—someone, perhaps long after his death, will find and disclose to the world the proofs of his innocence. Whence the counter-project to preserve and protect him at the end of the last dialogue, where "Rousseau" concludes: "The hope that his memory will be restored one day to the honor it deserves, and that his books will become useful by the esteem owed to their author is henceforth the only one that he can entertain in this world." (245).

"Have no doubt that heaven will bless such a just undertaking" (243): thus does "Rousseau" reassure the Frenchman. Innocence will someday be reestablished, and God is its ultimate guarantor, if not on earth then surely in the next life. At that time Rousseau will perhaps have no further care for the situation on earth, but everything is of a piece. Despite the failure, inscribed in his "History of the Preceding Writing" (246–57), of an appeal to God for temporal salvation, eschatology—which Rousseau normally disdains—is his ultimate recourse. The sort of cosmic menace represented by the conspiracy explains why the ultimate resolution of Rousseau's dignity takes on, as the dialogues come to a close, a quasi-metaphysical dimension. Having theoretically won his wager, a victory that is always inevitably refused him in the short run will at length be achieved, on condition that authentic documents survive to enlighten and back up his new defenders. For this ultimate reason, he is free, "released even from the anxiety of hope here below" (253).

Rousseau describes this new state only by its "complete tranquillity" (*pleine quiétude*) and "absolute calm." If there are vicissitudes in this constancy, they are no greater than variations of temperature from one day to the next. "Indignities" are now but scarcely perceptible.[12] But at the same time he still perceives himself as "a wretched stranger, alone, with no protector or defender on earth, insulted, mocked, defamed, betrayed by an entire generation, the victim of fifteen years of unlimited treatments worse than death and of indignities heretofore unexampled among men" and again one "who has been for fifteen years plunged and dragged by you through the mire of opprobrium and defamation, sees and feels himself endlessly covered with indignities unheard heretofore unexampled of among humans."[13] Rather than furnishing the very condition for serenity, solitude is cruel, even the most intense suffering that can be inflicted on him. It is the main feature of the landscape described at the beginning of the *Reveries of the Solitary Walker*:

> I stand here alone on earth, deprived of any brother, neighbor, friend, or society other than myself. The most sociable and the most loving of humans has been banished from society by a unanimous agreement. They have sought in the refinements of their hatred the torment which would be cruelest to my sensitive soul, and have violently broken all the ties that bound me to them. I would have loved men despite themselves. Only by ceasing to be such have they been able to evade my affection. Now they are unknown strangers, nonexistent for me since that is what they wanted. (*Reveries*, CW, 8:3)

The standard way of describing this final shift, because it is the one he himself recounted, is that after the conclusion of *Rousseau Judge of Jean-Jacques* Rousseau finally broke free from the whole vicious circle and left it behind. He identifies a particular event, seemingly one that took place the summer of 1776, that prompts this definitive renunciation.[14] This time he would really and without reservation turn inward:

> Such a singular situation surely deserves to be examined and described, and to this examination I consecrate my last moments of leisure. To succeed in this, I should have to proceed with order and method: but I am incapable of such work and it would even distract me from my goal which is to give myself an account of the modifications[15] of my soul and of their evolution. I will perform on myself in a way the same operations as physicists do on air to learn its daily state. I will apply the barometer to my soul, and these operations well executed and oft repeated might furnish me results as certain as theirs. (*Reveries*, CW, 8:7)

His enemies, he declares, have lost the power to "disturb [his] rest": "Let them enjoy my disgrace at will; they will not prevent me from enjoying my innocence and ending my days in peace in spite of them" (8).

And yet, embedded in this "in spite of them" there is still *them*: they are not as utterly forgotten as the discourse pretends.[16] Had Rousseau not assured Dusaulx as early as 1770 (and this is now at least 1776) that he had already entered into an era of calm?[17] In other words, it is not clear that there is any real temporal divide between these two discourses. The *avant-propos*[18] appended to *Rousseau Judge of Jean-Jacques* was according to all indications not yet written on February 26, 1776; the *Reveries* may have begun in September.[19] Yet in the interim and beyond he has continued the act of copying *Rousseau Judge of Jean-Jacques* (two more copies, apparently) during much of the period covered by composition of the *Reveries*.

Whatever shading of sincerity one chooses to ascribe in reading Rousseau, one must not so mistake the tone he adopts as to forget he is addressing a public on which he still hopes to have some effect. We should speak here not of a Rousseau who *has been* transformed (about which we know nothing) in the narrow valley that separates *Rousseau Judge of Jean-Jacques* and the *Reveries of the Solitary Walker*, but of one who has adopted a new discursive stance.

One could say that Rousseau finally won out; that even if he cannot savor it, he and particularly his life's work have prevailed: but only if one accepts literally in the first place his depiction of his existential situation in *Rousseau Judge of Jean-Jacques*—which no one really does. Throughout this period he underestimated his supporters, and they proved durable. If only he could have heard Victor-Donatien Musset-Pathay declaring in 1826: "I see Rousseau enjoying the esteem of men, to which he attached such a price, to which he was so entitled, and the deprivation of which was the torment of his life"![20]

NOTES

1. All references to *Rousseau Judge of Jean-Jacques: Dialogues* are to the CW edition, but translations have frequently been modified.

2. See also chapter 7 above, "The Madness of the Double: *Rousseau Judge of Jean-Jacques*," by Serge Margel.

3. I prefer not to refer to the work as "dialogues" (except generically to designate the chapter format) because that subtitle, though reproduced in CW and nearly everywhere, was in fact abandoned by Rousseau, as was the epigraph that appears with it on the two earliest manuscripts. The Pléiade edition is unreliable on this detail, since it does not in fact respect the manuscript of Geneva which it purports to follow.

4. "[Y]our Gentlemen . . . dispose as they wish of his reputation, his person, and his entire fate" (CW, 1:74); cf. letter *CC* 6504 from Rousseau to Paul Moultou (December 12, 1768): "those who dispose of me determine my conduct as God does that of the sea." All citations from Rousseau's correspondence (*CC*) refer to *Correspondance complète de Jean-Jacques Rousseau*, ed. R. A. Leigh (Geneva: Institut et Musée Voltaire, 1965–98). Translations are mine.

5. CW, 1:4, 91–94. The power of their leaders is sometimes ironically, even humorously hyperbolized: "If D'Alembert or Diderot had the nerve to assert today that he has two heads, seeing him pass down the street tomorrow everyone would see very distinctly that he has two heads, and each would be most surprised not to have perceived this monstrosity sooner" (233).

6. This is the single instance of the word "dignity" in *Rousseau Judge of Jean-Jacques*, whereas the negative form, "indignities," has on the contrary multiple uses, laying out a number of practices that rob a man of his dignity.

7. The implied comparison is to Diogenes of Sinope, who was said to walk about in the daylight carrying a lantern and replying to queries that he was just looking for an honest

man. Rousseau uses the same image in a letter to his friend Dusaulx, February 16, 1771 (*CC* 6837).

8. He has often in the past represented solitude as an ideal solution to protect himself, in particular when he recalls the island of Saint Pierre in book 12 of *Confessions*: "It seemed to me that on this island I would be better cut off from men, better sheltered from their attacks, better forgotten by them, in a word freer to indulge in the pleasures of indolence and the contemplative life. I wished I could be so confined to that island as to have no further dealings with mortals, and it is certain that I took every measure imaginable to avoid the necessity of maintaining any" (*Conf*, CW, 5:534–35).

9. *Mauvaise honte*, an expression used three times in *Rousseau Judge of Jean-Jacques* to designate shame that is not really shameful. The *Dictionnaire de Trévoux* gives this example: "There is some shame, some embarrassment in borrowing, but there is no infamy. Many people have false shame at not daring to inquire about things they do not know, because it is to confess they are in the dark about them."

10. See Marcel Raymond, *Jean-Jacques Rousseau: La quête de soi et la rêverie* (Paris: José Corti, 1962), and Arnaud Tripet, *La Rêverie littéraire: Essai sur Rousseau* (Genève: Droz, 1979).

11. Only once is even the devil indirectly invoked to describe their "sharp, diabolical, penetrating mind" (CW, 1:107); in one other passage the term is ironically and doubtless amusingly turned against the victim with his "irascible, diabolical pride" (74).

12. "Taking with me the witness of my conscience, I will despite them find consolation for all their indignities" ("History of the Preceding Writing," CW, 1:252).

13. These quotes are from "Document Entrusted to Providence" (CW, 1:247) and "To Every Frenchman who Still Loves Justice and Truth" (CW, 1:256).

14. "An event as sad as it was unforeseen has finally now snuffed out this feeble ray of hope in my heart and made me see my fate here below forever and irreversibly settled. Since then I have resigned myself unreservedly and found peace again" (*Reveries*, CW, 8:5). This blow has been possibly identified as the death of the Prince de Conti on August 2; this is plausible, but pure conjecture. See Rousseau, *Édition thématique du tricentenaire*, ed. Raymond Trousson and Frédéric Eigeldinger (Geneva and Paris: Slatkine and Champion, 2012), 3:466n3.

15. He had first written *dispositions*.

16. Similarly, I might point out, the desire for redress was still covertly acknowledged from the very beginning of *Rousseau Judge of Jean-Jacques*: his motives for writing no longer included, he asserted, "the hope *nor almost even the desire* to receive at last from those who have judged me the justice they deny me, and that they are quite determined to deny me forever" (CW 1:3, my italics).

17. "At ease for the future on earth, I aspire to the dwelling of peace where the works of iniquity cannot reach" ("Tranquillisé pour l'avenir sur la terre j'aspire au séjour du repos où les œuvres de l'iniquité ne pénètrent pas": Jean Dusaulx, *De mes rapports avec Jean-Jacques Rousseau*, ed. Raymond Trousson [Paris: Honoré Champion, 2012]), 161. As Frédéric Eigeldinger also points out in his annotation of the *Reveries*, the mentions of Mme d'Ormoy, l'abbé Rozier, la dame Vacassin (in Rousseau, *Édition thématique*, 3:479, 481, 501, 518, 513) deny the utter resignation declared in the first chapter. See Rousseau, *Édition thématique*, 3:454.

18. *Avant-propos* ("foreword") is Rousseau's term in the "History of the Preceding Writing," (whereas it is translated as "introduction" in CW, 1:246).

19. See Rousseau, *Édition thématique*, 3:441.

20. *Œuvres complètes de J. J. Rousseau, mises dans un nouvel ordre, avec des notes historiques et des éclaircissements par V. D. Musset-Pathay*, Paris: Dupont, 1823–24, 22 volumes; *Table générale* (separate unnumbered volume, 1826), viii.

CHAPTER 9

Rousseau and the Pursuit of Happiness

CHRISTOPHER KELLY

When one looks at the faces in the photographs in the DIGNITY exhibit one is more likely to think of qualities such as endurance than happiness. This is all the more true if one tries to think of a connection between the themes of this exhibit and the thought of Jean-Jacques Rousseau. Indeed, Rousseau may be best known as a thinker who argues for the social—not natural or divine—causes of human misery. The urban environments that serve as backdrops of many of the photographs in the DIGNITY exhibit certainly call this aspect of Rousseau's thought to mind. Nevertheless, Rousseau himself insists that we link the issue of the causes of human misery to the question of the possibility of happiness. He insists that we must investigate the possibility of happiness in order to understand the causes that prevent it, and it is upon this issue that I would like to focus.

Rousseau wrote so many things and so many sorts of things—discourses, treatises, plays, novels, operas, dictionaries, even a fairy tale—that it is hard to know where to begin to discuss his work. What I have chosen to do is to discuss a theme that runs through a large number of these different works. If some of these texts are little known even to many Rousseau scholars, my theme is certainly familiar to everyone: the pursuit of happiness. We are familiar with this from the Declaration of Independence, but also from popular books on economics or psychology and, most significantly, our daily lives.

I would like to approach this theme by means of my experience of traveling to the lecture at Notre Dame that was the basis of this essay. I am accustomed to getting up very early in the morning. Even when I have little inclination to do so, my dog makes sure that I do. Therefore, the day of my trip I got up at my home in Boston at 4:30. I spent some time getting ready to leave, took my dog for a walk, and left my house for the airport at 6:15. There I went through the experience with which everyone is familiar of checking in, going through security, and—most of all—waiting. I then spent hours in the confined space of the airplane and—after one connection and more waiting—arrived in South Bend hours later. None of this is at all remarkable, but I have to admit that the experience was something of an ordeal. It is not an experience that anyone would want to have without the prospect of something good coming at the end. I would certainly not have done it without a good reason. It is impressive that so many people willingly undertake such trips.

The experience makes me think about a conversation I once had with an American businessman and his wife who, for business reasons, had been living in Paris for a couple of years. Who would not like to live in Paris for a couple of years! This couple loved it, but what they did not love were their frequent trips back and forth across the Atlantic for business and family reasons. The wife told me that she wished she had a way of being rendered unconscious when she left her apartment and of waking up when she arrived at the end of her trip ten hours later. I suspect that we all have had experiences that make us sympathetic with this desire. We are eager to arrive at our destination, but we dread the experience of going there. We can even generalize beyond travel and say that the attainment of many of our goals is like this—we look forward to the result, but dread the process of going toward it.

What is very distinctive about modern Americans is that we freely chose to put ourselves in such situations over and over again. Indeed, we can even become uneasy when we are not in such situations. This feature of our lives and its distinctiveness was noticed almost two hundred years ago by Alexis de Tocqueville during the visit that led him to write his *Democracy in America*. One of the things that he says struck him was that although Americans are placed in what he called "the happiest condition that exists in the world" they do not, in fact, appear to be happy. The basic reason for this is that, instead of enjoying what is available to them, Americans are usually engaged in the serious and relentless pursuit of goods that they do not have yet. He describes one aspect of the restless activity that he observed this way: "When toward the end of a year filled with work some leisure still remains to him, [an American] carries his restive curiosity here and there within the vast limits of the United States. He will thus go five hundred leagues in a few days in order better to distract himself from his happiness."[1] Things have not changed since Tocqueville wrote this, or if they have it is only to intensify his observation. We all know people who return from a vacation ready to tell everyone about how many miles they covered each day rather than what interesting experiences they had or sights they saw. The task of my essay is to explain Rousseau's account of the significance of engaging in this sort of pursuit of happiness. To prepare for this I will turn away from my own travels and from the characteristics of American life and to Rousseau.

When Rousseau had reached his late thirties he had experienced many things but accomplished very little that was tangible. He spent his time doing unprofitable jobs, going to the theater and concerts when he had money, and hanging out with his friends at coffee houses. This is only one of the ways in which his life seems to exemplify certain possibilities of modern existence. During this same period he was also thinking and studying. Once he became active, within a few years he was immensely famous for his discourses, an opera, and a novel. He was one of the earliest examples we know of a literary celebrity. At the height of his fame he was inundated with letters from readers whom he had never met. Some sought letters of recommendation that would allow their hitherto unrecognized merit to be rewarded. Others hoped for a reply that would impress their friends with their intimacy with a famous man—think of what it would be like to get a letter from a famous writer. Some—mainly women and young men—however, wrote to Rousseau because they believed that he could give them something unavailable elsewhere. Near the conclusion of *Emile*, Rousseau's book on education, the tutor says to his fictional student who is named Emile, "You must be happy, dear Emile. That is the goal of every being which senses. That is the first desire which nature has impressed on us, and the only one which never leaves us. But where is happiness? Who knows it?"[2] Many of Rousseau's readers concluded from the study of his books that the answer to this final question—"Who knows it?"—was, "Jean-Jacques Rousseau." What was at stake in their reading of and correspondence with Rousseau was their life's happiness. For such readers Rousseau had either posed a question about which they had never thought or reopened a question they had been taught to regard as closed: the question of whether happiness was in principle possible. To raise such a possibility, as Rousseau had, is to create a longing that demands satisfaction. Feeling this longing, these readers demanded its satisfaction from him. Now, it happens that Rousseau's works provide a number of possible directions in which one could seek happiness—religion, politics, love, family, and so on. I am going to simplify my task by exploring only one of these directions, but I am not choosing it at random. I think it is the most distinctive and perhaps the most influential one that Rousseau presents as well as being the one that provides the standard that would allow us to judge the others. Let's approach Rousseau's position by reflecting on the problem it was meant to solve.

While Rousseau's readers responded to him as *the* expert on happiness he certainly was far from the only writer to discuss happiness in the eighteenth century. He himself complained, "All books speak to us about the sovereign good, all philosophers show it to us, each teaches others the art of being happy, none has found it for himself" (*Moral Letters*, CW, 12:180). The art of being happy as presented in all these books is empty because none of these philosophers have put the problem of happiness on the proper footing. As a very preliminary, but nonetheless necessary, step to grasping Rousseau's understanding of happiness, I would like to explore his analysis of one significant philosophic account with which he was confronted and against which he based his own. Then I want to look at the similar accounts of happiness given by some of Rousseau's contemporaries or immediate predecessors to which he responded. My goal is to shed some light on the problem he was attempting to solve and to identify some of the characteristic features of his solution. These are what made his account so appealing to his readers.

Now let me turn to some texts. A note to the *Discourse on Inequality* contains the first clear statement in Rousseau's writings that he had demonstrated what he later called his "great principle": "man is naturally good" (*Dialogues*, CW, 1:213). It is in this note that Rousseau gives his clearest and most forceful account of his claim that human misery has its source in social conditions rather than nature or God. This is the argument that I began by linking with the photographs in the DIGNITY exhibit. The note begins by describing one version of the position against which his doctrine of natural goodness stands: "A famous Author calculating the goods and evils of human life, and comparing the two sums, found that the latter greatly surpassed the former, and that all things considered life was a rather poor present to man" (*DOI*, CW, 3:74). The first meaning of Rousseau's own new doctrine of natural goodness, then, is not that human beings are naturally moral, rather it is that life is good for us, that it is not "a rather poor present." The famous author in question in this passage was Pierre-Louis Moreau de Maupertuis, whom Rousseau praises elsewhere in the *Discourse*. Rousseau praises Maupertuis for his scientific investigations, and Maupertuis was, indeed, a very prominent scientist. Today he is best remembered for an expedition to Lapland in which he took the astronomical readings and performed the calculations that proved that the earth was flatter at the poles than at the equator; in other words, it is not a perfect sphere. Like numerous scientists before and since, Maupertuis thought that the scientific method that allowed him to answer that sort of question could be extended to the solution of political and moral questions. Accordingly he did not restrict his investigations to the natural sciences and he attempted to bring his method of calculation to bear on other questions. He produced a series of works in which he used the methods of calculus to address a variety of problems. Some of these works were rigorously scientific and use the most sophisticated mathematical techniques available. When these techniques were beyond Maupertuis's own competence—he was a better researcher than mathematician— he consulted with the most able mathematicians in Europe. In other cases he used the language of calculus unaccompanied by sophisticated calculations to enhance the sense that he had deduced a rigorous conclusion.[3]

Maupertuis performed the calculation of goods and evils to which Rousseau refers in his *Essay of Moral Philosophy*, published originally in 1749 and republished shortly before Rousseau wrote the *Discourse*. Rousseau's passing reference may look like an attempt to provide a convenient and up-to-date foil for his alternative view, but as I will show the evaluation of human happiness in terms of the calculation of goods and evils is a recurring theme in his subsequent works. What are these calculations that led Maupertuis to his bleak conclusion that "all things considered life was a rather poor present to man"? In the *Essay* he gives a mathematical sounding definition of happiness as "*the sum of the goods* that is left after one has subtracted the *sum of evils.*"[4] One might think that different lives would yield very different sums, that lives of prosperity and health would be very different from lives of poverty and illness, but Maupertuis argues that he can arrive at a generally valid addition and subtraction by dividing life into moments of desire and of accomplishment of desire. Everyone experiences this division. We form a desire and later, if we are lucky, we satisfy it. In between these two moments there is a more or less long interval in which we are dissatisfied because we are striving to accomplish a desire that we have not yet satisfied. Maupertuis's focus is on this interval. He argues that we would wish to annihilate the interval between desire and satisfaction, saying, "Often we would want to have days, months, entire years suppressed" (*Maupertuis*, 202). If we, in fact, suppressed or subtracted the intervals—another mathematical term—we would find that "perhaps the entire duration of the longest life would be reduced to several hours." This is what the pursuit of happiness means, then—much tedious pursuit ventured for little tangible happiness.

Maupertuis confirms his argument about the interval by raising an interesting question: How many people would like to live their lives over again? By this he does not mean having a chance to use the knowledge we have acquired to correct all of our mistakes and make things turn out differently. Most of us would certainly want to do that. Rather, he means live it over again exactly as it was with all the pleasures and pains, brilliant actions and embarrassments. His conclusion is that if you ask anyone, "in any condition that one might take them," there will be few "who would want to begin their life over again as it has been, who would want to pass over again through all the same states in which they have found themselves" (*Maupertuis*, 204). Think of the many intervals of boredom and frustration and the few moments of genuine pleasure! This nearly universal unwillingness to relive one's entire life is, he says, "the clearest admission" that life is made up of far more evil than good.

One can now see the point of my story about my trip and my conversation with the businessman and his wife who were living in Paris with which this essay began. Maupertuis asks his readers to think about all the occasions in which they wished they could be knocked out for a few or many hours, or days, or months instead of having to be conscious while they wait to reach their destination. Think of the many devices—Rousseau with a great deal of foresight refers to them as "enormous machines for happiness or pleasure" (*Dialogues*, CW, 1:159)—we have invented to help us pass this time. The interesting question is whether we have invented these devices, such as cell phones or iPads, to give us something interesting and worthwhile to do during the intervals or whether we have invented them simply to distract us enough to make the interval more tolerable, in other words to stupefy us. Watching people in public transportation and university dining halls can give food for thought on this point.

Maupertuis does not shy away from the inescapable consequence of his argument. He praises the ancient Stoics for acknowledging that "as soon as the sum of evils surpasses the sum of goods, nothingness is preferable to being" (*Maupertuis*, 227; see also 224–25). Whatever the Stoics might have meant by "as soon as," Maupertuis says in his own name, "If there were nothing beyond this life, it would *often* be appropriate to end it" (*Maupertuis*, 189). Of course, he knows that most people do not act upon this conclusion. To explain why we continue to find such an existence tolerable he provides a further diagnosis of the human condition. The diagnosis is that all people, acting under the universal natural principle of the insatiable desire to be happy, spend their lives seeking what he calls "remedies to the illness of being alive" (*Maupertuis*, 204). When interrogated carefully they acknowledge that their lives have been spent futilely and even that the pursuit of pleasure has only aggravated this futility. In the end, for most people the desire to be happy leads only to indulgence in diversions that "prove the unhappiness of their condition" (*Maupertuis*, 203). Maupertuis's discussion of this is interesting and might strike a chord with some of you. He observes that some people play chess, others go hunting, all seek forgetfulness of themselves in serious or frivolous occupations. When these efforts at distraction fail, as they must in the long run, people seek to relieve or stupefy themselves, Maupertuis says, by drinking various liquors, smoking the leaves of a plant, or making use of a juice that puts them into a sort of ecstasy. These are Maupertuis's examples, not mine, but it would be hard for me to come up with ones that much more relevant today. The universal quest for distraction from oneself or relief in the form of stupefaction is proof that, try as they might to avoid facing Maupertuis's gloomy calculations, people do feel their truth.

To this diagnosis Maupertuis offers two palliatives that he knows fall short of being cures. Having praised the Stoics for their position on suicide, he also argues that this sect has seen the one possible alternative. They saw that the pursuit of happiness only increases the unpleasantness of the interval between desire and satisfaction and concluded that the strict limitation of desires is the one way to alleviate the illness of being alive. We should restrict our pursuit of happiness, not because moderation is a good thing in itself, but because the pursuit is so frustrating. Maupertuis endorses what we can call this stoic hedonism with the proviso that as soon as boredom with life takes over one should be prepared to end it.

Understanding that this recommendation would lead, as it in fact did, to the accusation that he had written "a work of impiety," Maupertuis concludes the *Essay* with two chapters on religion that led some readers to regard the work as "a book of devoutness," a charge which he also sought to avoid (*Maupertuis*, 182). He defends Christianity on entirely nonreligious grounds by arguing that it agrees with his view of the inherent misery of human life. Even its prohibition of suicide is an acknowledgment of the attractiveness of this remedy. He argues that the Christian view of providence is the only understanding that offers a plausible fulfillment of the desire for happiness. In fact, even if Christian hope for salvation were based on an illusion, it could add to the sum of goods in his calculation. Maupertuis implicitly recalculates

Pascal's famous wager by suggesting that a bet on Christianity wins whether this religion is true or false: if it is true we receive the reward for our faith, if it is false we have diverted ourselves from the misery of our condition almost as effectively as we would with the use of physical opiates.

Why have I spent so long tracing the argument of a thinker remembered mainly by historians of science rather than political scientists or philosophers? There are certainly eccentric elements in Maupertuis's *Essay*. Nevertheless, Rousseau's prominent reference to it clearly indicates that he thought that its analysis was symptomatic of more general tendencies. It is not hard to find evidence that this is true. One echo of his response to Maupertuis occurred a few years later when Rousseau addressed a much more famous author in the *Letter to Voltaire*. The identity of his concern in the two contexts is clear. In the *Confessions* Rousseau identifies the central issue at stake in his dispute with Voltaire. Comparing Voltaire's life of prosperity and glory—Voltaire had very shrewdly used his literary fame to make himself rich—with his own life of illness and poverty, he uses language very reminiscent of his discussion of Maupertuis's calculating the goods and evils of human life. He says, "Being more authorized than [Voltaire] was to count and weigh the evils of human life, I made an equitable examination of them, and I proved to him that out of all these evils, there was not one from which providence was not exculpated."[5] In the *Letter* itself he prefaces his affirmative answer to the question of whether "it is better for us to be than not to be" by stating the novelty of his position, "But on this subject it is difficult to find any good faith among men, and any good calculations among Philosophers" ("Letter to Voltaire," CW, 3:111). As in the *Discourse*, the issue here is one of *proper calculation*. In moving from the *Discourse* to the "Letter" and beyond, Rousseau broadened and deepened his target. It is no longer a single famous author who has made the error in calculation. Indeed, Rousseau's formulation indicates that the error made by Maupertuis is characteristic of philosophers in general: none of them make any good calculations on this question. Maupertuis's conclusion that life is "a rather poor present to man" is one that Rousseau saw as part of a general tendency, and he explicitly rejects it in the "Letter to Voltaire" when he says that "whatever ills might be spread over human life, it is all things considered not a bad present" ("Letter to Voltaire," CW, 3:112).

The error with which Rousseau charges Maupertuis and those who agree with him is neither that their calculations are simply wrong nor that their description of human life is simply false; it is, rather, that they have described something characteristic of the sorts of societies in which we live at present while thinking that they were describing the natural human condition and the way things must be for us. This is a very common theme in Rousseau's works. He makes the same charge against Hobbes and others elsewhere in the *Second Discourse*. Given the similarity of their errors, it is not surprising to find in Hobbes the classic statement, not of the precise calculations made by Maupertuis, but of their underlying premise. In one of numerous passages meant to discredit a traditional account of happiness, Hobbes says that "the Felicity of this life, consisteth not in the repose of a mind satisfied. For there is no such *Finis ultimus* (utmost aim) nor *Summum Bonum* (greatest Good) as is spoken of in the Books of the old Moral Philosophers. Nor can a man any more live, when desires are at an end, than he, whose Senses and Imagination are at a stand. Felicity is a continual progresse of the desire, from one object to another; the attaining of the former, being still but the way to the later."[6] This last statement is crucial, "felicity, or happiness, is a continual progresse of the desire from one object to another." There is no happiness that consists in genuine satisfaction. Hobbes and Maupertuis reject any account of happiness based on a conception of any good that offers enduring satisfaction.

The difference between them consists largely in Hobbes's willingness to characterize as happiness a condition in which we move from desire to desire without any enduring satisfaction. While Maupertuis might accept Hobbes's famous claim that life is nothing but "a perpetual and restlesse desire of Power after power, that ceaseth onely in Death," he refuses to concede that happiness is a term that can be applied to such an existence that, as I indicated earlier, he prefers to call the illness of being alive. Small as it might seem, this difference does lead to a practical conclusion in that Hobbes is both much more willing to tolerate perpetually unsatisfied desire and at the same time less optimistic about the palliative quality of even a hedonistic stoicism. He denies that it is possible for us to restrict our desires in order to prevent their frustration. Our desires are not subject to such rational control.

What Maupertuis and Hobbes have in common joins them in a thread that runs through a significant portion of Enlightenment thought. The bridge from Hobbes to Voltaire, for example, is found in John Locke, to whom we owe the phrases pursuit of property and pursuit of happiness, every bit as much as in Maupertuis. In discussing how it happens that men pursue happiness in such different ways, Locke argues that—contrary to what many philosophers in the past believed—this is not simply a result of the tendency of most people to make errors about what will truly make them happy. He asserts that "the Philosophers of old did in vain inquire, whether *Summum bonum* consisted in Riches or bodily Delights or Virtue or Contemplation: And they might have as reasonably disputed, whether the best Relish were to be found in Apples, Plumbs, or Nuts; and have divided themselves into Sects upon it."[7] In his article "Bien, Souverain bien," in the *Philosophic Dictionary*, Voltaire in effect translates this passage into his own style, making explicit his rejection of what Hobbes called the old moral philosophers and Locke called the philosophers of old. He proclaims, "Antiquity debated a good deal about the supreme good. It would have been just as well to ask, What is the supreme blue, or the supreme stew, the supreme walk, the supreme reading, etc."[8] He asserts that the greatest good is an illusion for two reasons: first, it varies according to persons and, second, cannot last for more than a moment in anyone. Voltaire, however, showed little sympathy for the

Stoic or Christian responses to the human condition that Maupertuis recommended. In fact, the approach of Voltaire and others could be characterized as an attempt to take advantage of the very symptoms that Maupertuis had identified as evidence that people unconsciously acknowledged the truth of his calculation about happiness: their attempts to find remedies for the illness of being alive in distraction from and relief of suffering. According to Rousseau, such an attempt only aggravates the problem.

Let's think about these two remedies of relief and distraction for a moment. Certainly a large part of our lives is devoted to relieving our own suffering and that of others. I will not devote much time to this issue and the related one of pursuit of comfort. We certainly see this everywhere around us in arguments about, for example, how to get the economy going and pleas for funding for medical research. The premise of these arguments is that comfort is good and discomfort is bad. One could question whether these are the only, or even the most important, goods and bads, but it is more useful for the purposes of my argument here to highlight the importance of distraction, or entertainment, a theme with which we are familiar today in our daily lives even if we reflect upon it less. Now, distraction or diversion was one of the issues separating Rousseau from Voltaire and d'Alembert in a dispute over the establishment of a publicly funded theater in Geneva, a dispute that began when d'Alembert (in part to gratify Voltaire who was living near Geneva) urged that city to establish a publicly funded theater. To be sure, d'Alembert, like many supporters of the arts, argued that the theater could be a source of moral improvement and it is important to note that it is he—and not Rousseau—who is the defender of censorship in their dispute. If the goal of the arts is moral improvement, it is hard, if not impossible, to argue against censorship to make sure they achieve that end. No one believes that everything that claims to be a work of art has a good moral effect. What are we to do with the ones that don't? Nevertheless, in addition to his argument for moral improvement, d'Alembert is also friendly to forms of entertainment that promise no moral improvement. When Rousseau attacked the theater as useless entertainment, d'Alembert responded, "Life is so unhappy and pleasure so rare! Why begrudge men, destined by nature almost only to weep and to die, some fleeting diversions that help them to bear the bitterness or the insipidity of their existence?" (*D'Alembert*, CW, 10:355). Indeed, he even insists that the theater is not *sufficiently* diverting. Facing up to the fact that life is composed of "discontent with ourselves and others, combined with a natural inclination for idleness in anxiety and activity in desires" would allow us to see that we should promote entertainment for its own sake and that we should seek entertainment that is particularly diverting (*D'Alembert*, CW, 10:356). It should act to alleviate "the agitation that torments us or the languor that consumes us by means of the distractions it offers us." Thus where Maupertuis had seen the symptoms of the illness of being alive, d'Alembert—and not only d'Alembert—sees the treatment for the illness. Indeed, d'Alembert's worry is that the theater is too tame to distract us. We really need more lively entertainment to distract us. One wonders what d'Alembert would have thought about football, NASCAR, and violent movies. In any event, his argument suggests that the proper role of intellectuals is to promote those entertainments that aid people in their quest for both relief of and distraction from the misery of their condition.

The thread formed by these related accounts of the impossibility of happiness as it is normally considered, of the futility of the pursuit of happiness, helps to show that the Enlightenment project that is often said to consist of the relief of man's estate by means of the progressive mastery of nature can manifest itself alternatively as the goal of relieving an essential dissatisfaction with existence by means of both material comforts offering temporary relief and entertainment that distracts us from ourselves and the insipidity of our existence. Rousseau, however, argues that the quest for a relief that can be only momentary and a distraction from ourselves that can be only incomplete merely aggravates the experience of illness. This is, however, not the illness of being alive, as Maupertuis would have it, but the illness of modern civilized life. Rousseau rejects the calculation on the basis of which these conclusions are reached. Let me now develop his alternative calculation.

Working for the sake of making ourselves comfortable later means orienting ourselves toward the future. Seeking entertainment for the sake of distracting ourselves from the tedium of our existence means orienting ourselves away from ourselves. Both of these involve turning attention away from ourselves to something outside. It is perhaps not surprising that the alternatives Rousseau suggests involve changing our orientation toward the present and toward ourselves. His opponents would claim that this could only make us miserable or more aware of our misery. What does Rousseau have to say in favor of this change? Briefly, his alternative is to replace the pursuit of relief with present enjoyment and to replace distraction from ourselves with a new focus on ourselves. I will try to explain these briefly.

Recall that the crucial element of Maupertuis's calculation is the "interval" between desire and satisfaction, the interval that we would want to see annihilated and that makes up almost all of our lives. Maupertuis established the existence and extent of this interval by appealing to an experience that Rousseau does not deny. In *Emile* Rousseau uses strikingly similar language: "Always occupied with the goal toward which they are straining, [men] regard with regret the interval separating them from that goal. One man wants it to be tomorrow, another next month, another ten years from now. None wants to live *today*" (*Emile*, CW, 13:593). In an earlier draft of this passage he makes an even more rigorous calculation specifically with regard to people who face a long commute to their employment. Once again we are back with the businessman and his wife whom I met in Paris. Rousseau says, "I assume that they put only one hour into each trip. I also assume that they are the masters of removing that hour from the day so that at the moment that they leave from one of the two cities they arrive at the other and the interval is suppressed, I say that perhaps there is not one of them who would not accept the offer and who would not believe he had gained a great deal. Now what would he have gained, I beg of you? To cut short his life by 360 hours a year, that is to say by one year every 24 years" ("Favre Manuscript," CW, 13:151). The conclusion Rousseau draws in the final version is even more extreme and, moreover, is also in perfect accord with that of Maupertuis. He says that "there is perhaps not a single one who would not have reduced his years to very few hours if he had been the master of eliminating, at the prompting of his boredom, those hours which were burdensome to him" (*Emile*, CW, 13:594). The existence of this interval, then, is the proof that the pains of life greatly outweigh the pleasures.

Rousseau agrees with Maupertuis that the pursuit of relief merely aggravates the experience of the interval. At times he also seems to agree in provisionally recommending a Stoic decrease of desire as a palliative. Desiring less will help us to avoid increasing the intervals between the formation of desire and its satisfaction. Nevertheless, Rousseau's occasional qualified Stoicism is more often supplemented by what could be called a refined Epicureanism. Rather than simply urging the reduction of desires in order to decrease pain, Rousseau argues that putting off rather than pursuing satisfaction can often increase pleasure. As one of his characters in his great novel, *Julie*, says, "Thus the sensuality of the sage is made more keen; abstaining the better to enjoy, that is your philosophy; it is the epicureanism of reason" (*Julie*, CW, 6:544). We enjoy dinner more by letting ourselves get hungry rather than by snacking all afternoon. I will leave other examples of how one could increase pleasure by delaying satisfaction up to the reader's imagination. In other words, Rousseau substitutes for the vain pursuit of happiness, the development of ways to increase the enjoyment of existence even in the absence of satisfaction of our desires. At the end of his calculation of the interval in *Emile*, Rousseau says, "If there is a single one among you who knows how to temper his desires so that he never wishes for time to pass, he will not regard life as too short. To live and to enjoy would be the same thing for him, and even if he were to die young, he would die full with days" (*Emile*, CW, 13:594). To live and to enjoy replace pursuit of happiness or distraction from misery. The person Rousseau describes would not simply reduce the interval by limiting desire, he would fill the remaining interval with enjoyment. Such a person is Rousseau's fictional student Emile whom Rousseau says he has raised not "to desire or to want but to enjoy." It is not surprising that Rousseau considered writing a work called "On the Art of Enjoyment." Unfortunately we have only a few fragments of this work.

As an aside I will mention that Rousseau is not unique in his judgment of Maupertuis's argument and its consequences. His great contemporary, Montesquieu, who was friendly with Maupertuis, made a similar objection quite independently in notes that he wrote that Rousseau would not have been able to read. He says, "M. de Maupertuis brings into his calculation only pleasures and pains, that is to say everything that informs the soul about its happiness or its unhappiness. He does not bring into it the happiness of existence and habitual felicity, which informs about nothing, because it is habitual."[9] This habitual pleasure or pleasure in simply existing, Montesquieu calls, "existence and nature." He concludes, "It is not necessary to say that happiness is that moment that we would not change for a different one. Let us say differently: happiness is that moment that we would not exchange for non-being." He is confident that we would seldom prefer non-existence to the pleasure of simply existing. Such considerations lead Montesquieu to a conclusion similar to Rousseau's about different social conditions and even the natural environment as promoting or inhibiting our experience of existence and nature, what Rousseau calls the "sentiment of existence."

Turning back to Rousseau, we can say that enjoying means learning to take pleasure in the interval between desire and satisfaction, to use the absence of satisfaction to make even limited enjoyment more keen. Rousseau says that Emile will learn to enjoy not only the satisfaction of desire but also desire itself as well as "going to the object of desire." Rousseau argues that it is possible to enjoy the longing even for imaginary objects. The possibility of enjoyment of the interval as well as the terms surrounding it shifts the balance of the calculation of the goods and ills of human life toward happiness. One example of this is that Rousseau suggests that we can and should travel in ways that make the trip itself enjoyable rather than in ways that make us wish that we could be unconscious or even simply distracted until we arrive at our destination. We should think about the scenery and talk with our neighbors.

This shift is seen in Rousseau's reply to the claim "few people would want to be reborn in the same condition in which they have lived," made by Voltaire and Erasmus, as well as Maupertuis. Remember that Maupertuis had said that his position that no one would want to live his life over again could be proven by polling people in any condition whatsoever. Rousseau argues that this is the experience only of the rich and of intellectuals: two groups that are chronically more miserable than they think they deserve to be and that chronically complain about this misery. As a college professor I have more exposure to one of these groups than the other, but my experience makes me trust Rousseau on this point. He appeals to different groups; referring to simple farmers living on the border between France and Switzerland, he says, "I dare to state that perhaps there is in the upper Valais not a single Mountaineer discontented with his almost automatic life, and who would not willingly accept, even in place of Paradise, the bargain of being reborn unceasingly in order to vegetate thus in perpetuity" ("Letter to Voltaire," CW, 3:111). To the testimony of these simple people he adds that of "an honest *bourgeois*," "a good artisan," and a peasant who lives in a free country. In these cases it is not a hypothetical Emile who has received a special education who serves as a counterexample, but a wide assortment of existing people who consider their lives to be "not a bad present."

Rousseau's recalculation leads him to reconsider the issue of suicide. Again, like Maupertuis, he endorses the Stoic position that the wise man will "depart voluntarily without a murmur and without despair, when nature or fortune very clearly brings him the order for departure" ("Letter to Voltaire," CW, 3:112). Nevertheless, unlike Maupertuis who said that these occurrences happen often, Rousseau insists that such situations exist very seldom "in the ordinary course of things." Indeed, if Maupertuis's calculation were accurate, suicide would be epidemic given the limitations of relief, distraction, and stupefaction, and thus "the human race could not long subsist." Fortunately for the continuation of the species, "however ingenious we may be in stirring up our misfortunes by dint of fine institutions, we have not been able, up to the present, to perfect ourselves to the point of generally rendering life a burden to ourselves and to prefer nothingness to our existence" ("Letter to Voltaire," CW, 3:111). Again, Rousseau claims that most people do, in fact, replace the quest for relief with the experience of enjoyment. They can do so, as he later wrote, because, "the sweet enjoyment of life is permanent; to taste it, it is sufficient not to suffer" ("Letter to Franquières," CW, 8:265). In short, enjoyment, not uneasiness or suffering, is the underlying, if too often invisible human condition. It is in large part our failure to appreciate this fact that leads us to do the things that stimulate rather than relieve our uneasiness.

What distinguishes the rich and the intellectuals from those capable of enjoyment is that they are "of all the orders of men the most sedentary, the most unhealthy, the most reflective, and consequently the most unhappy" ("Letter to Franquières," CW, 8:265). These are people who, like Voltaire himself, are "loaded with good things of every sort," but who are miserable nonetheless. Because they have the means for satisfying their desires at hand, the interval between desire and satisfaction should be short. Even so, they are the most active seekers of diversions from themselves in the form of entertainment or stupefaction. It appears to be their reflective character that causes this intense dissatisfaction with existence.

That the possibility of happiness is most problematic for reflective people is apparent in the one passage in Rousseau's works in which he comes closest to endorsing Maupertuis's calculation. Early in book 2 of *Emile* he asserts that the very meaning of absolute happiness is simply inaccessible to us to say nothing about the experience of this happiness. In considering even relative happiness, he says, "The happiest is he who suffers the least pain; the unhappiest is he who feels the least pleasure. Always more suffering than enjoyment" (*Emile*, CW, 13:210). Here Rousseau holds out only the hope of being "not unhappy" or being "less removed from being happy," although even here his claim that the unhappiest is the one who feels the least pleasure implies that some positive enjoyment is possible. While he does not endorse suicide here, he says that the wise man finds the inevitability of his death to be a consolation for bearing the pains of life. Outdoing his characterization of Maupertuis's account of life as "a rather poor present," he even says, "If we were to be offered immortality on the earth, who would want to accept this dreary present." Is Rousseau contradicting here what he says later in the book? Considering that this endorsement of the calculation of the philosophers might be misunderstood, for later editions of *Emile* Rousseau added a note reading, "It is understood that I speak here of men who reflect and not of all men" (*Emile*, CW, 13:742). Does this mean that there is no form of happiness available to those who reflect and that Rousseau concedes that distraction and stupefaction are the right courses for them? Where can such people find enjoyment?

I began by talking about the many readers who wrote to Rousseau looking for guidance about how to be happy. One of these, who called herself "Henriette," was afflicted with an unusually strong case of this reflective version of what Maupertuis called the illness of being alive. She wrote to Rousseau that every morning she awoke with an overwhelming sense of dread at facing her existence. She said that she sought relief from this sense of dread in pursuing the sort of intellectual and social activities that Rousseau tended to criticize. In effect, she asked Rousseau both for help and for an endorsement of her way of life. Often people who say they are asking for advice are in fact looking for an endorsement of what they already intend to do. Rousseau responded that, for reflective people like her, the greatest misfortune of their condition is that "the more one feels its ills, the more one increases them, and all our efforts to leave it do nothing but bog us down more deeply in it."[10] While he does urge her to engage in a more active life, to "get a life" as we might say, he does not urge her simply to stop thinking and enjoy life as the mountaineers do since "one does not take off one's head like one's bonnet, and one does not return to simplicity any more than to childhood."[11] Following the pattern described by Maupertuis, "Henriette" desperately seeks to escape her feeling of dread by looking for distraction from herself. Her distinctiveness lies in the fact that she seeks distraction in neither the theater nor strong drink. Rousseau observes, "You want to distract yourself from yourself by means of philosophy."[12] He argues that, rather than distracting herself from herself this way, she must find her way back to herself. This is what he calls "gathering oneself together into oneself," which he presents as a precondition for enjoyment for reflective people.

Prior to Rousseau, and indeed after him, the term he uses here that I have translated as "gathering oneself together," *recueillement*, was a term used primarily in connection with religious meditation or contemplation, as in putting oneself into the proper state of mind to receive a sacrament. Rousseau makes use of these connotations, but in a quite unreligious way. Perhaps his most distinctive use of the term is one identified in dictionaries as unique in the French language. One of his characters in his novel *Julie*, an English nobleman named Lord Edward, has spent years torn between his virtue and his love for not one, but two women: a married Italian noblewoman and a reformed prostitute. It would be hard to combine virtue with either of these loves. He has spent his time traveling back and forth between Rome where these women live and his home in England. In these lengthy travels he certainly would have experienced the desire to eliminate many tedious hours. On the verge of deciding to abandon his pursuit of these women Edward declares to his friend that "it is time for me to gather myself together into myself" (*Julie*, CW, 5:534), by which he seems to mean retire from this life of endless vacillation and travel. By this he does not mean that he will withdraw into a life of monastic meditation, but that he will withdraw to his estate, sharing its solitude with his friends. The distraction from himself caused by his frantic love life, which drives him from England to Rome and back, leaving him with many intervals between desire and satisfaction, will be replaced by an absorption in a domestic life centered on friendship. Thus, while this term suggests a retreat into oneself, it is quite compatible with, indeed requires a sort of social existence.

Just as Rousseau opposes "the art of enjoyment" to relief from suffering, he opposes gathering oneself into oneself to distraction from oneself of the sort found in entertainment. A full evaluation of his account of happiness would require giving some more substance to these terms than I have done here and comparing his account with genuine alternatives. For those who would like to see Rousseau's description of such a condition I recommend the account he gives at the end of book 4 of *Emile* where he discusses how he would live his life if he were rich. A full treatment of this issue would also require giving an account of the limits that Rousseau sees in this new way of seeking happiness. What I have tried to show is that his focus on these precise elements results from his effort to reopen the question of the possibility of happiness against the foreclosure of this possibility, which he saw as characteristic of the thought of his contemporaries as represented in their emphasis on the pursuit rather than the attainment of happiness.

NOTES

1.   Alexis de Tocqueville, *Democracy in America*, translated and edited by Harvey C. Mansfield and Delba Winthrop (Chicago: University of Chicago Press, 2000), 512.

2.   *Emile*, CW, 13:630. All quotations from *Emile* refer to this edition. One should not simply assume that this is Rousseau's opinion. See Fragment 21, in CW, 12:279.

3.   For an account of Maupertuis's career, see Mary Terrall, *The Man Who Flattened the Earth: Maupertuis and the Sciences in the Enlightenment* (Chicago: University of Chicago Press, 2002). It is somewhat surprising that Terrall says nothing about Maupertuis's *Essay* (discussed below) in this very comprehensive study.

4.   *Essai de philosophie morale* in *Œuvres de M. de Mauperuis* (Lyon: Chez Jean-Marie Bruyset, 1756), 1:197. Cited in this chapter as *Maupertuis*.

5.   *Conf*, CW, 5:360–61. See also *Letter to Voltaire*, CW, 3:120.

6.   Thomas Hobbes, *Leviathan*, Chapter 11.

7.   John Locke, *An Essay Concerning Human Understanding*, 2.21.55. Stephen Eide has pointed out to me that Locke is very cautious about denying the existence of a summum bonum. See ibid., 4.12.11.

8.   Voltaire, *Philosophical Dictionary*, trans. Peter Gay (New York: Basic Books, 1962), 114.

9. Montesquieu, *Mes Pensées* in *Œuvres complètes*, ed. Roger Caillois (Paris: Gallimard, 1949), 2:1267.

10. "Letters to Henriette" in *Rousseau on Women, Love, and Family,* ed. Christopher Kelly and Eve Grace (Hanover, NH: University Press of New England, 2009), 150.

11. Ibid., 149–50.

12. Ibid., 152.

CHAPTER 10

From Rousseau to Occupy

Imagining a More Equal World

C h r i s t i e   M c D o n a l d

We came to the tercentennial anniversary of Rousseau's birth with a lot on our minds: a heightened consciousness of change and human suffering globally (from whatever space we occupy in the information revolution), perhaps a sense of helplessness and even triviality (what got reported, for example, in the high stakes primary campaign of spring 2012); often an understandable desire to look away from the harsh realities that have followed in the wake of the 2008 economic crisis. One of the questions we need to ask is what Jean-Jacques Rousseau has to say to us today in such circumstances and whether we still look to the humanities for guidance in a world jouncing with technological advances and scientific inventions. In thinking about Rousseau and human rights, two main lines of discussion will be followed here: the first draws on the anthropological and political works by Rousseau (*The Discourse on the Origin of Inequality* and the *Social Contract*) looking to the definition of what constitutes the individual and social existence, the dignity of humankind, their natural and inalienable rights. The second focuses on discourses of sentiment and sensibility primarily in *Julie, or, The New Heloise*, to open up issues around empathy and the body that affect a sense of rights within community: the family, the small society, and a sense of humanity worldwide.[1]

How is it possible to put together Rousseau's anthropological thought about self and other, his political theory about the individual and society, and the question of human rights at its root? This is what I would like to look at briefly. To do so, I will first locate some of the ways in which Rousseau has been read; then, I will outline schematically the principles of human rights in Rousseau's thought, taking examples from the *Discourse on Inequality*, the *Social Contract,* and his novel, *Julie, or, The New Héloïse*; finally, I will fast-forward to the Occupy movement and suggest the kind of theoretical continuity we might see there. The question I am asking then is: how do we read Rousseau today and how does his work help us read our own era?

ROUSSEAU AND ENLIGHTENMENT: BETWEEN INDIVIDUAL RIGHTS AND A "SOCIAL CONTRACT"

Lévi-Strauss

The mid-twentieth century was a key moment in reading Rousseau across the disciplines of anthropology, political science, and literature. Rousseau's work loomed large in anthropologist Claude Lévi-Strauss's writing as Lévi-Strauss laid out the structural basis upon which the binary of nature and culture could be analyzed. In 1962, upon the occasion of Rousseau's 250th birthday, Lévi-Strauss saluted Rousseau not just as the precursor of modern ethnography; "Rousseau did not restrict himself to anticipating ethnology; he founded it."[2] Lévi-Strauss goes on, as though this statement were not surprising, to evoke the problem of how Rousseau adopted a method to relate nature and culture in the *Discourse on Inequality*: "When one wishes to study men, one has to look close by; but in order to study man, one has to learn to cast one's eyes far off; first one has to observe the differences in order to discover the properties."[3] In *Tristes Tropiques* (1955), his intellectual autobiography, Lévi-Strauss had suggested, "It would be gratifying to be able to show the considerable support given . . . by contemporary anthropology to the theories put forward by eighteenth-century thinkers."[4] For Rousseau and his contemporaries, it was the notion that "cultural attitudes and features such as the 'contract' and 'consent' are not secondary creations . . . they are the basic material of social life, and it is impossible to imagine any form of political organization in which they would not be present."[5] There is a very curious kind of haunting that Rousseau exerts upon Lévi-Strauss, whose magisterial homage to him as "the most anthropological of the *philosophes*" includes the quite pertinent fact that Rousseau's travels were pretty much limited to trekking across mountains between Paris and Geneva. But beyond firsthand documentation (or its lack), what is important to me is that both thinkers looked to *hypothesis*: for Rousseau, hypothesis became the model for truth while for Lévi-Strauss, it was the model for structural knowledge and understanding. Rousseau turned away from the facts of history in the *Discourse on Inequality*, creating a narration of the hypothetical origins of humankind: an imagined history to counter what he saw everywhere as the moral degradation in society. The need to step back and challenge the status quo was key to Rousseau's entire work, and it is what also brought him celebrity (or notoriety). Lévi-Strauss saw Rousseau less as a removed, contemplative thinker and more "as the involuntary agent of a transformation conveyed through him. In Jean-Jacques Rousseau, the whole of mankind learns to feel this *transformation*."[6]

In discussion about the diverse readings of Rousseau in the 1960s, and in particular Kantian readings, Peter Gay pointed to the importance of the German philosopher Ernst Cassirer (1874–1945), who effected an idealist reevaluation of Rousseau. "For Cassirer, Rousseau was a rational philosopher, the roots of whose thought were deeply buried in his complex character and his varied experience, and whose ideas display a consistent development and rest on a consistent principle."[7] Gay, himself a distinguished historian of the eighteenth century, pronounced this the "best current understanding of Rousseau," just two years short of the breakout publication of *Of Grammatology* in 1967 by Jacques Derrida. Cassirer understood that Rousseau was having a "passionate quarrel with his epoch."[8] He wrote that Rousseau's sentimentalism was no "mere 'sensibility,' but an ethical force and a new ethical will."[9] Yet he saw Rousseau's work in a linear progression, which had prepared Kant's thinking, and he viewed the Enlightenment as a *unified* movement toward secular rationality. This was a transitional moment in thinking about Rousseau, reevaluating many models of interpretation (during the "linguistic turn"). *Of Grammatology* opened up new ways of reading and thinking about Rousseau, not seeking to find a unity of Rousseau's thought, but maintaining the tensions between the binaries of nature and culture, presence and absence, sentiment and reason. Derrida offered a model for reading the contradictions rampant in Rousseau's works without resolving them into a synthetic meaning, as part of what would become widely known as a deconstructive strategy of reading and writing.

In 1962, Michel Foucault prefaced an edition of Rousseau's strange and anguished work, *Rousseau Judge of Jean-Jacques: Dialogues*.[10] What interested him at the time was bringing out this forgotten text about a language of failure and a system of surveillance signs. In a short but important piece written in 1982, Foucault addressed Kant's important, short text of 1784, "Was ist Aufklarung?" ("What Is Enlightenment?"), remarking: "It is neither a world era to which one belongs, nor an event whose signs are perceived, nor the dawning of an accomplishment."[11] If Kant viewed Enlightenment as an "'exit,' a 'way out'" (the escape from immaturity), for Foucault, the important question was: "what difference does *today* introduce with respect to yesterday?" defining Enlightenment "by a modification of the preexisting relation linking will, authority, and the use of reason."[12] Foucault focuses on the present, "today," and there locates modernity as an attitude rather than a particular moment in history.[13] "The thread," he writes, which may connect us with the Enlightenment is not faithfulness to doctrinal elements but, rather, "the permanent reactivation of an attitude—that is, of a philosophical ethos that could be described as a permanent critique of our historical era."[14] Criticism is thus historical ("genealogical in its design and archaeological in its method"), allowing for the understanding of what has led to "constitute ourselves and to recognize ourselves as subjects of what we are doing, thinking, saying."[15] Setting aside questions about whether one should be for or against Enlightenment, Foucault concludes: "I continue to think that this task requires work on our limits, that is, a patient labor giving form to our impatience for liberty."[16] If Foucault's interpretation of Kant situates the present and its critique, it is in a pre-Kantian view that rationalism is not what most significantly defines Enlightenment.

Rousseau is very much an Enlightenment thinker in the sense of taking stock of the present with a critical eye, drawing attention to humans as sentient beings, and asking what grounds and structures contemporary society. It is feeling (*sentiment*) that defines the existence of the subject, not reason, and the possibility of seeing failure as a testing of limits. I have made the case elsewhere[17] that failure is not merely the sense of inadequacy for Jean-Jacques Rousseau, as the first line of the *Social Contract* makes clear: "Man is born free, and everywhere he is in chains" (*SC*, CW, 4:131). Failure is the basis on which his social, political, and personal thought rests. Yet Rousseau's interpretation of failure is as complex as his ideas about equality and freedom. A disjunction occurs between the failure of facts and the concrete, on the one hand, and a utopian vision, on the other, that galvanizes Rousseau's political and social thought. These principles define equality and freedom not just to change or reform thought, but to inaugurate a sense of self and society different from what had preceded him.

Locating Inequality

In the early anthropological works, Rousseau reimagines the history of humankind emerging from nature to culture, in a precontractual world moving from isolation in nature to nascent society. The task he gave himself in the *Discourse on Inequality* was to answer the question: "How [might] the source of inequality among men be known unless one begins by knowing men themselves? And how will man manage to see himself formed, through all the changes that the sequence of times and things must have produced in his original constitution, and to separate what he gets from his own stock from what circumstances and his progress have added to or change in his primitive state?" (*DOI*, CW, 3:12).

In looking to trace the infinitesimal changes of a hypothetical history, Rousseau designated two principles prior to reason and the development of culture that defined human nature: the first principle is self-preservation within every human being (*amour de soi*); the second "inspires in us a natural repugnance to see any sensitive Being perish or suffer, principally like ourselves" (*DOI*, CW, 3:15). This is the basis for commiseration, or what Rousseau called "pity": the ability to empathize with another and thereby to *feel* for and with her or him. This unwarlike feeling becomes the foundation of pacific relations among all sentient beings. Love is a derivation of pity as it localizes the feelings of one being for another. *Amour-propre*, on the other hand, "is only a relative sentiment, artificial and born in Society, which inclines each individual to have a greater esteem for himself than for anyone else, inspires in men all the harm they do to one another, and is the true source of honor" (*DOI*, CW, 3:91n12). Rousseau, that is, conceived *amour propre* as the degeneration of early self-sufficiency and independence in nature to unhealthy comparisons between self with others.

While Rousseau argued the question of natural law here (prior to civil law), sociability would be nevertheless derived from *pitié* and set the stage for creating a theory of social conventions not based hierarchically on force or rank (in the *Social Contract*). The rhetorical and historical strategy that paved the way for remaking society was located in his method: "Let us . . . begin by setting all the facts aside, for they do not affect the question. The Researches which can be undertaken concerning this Subject must not be taken for historical truths, but only for hypothetical and conditional reasoning better suited to clarify the Nature of things than to show their genuine origin, like those our Physicists make every day concerning the formation of the World" (*DOI*, CW, 3:19). History, "when it exists," he writes, can "present the facts that connect [the different stages]. It is up to philosophy, when history is lacking, to determine similar facts that might connect them" (*DOI*, CW, 3:42). This allowed Rousseau to retreat from the politics of his day and challenge the very basis of his contemporary society. It was this abstract quality of his thinking that reverberated through the French Revolution and beyond.

Rousseau begins part 2 of the *Discourse on Inequality* with the following statement: "The first person who, having fenced off a plot of ground, took it into his head to say *this is mine* and found people simple enough to believe him, was the true founder of civil society" (*DOI*, CW, 3:43). The development of human "progress" for Rousseau turns out to be based on a shaky metaphysical, moral, and economic basis that will only increase rather than decrease inequality. He laments: "What crimes, wars, murders, what miseries and horrors would the human Race have been spared by someone who . . . had shouted to his fellows: Beware of listening to this impostor; you are lost if you forget that the fruits belong to all and the Earth to no one!" (*DOI*, CW, 3:43). The quality of becoming a free agent, endowed with a conscience, a perfectible being, leads not to a good society but inevitably to the one Rousseau sees around him, filled with social and economic inequality. No reform appears to Rousseau to make this better.

Rousseau proposes a more radical change in the *Social Contract* as he describes the "general will":

One who dares to undertake the founding of a people should feel that he is capable of changing human nature, so to speak; of transforming part of a larger whole from which this individual receives, in a sense, his life and his being; of *altering man's constitution in order to strengthen it; of substituting a partial and moral existence for the physical and independent existence we have all received from nature. He must, in short, take away man's own forces in order to give him forces that are foreign to him and that he cannot make use of without the help of others. (SC, CW, 4:155)*

Somewhere then between the *Discourse on Inequality* (1755), the *Social Contract* (1762), and the "Declaration of the Rights of Man and Citizen" (1789), rights emerge as one of the most important legacies of Enlightenment. Article 1 of the "Declaration of the Rights of Man and Citizen" reads: "Men are born and remain free and equal in rights. Social distinctions may be founded only upon the general good."[18] Finding the balance between the rights of the individual and the good of the whole is what Rousseau proposes to create in his notion of the social contract: "Find a form of association that defends and protects the person and goods of each associate with all the common force, and by means of which each one, uniting with all, nevertheless obeys only himself and remains as free as before" (*SC*, CW, 4:138). This is the fundamental problem to which the social contract holds the solution.

Human Rights in the Eighteenth Century

Among the many interesting works on human rights, Lynn Hunt traces the emergence of the terms and the concept of "human rights" in her outstanding book *Inventing Human Rights: A History*. In France, Voltaire used the term "human rights" in his *Treatise on Tolerance* (1763) involving a case of religious intolerance and torture (in French *droit* means both "right" and "law"). It was Rousseau's *Social Contract* however that gave the term wide traction when he used it for the first time (appearing without specific definition, alongside "rights of humanity," "rights of the citizen," and "rights of sovereignty"). This usage associated "rights" thereafter with Rousseau.[19] Three related elements define human rights: that rights be natural (all humans are endowed with them), equal (for all), and universal (globally for all humans). The first is the easiest one around which to find consensus, a natural right. Hunt further points out that these rights had to become political, to be located not only in nature but in society, to have an important effect. One may distinguish human from divine or animal rights, but they must be further defined laterally with the society of humans.

Despite the clear principles of the "Declaration of the Rights of Man and Citizen" at the start of the French Revolution, an unequal or exclusive basis on which the rights could be exercised persisted: only those who were equal and free were considered active citizens—that is, property owners and not women. The gender bias in name and substance prompted Olympe de Gouges to rewrite the articles of the Declaration in her "Declaration of the Rights of Women" (1791): "Woman is born free and lives equal to man in her rights. Social distinctions can be based only on the common utility."[20] We know that the ideals of freedom, equality, and fraternity were quickly betrayed during the Terror, and Gouges herself was guillotined. Looking at how these ideas emerged in such unlikely places, Hunt asks: if rights are self-evident, why does everyone not recognize them and why do they arise in specific times and places (the eighteenth century) from the American Bill of Rights to the "Universal Declaration of Rights" adopted by the United Nations General Assembly in 1948?

Along with the concepts of liberty and equality, the notion of autonomy of the individual, in particular moral autonomy, became important. Although a promise could be held out for the potential of moral autonomy for children, servants, and even slaves, such was not the case for women who remained dependent on fathers and husbands. "Human rights depend both on self-possession and on the recognition that all others are equally self-possessed. It is the incomplete development of the latter that gives rise to all the inequalities of rights that have preoccupied us through-out all history" (Hunt, *Inventing*, 29). That history did not progress in a linear fashion to the universal enactment of such ideals has led to questioning how "emancipatory" the principles of such rights have been. The question of who can or cannot speak for and exercise rights remains problematic today, as the Amnesty exhibition DIGNITY attests.

Autonomy and the role of empathy (what Rousseau called *pitié*) are not only ideas but also cultural practices. Exposure to new experiences—whether reading epis-tolary novels about changing views of marriage and love for the eighteenth century or photographic exhibits for the twenty-first—helps "spread the practices of au-tonomy and empathy" (Hunt, *Inventing*, 32). They foster a kind of inward looking: a kind of "imagined empathy," that writers and artists set out to explore.

Transforming the Contract: Julie

In the wildly popular epistolary novel *Julie, or, The New Heloise*, Rousseau dramatizes a process leading from a love story to the creation of a utopian society. In this novel, Rousseau tested the ideas of the *Social Contract* by examining how, if the family was understood as a model for society, individuals sorted through the problems of their own self-interest, their own good and well-being, and the good of society as a whole. Sexuality, love, and marriage stand on the battleground of life narratives and trans-formative principles.

To recap the story: the young love-struck hero, Saint-Preux, comments on the relationship of the family and society (in a rural area near Geneva): "the same freedom reigns in homes as in the republic, and the family is the image of the State" (*Julie*, CW, 6:66). The heroine, Julie, at first protests loudly about the legitimacy of her re-lationship to Saint-Preux in which love is to guarantee virtue. But soon she writes to her friend Claire that her father has turned down the proposal of marriage put forth by a benevolent Englishman, Milord Edouard, on behalf of herself and Saint-Preux. Her father objects on the basis of unequal social standing; her mother defends the situation weakly. If this were the right match, the relationship between them would promise a future in family and society (the father does not yet know that Julie is pregnant with a child by Saint-Preux). Julie however (as now uncertain guarantor of the future) cannot reconcile the sense of the bond she considers sacred with her lover and her father's social interdiction, and he is determined to maintain the power to determine her future and his succession. When Julie dares to respond to her father's invectives about Saint-Preux (in words that she does not report), he loses rational control, and "beat[s] [her] mercilessly"; her mother throws herself in between the two of them and receives some of the blows. At this moment, Julie falls and hits her head against a table. "Here ended the triumph of anger and began that of nature," causing an abrupt change in which the father whose "dignity" (in the older, here more ironic sense of honor) does not permit him to apologize. Julie exclaims: "there is no mortification as touching as that of a tender father who thinks he has put himself in the wrong. The heart of a father feels it is made for forgiveness, and not to have need of forgiveness" (*Julie*, CW, 6:174–75). Julie ultimately melts as her father sits her on his knee and they embrace like lovers as the mother looks on tenderly; the description is a sentimental scene.

Yet the transformation from paternal violence and anger to paternal tenderness provides a turning point, a revolution within Julie: "I cannot well express the revolution that has taken place in me, but since that moment I find myself changed" (*Julie*, CW, 6:145). She is reminded of a golden age when nothing disturbed her own innocent natural family. Remorse and tenderness, however, do not change her father's mind. He prohibits her from marrying Saint-Preux, projecting hatred onto him for the excesses he suggests "forced" his own brutality. A post scriptum follows in which Julie describes her subsequent miscarriage.[21] As the presumed physical cause of the miscarriage, the father's blow at the same time violently aborts an attempt at individual freedom, however underplayed, in making sure that the family continues through paternal power.

Speaking for the lovers and the Englishman, Julie asks, should marriage not be the "Freest as well as the most sacred of engagements? . . . Indeed, all laws that constrict it are unjust; all fathers who dare create or break it are tyrants."[22] When Julie "chooses" to give up her independent, passionate life, none of the arguments about fortune, nobility, prejudice, or titles, nor the continuation of the paternal line (all rehearsed in a letter from her friend) can sway her. Two opposed discourses operate within Julie simultaneously: the one individual, the other collective. "Do you know what is produced in me by so many contrary movements that cancel each other out? A sort of stupor that renders my soul almost insensible, and leaves me without the use of either passions or reason. The moment is critical . . . yet, I was never less in a condition to guide myself" (*Julie*, CW, 6:145).

In the end, Julie bends to her father's will, taken as a sign of true benevolence; she renounces Saint-Preux and marries her father's choice, the older, rational Monsieur de Wolmar. She does however not abandon her passion; cleaved in the temporal world, she will go on to live an exemplary moral life, but within her heart the two souls, hers and Saint-Preux's, remain indivisible. So Julie will ostensibly give up choice and individual freedom to become a part of the social web inherited from a tradition of social hierarchy, which she will transform not from without but within. The revolution of which she speaks is personal and internal, and it allows her to found a new social contract. Hers will be a movement of reform in creating Clarens, a waypoint on the way to democracy through the extended paternalism of the family. As a woman, Julie wins and loses in the newfound power she will gain when she marries for reason. She wins because she has followed her ethical sense and given herself to society in her relationship to otherness; she loses because her freedom is an illusion, and although women were essential to both marriage and the development of democracy, they were included in the contract of neither (*Julie*, CW, 6:329). Julie's internal virtue is deeply linked to her "sentiment" and her sense of marriage and domesticity.[23] She is a complex character who is both submissive daughter and wife, and active as a letter writer within the genre of the novel of letters. Does her power and influence come, as some have argued, from her subjection to men's desire?[24] What I take from this scene has less to do with the gendered question of seduction and equality than with the importance of the example for all. As Interlocutor N states in the prefatory "Conversation About Novels": "In Tableaux of humankind, Man must be recognizable to everyone" (*Julie*, CW, 6:8).

The artist Gravelot and the engraver Ahmet designed the engraving in figure 3 that accompanies this scene; it was one of twelve produced for Rousseau's editions. Gravelot respected Rousseau's elaborate instructions, which were as follows:

> The scene takes place in the room of the Baron d'Étange, Julie's father. Julie is seated, and near her chair stands an empty armchair; her father who occupied it is kneeling in front of her, pressing her hands in his, shedding tears, and in a suppliant and pathetic posture. One perceives, from a certain air of lassitude, that she has tried every way to make her father rise or to get free of him; but failing to do so, she lets her head lean back against the chair, like a person about to swoon, while her two hands still extend forward and rest on her father's arms. The Baron should have a venerable physiognomy, white hair, a military bearing, and, although suppliant, something noble and proud in his demeanor.[25]

The title of the engraving is *Paternal Force* and it renders an already complex scene even more complex (*Julie*, CW, 6:624). In fact, this is a stunning reversal of what happened earlier when the father struck Julie physically; this scene, as dictated by Rousseau, takes place after the fact. The concept of "force" is no longer to be understood, or accepted by Julie, as authority or violence, but rather as feeling.[26] Yet in the engraving, we can see the body language of a woman not only resigned but also

Figure 3. *Paternal Force,* from *Recueil d'estampes pour la Nouvelle Héloïse avec les sujets des estampes, tels qu'ils ont été donnés par l'éditeur.* Drawing by Gravelot; engraving by Ahmet. Paris: Duchesne, 1761. [715.61.753]. Courtesy Houghton Library, Harvard University.

resisting through her quasi-illness, leaning back to find a way out of her own. Rousseau in fact sets up multiple perspectives, first in the letters, then by the gloss (or directive) he writes about the engraving. Almost as though he had put himself in the position of Saint-Preux, who responds to the father's decision with outrage in the language of rights: "Nay, nay, Monsieur, whatever opinion you may have of your acts, they do not oblige me to renounce for your sake rights so dear and so well deserved by my heart" (*Julie*, CW, 6:267). It is now accepted, writes Philip Stewart, that the legends written by Rousseau for the engravings cannot only be read separately, but also can be read as though Rousseau were himself displaced into a reader of the novel, as well as being its author.

The engraving by Moreau le jeune entitled *Le Soufflet* or "The Slap" (fig. 4) situates the scene at the moment of violent conflict between Julie and her father, rather than, as Rousseau dictated to Gravelot, in the follow-up moment of reconciliation.[27] As the only other artist to publish these engravings during Rousseau's lifetime, Moreau's illustrations had more impact than Gravelot's did throughout the nineteenth century. While Rousseau focused Gravelot's engraving, as a visual spectacle, on the transformation of the father, Moreau shows that force is indeed force between father and daughter. Authority and force are not so easily undone through reconciliation.

There is then a crossover from letter and reader to theatrical image and spectator.[28] I believe that we can perceive something like what Jacques Rancière calls the "redistribution of the sensible" cutting across the oppositions of strong and weak and asking the viewer, who is also a reader, to become active in the interpretation of the scene. Commenting on the novel, and this scene in particular, Mme de Staël exclaims in her *Letters on the Writings and Character of Jean-Jacques Rousseau*: "Woe to any woman who would have the courage to resist her father."[29] What can we say then about Julie? Is she what Rancière dubs an "embodied allegor[y] of inequality" here?[30] Can we not see in the novel and its engravings as visual complements how Rousseau's novel leads the reader to understand that "the relations between saying, seeing and doing themselves belong to the structure of domination and subjection?"[31] Ironically, having condemned theatre in the *Letter to d'Alembert*, Rousseau presents this as one of the most dramatic visual moments of the novel (reminiscent both of Greuze's moral tableaux and Diderot's theory of sentiment in drama). As one of his most complex characters, Julie stands between lover and wife/mother, activity and passivity. We see Rousseau seeking at some level to create in the reader as viewer an "emancipated spectator," one for whom the limit between looking and acting, between the individual and the members of a social collectivity becomes shaded.

In the interstices between the old and the new, between reproduction and sexuality, compassion and authority, it was necessary for Rousseau to maintain the story of the family, albeit a paternalistic one, in order to make the transition to a new order. Julie has understood something quite unique in the thought process toward the social

Figure 4. *Le Soufflet (Julie frappée par son père)*. Drawing by Moreau le jeune; engraving by Noël Le Mire. [715 .L516.74s.sz2]. Courtesy Houghton Library, Harvard University.

contract: that desire is the expression of the individual while the family exacts a relationship to the other. And I believe the end of the novel needs to be read (as I have elsewhere tried to do) in that light.[32] Rousseau ventriloquizes Julie at the end of the novel where, having become a model of virtue and raised a family as a precursor to the social contract, she reclaims her right as an individual in announcing that her love for Saint-Preux never truly ceased. Whatever the public part of her that was given over to society, a private part remained—despite her best efforts—unrelenting.

Retention of a private, inner world for Julie is consonant, I believe, with Wayne Booth's assertion, in his Amnesty Lecture in Oxford in the 1990s, that human rights should be understood as protection of an individual's "freedom to pursue a story line, a life plot."[33] The epistolary novel allows such a right, as do the myriad forms of autobiography within and outside fiction.

HOW CAN ONE PROTECT THE FREEDOM TO PURSUE ONE'S OWN STORY AS A LIFE WITHIN A WORLD SO UNEQUAL?

Fast forward to the year 2011, if you will, and two examples from the press raise similar problems, despite the change of century and context.

Occupy

The Occupy movement was an active and visible force beginning in September 2011; its symbolic power, against the odds, grew through that eventful autumn and has left its mark. It was a movement that carried Rousseau's thought into the present through issues of dignity and human rights.

The main issue around which Occupy Wall Street, and all of the other Occupy groups, rallied was inequality, mostly economic, but also social and political: "We are the 99 percent; they are the 1 percent." *Le Monde* and other news journals quickly understood that this slogan was a stroke of genius pitting the people in the 99 percent against the economic aristocracy in the 1 percent.[34] Given the economic and political structures in place, and the seeming impossibility for the 99 percent to change them through democratic processes (the vote, Congress, etc.), the movement called Occupy erupted—another brilliant if controversial strategy to take over important urban spaces. Issues of free speech and free assembly were paramount in relation to symbolic location: Occupy Wall Street, near the financial center of corporate America, Wall Street; Occupy Harvard was situated in Harvard Yard—not at the Harvard Business School—near the iconic statue of John Harvard.

It is not surprising that one blogger read from Rousseau's *Discourse on Inequality* to characterize what was crucial in the Occupy movement, including, significantly, what defines natural and social inequalities, as well as how Rousseau's words could describe contemporary inequality: "I would prove that if one sees a handful of powerful and rich men at the height of grandeur and fortune, while the crowd grovels in obscurity and misery, it is because the former [the powerful and rich] prize the things they enjoy only insofar as the others [the poor and invisible] are deprived of them; and because, without changing their status, they would cease to be happy if the People ceased to be miserable."[35] It is this tone of outrage at the inequities and injustice that binds together the Occupy movements and links them to Rousseau's thought. Although no one agenda dominated, issues of debt and unemployment, a more equal level of income, and reducing the power of wealth in politics form the core issues. For a generation gravely concerned about its future during the period of recovery from the "Great Recession" of 2007–2009, corruption of the global financial and economic system needed to be addressed. On January 16, 2012, Martin Luther King Day, the Occupy Wall Street website posted the following: "We are using the revolutionary Arab Spring tactic to achieve our ends and encourage the use of nonviolence to maximize the safety of all participants. This OWS movement empowers real people to create real change from the bottom up. We want to see a general assembly in every backyard, on every street corner because we don't need Wall Street and we don't need politicians to build a better society."[36]

The sense that the "social contract" had been broken in a fundamental way was key to the Occupy movement. Access to information, safety, education, and health care figured prominently among the many and diverse demands. The term "social contract" still owes much to Rousseau, as it did during the French Revolution. Its use by Occupy was both symbolic and procedural (in the general assemblies). Symbolically, it targeted not only the economic inequality but as well the moral degradation of corporate, financial, and political leadership. Elizabeth Warren, for example, spoke about the underlying social contract (relying on the concept of the individual) that has facilitated the success of the wealthy, with the sense that they, in turn, should be made to give back; to which George Will retorted in a piece titled "Elizabeth Warren and Liberalism, Twisting the 'Social Contract'" in the *Washington Post* stating: "The collectivist agenda is antithetical to America's premise, which is: Government—including such public goods as roads, schools and police—is instituted to facilitate *individual* striving, a.k.a. the pursuit of happiness."[37] Where Occupy signaled a broken social contract in contemporary society, conservatives like Will saw Occupy (and liberalism) breaking the contract. The battleground became, among other things, the definition and implementation of a social contract, a kind of open signifier with people fighting despair to reclaim a vision of democracy and assume an active role in making their future.

A thoughtful blog, noting the discussion of Rousseau's *Social Contract* at the Amsterdam Occupy, summed up the open-endedness of notions like social contract and general will thus: "Basically, Occupy's performative claim is that the conventional structures no longer serve the general will, but that they serve particular wills instead. To this, Occupy opposes a new Universalist politics, one of shared opinion. This reflects Rousseau's critical use of the term—general will was an antidote to absolute monarchy."[38] If some saw the human mic(rophone) as a sign of the imposition of an oppressive, forced consensus (Rousseau's tyranny of the majority), and not as a practical solution to the lack of amplification, others viewed it as part of the experiment in extreme democracy: "We amplify each other's voices, so we can hear one another. There is no hierarchy."[39] We can think of Rousseau's melodic line in unison, a sign of transparency reminiscent of the festival gathering in proximity of early societies described in the anthropological works. So too the general assemblies could be viewed alternatively as completely inefficient or an example of how a grassroots movement could operate differently through participation in decision-making processes: a leaderless movement of resistance. The process of the movement was part of the protest itself. In the Occupy Harvard movement, which occasioned discussions about the administrative view and the academic opening to teach, problems of democracy, participatory governance, and elitism came together in difficult but important ways. The bridge between what constitutes authority and how it is used; the way in which individuals think about institutions and operate within them; the articulation of a future based not on the imperfections of the present; all these moves could be found in the tenets of Rousseau's own theoretical position, based on failed structures that suggest through abstract thought a way to a more just world. As equality and rights within the social contract remain values to be fought for and reimagined within political contexts, they take on their full meaning.

Universal Human Rights

Eleanor Roosevelt, chair of the Universal Declaration of Human Rights drafting committee, stated the continuity from the French Declaration of Rights to the proposal put forth to the United Nations General Assembly in 1948: "We stand today at the threshold of a great event both in the life of the United Nations and in the life of mankind. This declaration may well become the international Magna Carta for all men everywhere. We hope its proclamation by the General Assembly will be an event comparable to the proclamation in 1789 [the French Declaration of the Rights of Citizens], the adoption of the Bill of Rights by the people of the US, and the adoption of comparable declarations at different times in other countries."[40] Linking the global and the local, she said at the tenth anniversary of the adoption of the Universal Declaration of Human Rights:

> Where, after all, do universal human rights begin? In small places, close to home—so close and so small that they cannot be seen on any maps of the world. Yet they are the world of the individual person; the neighborhood he lives in;

the school or college he attends; the factory, farm, or office where he works. Such are the places where every man, woman, and child seeks equal justice, equal opportunity, equal dignity without discrimination. Unless these rights have meaning there, they have little meaning anywhere. Without concerted citizen action to uphold them close to home, we shall look in vain for progress in the larger world.[41]

The question of how to argue universal values in the context of local situations remains one of the vexed problems of our current world: individuals live in societies and nations where their rights may not be respected. In fact, the explicit discourse of human rights became prominent when the Occupy movement was being threatened around the country with eviction: the freedoms of speech, peaceful assembly, and association were at issue for many. And so the United States Human Rights Network took a stand and declared: "Due to the Network's firm belief that economic rights are also human rights, the USHRN stood in full support of the Occupy Movement in Los Angeles and other cities since their inception, protesting the collusion of government and economic elites."[42]

The follow-up to the Occupy movement is still unfolding, as I revise this chapter for publication. During the primaries for the 2016 presidential election, strands of anti-establishment, anti-elite, and populist forces were at work in the campaigns of Bernie Sanders and Donald Trump.[43] The Black Lives Matter movement became heir to Occupy through its protest, use of the media, and "opaque leadership structures to challenge state power."[44] There was a good deal of disagreement about the way forward, but many agreed that the Occupy breakthrough made a difference in conceiving the future, not simply linked to space but also to imagination, "identifying injustice and conceiving of another world."[45] This is where the legacy of Rousseau's work again becomes pertinent: by first thinking what is wrong, it is possible to acknowledge what needs to be rethought and changed.[46] Rights and democracy are not fixed; they are ongoing projects. You truly cannot evict an idea: indeed "You Can't Evict an Idea" was a slogan mounted on a poster at Occupy Boston in December 2011. By reexamining the attitudes today toward the social contract within the nation (the 1 percent to the 99 percent), by calling upon a discourse of empathy globally (in relation to all others), the individual may reclaim the right to respect and dignity, to her or his individual narrative, and the potential not only to hope but to act within and beyond one's own borders.

NOTES

1. There is a vast literature on human rights, going back to Antiquity; this essay looks to the eighteenth century as an important turning point in discussions around rights with

respect to Rousseau in particular and to an extent his impact on the "Declaration of the Rights of Man and Citizen" and the French Revolution. The following is a brief bibliography dealing with human rights: Antoine de Baecque, *L'An 1 des droits de l'homme* (Paris: Presses du CNRS, 1988); *Le Fondement des droits de l'homme: Actes des entretiens de l'Aquila, 14–19 septembre 1964,* Institut international de philosophie (Florence: La Nuova Italia, 1966); Marcel Gauchet, *La Révolution des droits de l'homme* (Paris: Gallimard, 1989); Lynn Hunt, *Inventing Human Rights: A History* (New York: W. W. Norton, 2007; see especially chapter 1: "'Torrents of Emotion': Reading Novels and Imagining Equality"); Micheline R. Ishay, *The History of Human Rights: From Ancient Times to the Globalization Era* (Berkeley: University of California Press, 2004); Nwachukwuike S. S. Iwe, *The History and Contents of Human Rights: A Study of the History and Interpretation of Human Rights* (New York: Peter Lang, 1986); Jack Mahoney, *The Challenge of Human Rights: Origin, Development, and Significance* (Malden: Blackwell Publishers, 2007); Terence E. Marshall, "Poetry and Praxis in Rousseau's *Emile*: Human Rights and the Sentiment of Humanity," in *Modern Enlightenment and the Rule of Reason*, ed. John C. McCarthy, 187–212 (Washington, DC: The Catholic University of America Press, 1998); Arthur P. Monahan, *The Circle of Rights Expands: Modern Political Thought after the Reformation 1521 (Luther) to 1762 (Rousseau)* (Montreal: McGill-Queen's University Press, 2007); Joseph Slaughter, *Human Rights, Inc.* (New York: Fordham University Press, 2007). I wish to thank Tali Zechory, a graduate student in the Department of Romance Languages and Literatures at Harvard University, for her initial research into this topic and for the discussions we have had around these questions since.

2. Claude Lévi-Strauss, "Jean-Jacques Rousseau, Founder of the Sciences of Man," in *Structural Anthropology II,* 33–44 (Chicago: University of Chicago Press, 1962), 35.

3. Jean-Jacques Rousseau, *Essay on the Origin of Languages and Writings Related to Music,* in The Collected Writings of Rousseau, vol. 7, ed. and trans. John T. Scott (Hanover: Dartmouth University Press, 1998), 7:305.

4. Claude Lévi-Strauss, *Tristes tropiques* (New York: Penguin, 1992), 314.

5. Ibid., 315.

6. Lévi-Strauss, "Jean-Jacques Rousseau, Founder," 35.

7. Peter Gay, "Introduction," in Ernst Cassirer, *Rousseau, Kant, Goethe* (New York: Harper and Row, 1965), xi.

8. Ernst Cassirer, *The Philosophy of the Enlightenment* (Princeton: Princeton University Press, 1951), 273.

9. Cassirer, *Philosophy,* 274.

10. Michel Foucault, "Introduction," in Jean-Jacques Rousseau, *Rousseau juge de Jean-Jacques: dialogues* (Paris: A. Colin, 1962).

11. Foucault, "What Is Enlightenment?" in *Ethics, Subjectivity and Truth: Essential Works of Foucault 1954–84,* trans. Catherine Porter, ed. Paul Rabinow, 303–9 (New York: The New Press, 1997); Emmanuel Kant, "An Answer to the Question: What Is Enlightenment?" trans. James Schmidt, in *What Is Enlightenement?* ed. James Schmidt, 58–64 (Berkeley: University of California Press, 1996).

12. My emphasis. As "a reflection on history and a particular analysis of the specific moment at which he is writing and because of which he is writing," Foucault, "What Is Enlightenment?" 305.

13. Ibid., 309.

14. Ibid., 312. Foucault separates the "theme" of humanism (based on varying notions of "man" taken from "religion, science, or politics") from Enlightenment, and he reformulates Kant's question, sidestepping the complex history of humanisms: "this thematic . . . can be opposed by the principle of a critique and a permanent creation of ourselves in our autonomy: that is, a principle at the heart of the historical consciousness that Enlightenment has of itself" (314). "It seems to me dangerous to confuse them; and further, it seems historically inaccurate. If the question of man, of the human species, of the humanist, was important throughout the eighteenth century, this is very rarely, I believe, because the Enlightenment considered itself a humanism" (314). "I think that, just as we must free ourselves from the intellectual blackmail of 'being for or against the Enlightenment,' we must escape from the historical and moral Confucianism that mixes the theme of humanism with the question of Enlightenment. An analysis of their complex relations in the course of the last two centuries would be a worthwhile project, an important one if we are to bring some measure of clarity to the consciousness that we have of ourselves and of our past" (314–15).

15. Ibid., 315.

16. Ibid., 319.

17. See my chapter, Christie McDonald, "Fail Better: Rousseau's Creative *Délire*," in *Rousseau and Freedom,* ed. Christie McDonald and Stanley Hoffmann, 274–92 (Cambridge: Cambridge University Press, 2010).

18. Available at http://avalon.law.yale.edu/18th_century/rightsof.asp.

19. Hunt, *Inventing,* 22–24.

20. Olympe de Gouges, "Declaration of the Rights of Woman," 1791, article 1. Available at http://csivc.csi.cuny.edu/americanstudies/files/lavender/decwom2.html.

21. "After writing my letter, I went into my mother's room, and I came so sick that I am obliged to come put myself back to bed. I even can detect . . . I fear . . . ah, my dear! I do fear that my fall yesterday may have some more fatal consequence than I had thought. So then all is finished for me; all my expectations abandon me at the same time" (*Julie*, CW, 6:146).

22. "That chaste bond of nature is subject neither to sovereign power nor to paternal authority, but to the sole authority of the common father who has the power over hearts, and who by ordering them to unite can force them to love each other" (*Julie*, CW, 6:158). In addition, Saint-Preux writes in part 1, letter 23: "The same freedom reigns in homes as in the republic, and the family is the image of the State" (*Julie*, CW, 6:66).

23. See Christine Roulston, *Narrating Marriage in Eighteenth-Century England and France* (Burlington, VT: Ashgate, 2010); Nadine Berenguier, *Conduct Books for Girls in the Enlightenment* (Burlington, VT: Ashgate, 2011).

24. See Joan W. Scott, "Féminisme à la française," *Libération* (June 9, 2011): 18. In this article about the Dominque Strauss-Kahn affair of 2011, Scott points to a debate about equality and seduction in which she cites controversial statements by Philippe Raynaud about seduction as "une forme particulière d'égalité" (*Le Débat*, no. 57, 182), Mona Ozouf, *Les Mots des femmes: Essai sur la singularité française* (Paris: Fayard, L'esprit de la cité, 1995), and Claude Habib, *Le Consentement amoureux et la Galanterie française* (Paris: Hachette, 2001).

25. Jean-Jacques Rousseau, *Sixth Engraving* for *Julie,* part 3, letter 48 (*Julie,* CW, 6:624).

26. I thank Philip Stewart for email exchanges and discussions about the engraving and the scenes from *Julie* to which it refers. See Philip Stewart, "*Julie* et ses légendes," *Studies on Voltaire and the Eighteenth Century* 260 (1989): 257–78; and "Rousseau, Boucher, Gravelot, Moreau," *LIT (Literature Interpretation Theory)* 5 (1994): 261–83.

27. Others were published later by Chodowiecki, Monsiau, Devéria, Marckl, Desenne, Prud'hon, Manceau, Schall, and Johannot.

28. See Stewart, "*Julie* et ses légendes," 3.

29. Madame de Staël, *Œuvres complètes* (Paris: Honoré Champion Éditeur, 2008), 1:61. Staël herself read Rousseau's life more actively than the novel when it came to letting him off the hook for giving away his five children to the *enfants trouvés,* as he admits to doing in the *Confessions.* Although she saw in him the genius who "dreamed more than he existed," someone for whom observation was near impossible, she could not abide his rationale for abandoning paternity. Rousseau told his contemporaries they most needed mothers to restore the natural and social order. What he needed to do away with was fatherhood, as much viscerally as conceptually. In giving the care of his children to the state, Rousseau writes, "by destining them to become workers and peasants instead of adventurers and fortune hunters, I believed I was performing an action of a Citizen and father, and I looked at myself as a member of Plato's Republic" (*Conf,* CW, 5:299). Rousseau discarded the facts, remaking his own failure into a theoretical triumph—untenable he admits in the position of father protecting his children from himself (and society)—and also writing a pedagogical tract on educating the young within the context of contemporary society.

30. Jacques Rancière, *The Emancipated Spectator* (New York: Verso, 2011), 12.

31. Ibid., 13.

32. See Christie McDonald, *The Extravagant Shepherd: A Study of the Pastoral Vision in Rousseau's Nouvelle Héloïse,* Studies on Voltaire and the Eighteenth Century, 105 (Banbury: The Voltaire Foundation, 1972; 2nd ed., 2007).

33. Wayne Booth, "Individualism and the Mystery of the Social Self; or, Does Amnesty Have a Leg to Stand On?" in *Freedom and Interpretation: The Oxford Amnesty Lectures, 1992,* ed. Barbara Johnson, 69–102 (New York: Basic Books, 1993), 89.

34. Kalle Lasn, a former publicist retired in Vancouver, Canada, is credited with both the slogan of the 99 percent to the 1 percent and the call to Occupy Wall Street, thus giving the movement its name.

35. *DOI,* CW, 3:63. The blogger is Jason J. Campbell, available at http://nova .academia.edu/jasonjcampbell/Teaching/27840/A_Discourse_on_Inequality_and_Occupy _Wallstreet.

36. See http://occupywallst.org/.

37. The context for Warren's comments is available at http://www.cbsnews.com /8301-503544_162-20110042-503544.html. George Will's response was in "Elizabeth Warren and Liberalism, Twisting the 'Social Contract,'" *The Washington Post,* October 5, 2011.

38. See the post at Reading At Occupy Amsterdam from November 13, 2011, titled "'The social contract may look like a finished text, but should not be read that way':

Reading Rousseau." Available at http://readingatoccupyamsterdam.blogspot.com/2011/11/social-contract-may-look-like-finished.html.

39. "Consensus (Direct Democracy@Occupy Wall Street)" video, cited in Rakesh Khurana and Eric Baldwin, "Occupy Wall St.," unpublished draft of a case study for the Harvard Business School (October 18, 2011), 6. I am grateful to my colleague Rakesh Khurana for a series of email exchanges about the Occupy movement in general and the Harvard Occupy movement in particular and for allowing me to read the draft of the case study.

40. Mrs. Franklin D. Roosevelt's speech was originally published by the Department of State in *Human Rights and Genocide: Selected Statements*; *United Nations Resolution Declaration and Conventions*, 1949.

41. Excerpt from a speech by Eleanor Roosevelt at the presentation of "IN YOUR HANDS: A Guide for Community Action for the Tenth Anniversary of the Universal Declaration of Human Rights" (United Nations, New York), Thursday, March 27, 1958.

42. "The primary goal of the United States Human Rights Network, an Atlanta-based coalition of more than 300 organizations from around the country, is to increase the visibility of the U.S. human rights movement and link U.S.-based human rights activists with the global human rights movement. Its National Conference and Members Meeting [was] . . . held Dec. 9. . . . The Network's biannual conference comes to the city during a time of unprecedented discontent with the nation's Depression Era–level joblessness and growing economic inequality" (www.ushrnetwork.org).

43. Martin Levitin, "The Triumph of Occupy Wall Street," *Atlantic* (June 10, 2015), available at theatlantic.com; Euel Elliott, "How Occupy Wall Street Led to the Rise of Donald Trump," *Fortune* (March 23, 2016), available at Fortune.com.

44. Arun Gupta, "From Occupy Wall Street to Black Lives Matter: Where Does Radical Protest Go from Here?" November 13, 2015, available at occupy.com.

45. Bill Fletch Jr., "Occupy the Imagination," *The Nation* (April 2, 2012): 15.

46. See Jacques Rancière, "Who Is the Subject of the Rights of Man?" *South Atlantic Quarterly* 103, no. 2/3 (Spring/Summer 2004): 297–310.

Part Three

DIGNITY @ ND: THE EXHIBIT AND THE CAMPAIGN
BY AMNESTY INTERNATIONAL

Editor's Introduction to Part Three

JULIA V. DOUTHWAITE

This section contains material from the exhibit catalog of the original DIGNITY show, as prefaced by some reflections by the photographers on what dignity means to them. First of all, let us explain the Demand Dignity campaign. The campaign, launched by the Amnesty International annual report of May 2009, was designed with multiple issues in mind, including maternal mortality, corporate accountability, slums, and making rights law.[1] The website of Amnesty International USA featured a group of enthusiastic Africans at a gathering of some kind and the caption: "In 2009, Amnesty launched a campaign across Sierra Leone with activists, musicians and a drama group to engage with local communities on maternal health. The campaign encouraged people to become active in 'demanding their rights and accountability from the authorities.'" The website laid out goals—improving people's access to housing, health care, and safety from environmental dangers—and presented a powerful description of horrors that visit the poor: "A family is evicted without warning, losing their home and community. A woman isn't given the information or health care she needs, and suffers serious injuries in childbirth. An oil company fails to clean up pollution, destroying the land and livelihoods of thousands. For people living in poverty, facing discrimination and struggling to access justice, violations of their basic human rights—to housing, health, education and more—can lead to a devastating downward spiral."

Interestingly, the campaign's slogan had a distinctly Rousseauian ring to it: "We are all born free and equal in dignity and rights—yet everywhere, these rights are being denied." Compare that to the first words of the *Social Contract*: "Man is born free; and everywhere he is in chains."

These issues mobilized the work of activists in France too, although the recourse to photojournalism was a unique approach, the brainchild of organizer and curator Yves Prigent. Their recourse to the visual arts was a novel approach for an organization that usually operates in a more scholarly mode through written texts and diplomacy. But it made sense for this campaign. As Prigent and other members of the Paris bureau wrote in the preface to the French catalog, "If we are to break power relations and incite a much-needed turn-about in attitudes and practices, we must start by raising people's awareness on an individual and on a collective level. Amnesty International's work has always been rooted in that conviction. It was nonetheless an unprecedented idea to ask politically active photographers to join the effort. . . . [Their photographs] reveal abuses denounced by Amnesty International and incite a thoughtful response."[2]

In looking through the chapters in this part of the book, readers will see how each photographer interpreted the campaign on the ground in some of the world's most depressed areas: from the shantytowns of Lagos, Nigeria, to the outskirts of Skopje, Macedonia; from the hills of Mexico's hinterland to the crumbling high rises in Cairene slums and the remote forest villages of Northeastern India. Everywhere the poor live in danger for their lives and well-being. Industrial pollution, open sewers, and corporate greed threaten people's homes in Nigeria and India. Soldiers and drug traffickers routinely massacre human rights activists in Mexico and rape their wives into submission. Apartment dwellers in Cairo suburbs risk electrocution, landslides, or summary eviction from their illegal squats, while the Roma of Macedonia barely exist in the eyes of their fellows, being as they are excluded from the right to citizenship, education, work, or reparation for the war crimes that made them homeless in the first place. Although many of the photos adopt conventions of classical portraiture and what appear to be formal, staged poses (by design or because the sitters chose them), the concentrated energy on the faces of the subjects is arresting and makes for a psychologically gripping experience.

Readers seeking background detail on the five countries, such as one typically finds in an Amnesty International annual report, will not be disappointed here either. Each photographer presents requisite background information on the country, its governance, economics, and recent politics to help readers understand the evolution of the problems in view. But the best part of DIGNITY for many of us is the stories: the personal anecdotes relayed to the photographers by unforgettable girls and boys, men and women, who seem to transcend their poverty with intelligence, grace, and the sheer force of will, that is, with dignity.

WHAT DOES DIGNITY MEAN TO YOU?

Prior to the opening of DIGNITY at Notre Dame, we interviewed Yves Prigent, who conceived and organized the exhibit for Amnesty International France, and the five photographers he chose to realize the vision. We asked what the term "dignity" meant to them.

Yves Prigent (Amnesty International France)

Way too many times when we refer to the fight against poverty or to poverty as a whole, it's considered from economic angles or approaches. Which is not taking into account the fact that poverty is a result of massive and multiple violations of human rights. We needed more than just reports. We needed to have strong images to reach out to the public, to help the people to understand what it takes, what were the goals of the campaign, and what were the personal stories behind it. I think after you see this kind of exhibit or after you read an Amnesty report on these kinds of issues, then you don't have any excuses for not doing anything. Just to talk about it is the first step.

Guillaume Herbaut (Mexico)

Dignity is to feel human, upright, respected, that's it, to really be yourself. And I realize, the more that I work and go into complicated situations, the more I realize that this DIGNITY campaign is even more important today, because things are speeding up and I have the impression that dignity on earth is being crushed. Dignity, it's human rights, it's being able to live, simply, without being crushed by people who want to use you. It's huge. But I think that it is the essence of humanity. If you lose your dignity, you lose a lot of things, and you don't want to live anymore.

Jean-François Joly (Macedonia)

Today I am never surprised anymore by what I see. And sometimes that makes me sad. Because I would very much like to see that change, and I'd like to participate myself in the process of changing the way people look [at each other]. Because I think that poverty is directly tied to the *regard* [or gaze] that is cast upon these people. Even here when you take the metro or the RER [interurban train], as soon as you see somebody coming around begging in the metro, observe how people look at him. Either they don't look at him, or else by the way that they look at him, they push him deeper into failure. So for me, as a photographer, it's also a way to re-integrate these people in the regard of others. All these pictures are taken vertically. For me the vertical angle, it is about human dignity. Even if he doesn't have anything else, he is standing. Dignity, that's it, it's the fact of standing up. And thus standing up in the regard of others also.

Johann Rousselot (India)

You talk about dignity? I mean every human being deserves a minimum of dignity. When you lose dignity it's like losing your identity. These kinds of things are not acceptable. And why is it so hard to give to these people? Especially the tribal people, they are not asking much. And even the little part can't be given to them. Why is that so difficult? Please don't destroy this world. They want to replace this with factories. You know, boot it with pollution and death that will just pour into the whole landscape. So the whole point I was trying to make is to preserve and conserve, you know, places that are still untouched and wide. Just beautiful. Where beauty is.

Michaël Zumstein (Nigeria)

It was a question of humanity. I mean when you see in the shantytown of Makoko, what is happening here? Where is the humanity here? It's horrible. I mean it was very difficult to hear and to see. And that's why it was very important for me to work for Amnesty and to tell and to show what is happening there. Dignity is not a simple word. It is very important. It's the way you behave in front of your children, by example. When you are living in some very bad conditions, and your parents cannot provide you with food and a good education, I can see that in the next generations they will not respect their society. That's why we need to improve the living condition of people who are in Lagos, or in India, or everywhere, because we cannot separate all these rights. They need to be defended all together.

Philippe Brault (Egypt)

Brault reformulated the question to reflect on why he works as a photojournalist. He chose that vocation during the years when he served as a soldier in Lebanon, fulfilling his obligatory military service for France. As Brault said, "I carried a weapon and, by choice, a camera." In order to make the photos of the DIGNITY exhibit, he explained: "When you work as a photojournalist, the rule is to stay very close to the story. If you can express your feelings through photography, you are an artist. I would like to tell the story of how people live in a slum area. If you think you are going to find them very weak, you are wrong. People stay very strong when they have dignity."

NOTES

1. The broad scope of this campaign, as compared to the focused actions that have characterized Amnesty International's work in the past, has led some critics to diagnose an organization at a crossroads. See Stephen Hopgood, "Dignity and Ennui," Review Essay of *Amnesty International Annual Report 2009: The State of the World's Rights, Journal of Human Rights Practice Advance Access* (Jan. 19, 2010): 2, 13. The word is still out on DIGNITY's ability to raise funds for Amnesty, but as conceived in France, the DIGNITY campaign had a stunning impact. After a début in the Hôtel de Ville in Paris, it was featured in a dozen traveling shows, from Marseille to Mâcon.

2. Amnesty International, "Plus de droits, moins de pauvreté" in *DIGNITÉ: Droits humains et pauvreté. Un document de l'Œil public et d'Amnesty International* (Paris: Éditions Textuel and Amnesty International, 2010), 6, my translation.

CHAPTER 11

Economics

A Tool in the Fight against Injustice

ESTHER DUFLO
Translated by Julia V. Douthwaite

Political goodwill is essential to waging a successful war against poverty, but it alone is not enough. Given the enormity of the challenge and the limited means at their disposal, even the most well-intentioned authorities must make choices, choices about where to spend taxpayers' dollars and which issues to invest in for the greatest impact.

Yet the rhetoric of development often simplifies the situation. Some writers claim that poverty could be eliminated in twenty years, if wealthy countries agreed to invest enough funds into poor economies to launch targeted actions, such as the wide-spread availability of fertilizer and mosquito netting, or the establishment of micro-lending operations and free schools. Others argue that foreign aid actually fosters existing problems and creates new ones, such as corruption and misdirection of state priorities. According to this school of economic thinking, the natural play of market forces and competition will eventually right wrongs, if left to themselves.

These debates could go on indefinitely in the absence of real evidence of policy results. The poor will bear the brunt, no matter what style of economics are in vogue. An iron-clad justification is always available to citizens of wealthy, developed countries: after all, what is more obvious than the waste involved in fighting poverty abroad? It is more reasonable to keep one's wealth at home.

This essay was commissioned specially for the French catalog entitled *DIGNITÉ: Droits humains et pauvreté; Un document de l'Œil public et d'Amnesty International* (Paris: Éditions Textuel and Amnesty International, 2010).

Nevertheless a third current of economic thinking makes common cause with human rights activism to insist on humanitarian concerns and the dignity that is due to all people. Amartya Sen, Nobel Laureate for Economics in 1998, was a pioneer in this development. He was one of the first to argue that equal rights will never exist as long as access to those rights is limited by poverty. For him, health and education are essential *capabilities* without which human life is stunted. Access to health and education must therefore lie at the heart of any plan for human development.

This attitude seems to be gaining ground, not only among funding agencies, but also among the governments of developing countries that receive such aid: universal education and health care are now considered essential rights. Three out of the eight Millennium Development Goals agreed upon by the United Nations for 2015 concern health: they include commitments to reduce infant mortality, improve maternal health, and to continue the fight against AIDS, malaria, and other diseases. Two of the objectives involve education: demands for universal primary education and the promotion of gender equality especially in schools. Real advances are being made: more children are enrolled in primary schools, and improvements have been realized in some African nations as regards access to health care, particularly through the distribution of mosquito netting and measles vaccinations.

In spite of these advances, however, the state of public education and health in the developing world does not inspire optimism. In 2007, 9 million children died before the age of five from illnesses that could have been prevented or cured. Every year, 500,000 women die in childbirth. And even if more children are going to school, many do not learn much there. These failures, and the general slowness of progress, have been interpreted as proof by so-called "aid skeptics" of the idea that it is useless or even dangerous to try and intervene in such fields. In the absence of a real demand articulated by inhabitants of developing countries, spending more does not mean doing better.

A superficial yet seductive logic lies behind such reasoning: it seems to restore autonomy to people of developing countries, an autonomy stolen by international aid organizations. In the name of our respect for humanity and fundamental freedoms, we should abandon all efforts to help unless the people in question generate their own ideas by themselves. This analysis ignores the crucial teachings of Amartya Sen. He taught that freedom, which he understood as the absence of hindrances, is worth nothing if the individual does not have the wherewithal to act (this is what Sen calls "capability").

It follows, then, that the peasants who did not survive the great famine in Bengal were free to buy food, but their buying power was so limited by inflation that they were incapable of doing so. Similarly, a mother who has received no education and whose neighbors are also illiterate will likely be unable to imagine a different future for her child, even though she is free to do so. By the same token, vaccinations are rarely requested, even though they are the most efficient means of saving lives.

The extension of such capabilities cannot be entirely left up to the requests of peoples whose freedom is already limited by countless obstacles, whether it is their inability to imagine another future or the impossibility of saving money for a child's schooling. In the name of justice, Amartya Sen declares, education and health must remain societal obligations.

What can we do to make these social responsibilities carry meaningful weight in poor countries? To the extent that a society encourages education and health care beyond the minimum, it is solely responsible for providing those services. We cannot legitimately claim to support the people's right to health and education, then, unless we are willing to investigate the practical organization of such services.

It is crucial to keep such issues in the public eye; access to health and education must not be left to circumstance or improvisational techniques, even if aid is meant to be generous. Because when failures happen, they threaten the whole structure of efforts behind such aid. The fight against poverty requires bold solutions and systematic experimentation: we must continue coming up with new approaches, recognize errors as they arise, and learn from them to design better policies going forward. Experimentation must be conducted under rigorous, scientific methods.

Economists often make themselves unpopular when they force people to make choices. But making choices based on experimental methods, and using the most efficient results, is the only practical means we have to start making respect for human rights a worldwide reality.

CHAPTER 12

Mexico

GUILLAUME HERBAUT
Translated by Lauren Wester

The state of Guerrero in southern Mexico is one of the most remote regions in the country. Its mountainous area, La Montaña, houses mainly indigenous communities. This cut-off region is plagued by endemic violence, and the people, caught in a stranglehold between army, paramilitaries, guerrillas, and drug traffickers, try to maintain a traditional way of life. Since the uprising in neighboring Chiapas in the 1990s, the government has increased military presence in Guerrero considerably, especially to fight the guerrilla movements. The army has been charged with brutally repressing these movements. But in reality, the repression has been mainly against the civilian indigenous populations, who have been subject to forced abductions, arbitrary arrests, acts of torture, and assassinations. As for the nonindigenous landowners, they maintain paramilitary militias in order to protect and expand their property while the drug traffickers—who also claim to control a part of the region—arm their own men. It is not unusual for landowners to have relationships with drug cartels or even be members of them.

In such a violent environment, the indigenous populations attempt to survive in villages that are quite far from urban areas. The region's isolated position makes access to a certain number of basic services (for example, health care and education) very difficult. Those who do not emigrate to the northern part of the country or to the United States often have no choice but to join the guerrillas or to seek work on one of the plantations controlled by traffickers. Out of fear that the region might fall permanently under the control of drug traffickers, the government has increased repression of the locals. Far from taking measures to guarantee people's access to essential services, the authorities abuse the legal system. This hinders the work of activists who fight on behalf of the communities and who dare to denounce breaches of human rights. Threats, intimidation, and even murders frequently go unpunished.

The members of the OPIM (Organization of the Indigenous Me'phaa People), an association founded in 2002 to defend and promote the rights of the natives of Guerrero, regularly bear the brunt of this violence. A number of them have been placed under surveillance, and one of their leaders, Lorenzo Fernández Ortega, was assassinated in 2008. Yet defending and asserting the social and environmental rights of indigenous populations remains crucial. Recent investment projects have sparked worries, protests, and increased reprisals against those who dare express reservations.

The Mexican authorities are, however, committed—especially with the backing of the United Nations Human Rights Council—to protecting the life and the physical integrity of human rights defenders. It is imperative for the international community to remind the authorities of their responsibilities and to hold them accountable.

LA MONTAÑA

"Here, everybody distrusts everybody. Everybody is afraid of dying."

"Here" is the region of La Montaña in the state of Guerrero, less than 190 miles from Acapulco and its luxury hotels, yachts, and tourists. The person who told me this in his small office had just hidden a revolver under a newspaper. He's the local journalist. He has received death threats. This is *normal*, he says, because elections are coming up.

It's a violent, wild, and desperate region. Homicide is the number one cause of death. It is not recommended to go out at night, and you have to be careful of gangs that might rob you. "Yesterday near the village of Ayutla, an armed masked man stopped a bus. He made the driver get out and shot him with a bullet to the head." A police inspector who seemed really nice told me this. I later learned that he is strongly suspected of having tortured a young woman, simply to obtain information about a murder witness.

Figure 5. *Maria*. Photograph by Guillaume Herbaut, 2008.

La Montaña is a region with a large indigenous population. The state of Guerrero has the highest rate in the country of human rights violations. For example, one death in every three is a violent one.

Figure 6. *La Montaña Landscape*. Photograph by Guillaume Herbaut, 2008.

TESTIMONY OF TERESA JESÚS CATERINA

Teresa Jesús Caterina is an indigenous Me'phaa. She lives in the region of La Montaña in the village of Barranca Guadalupe.

December 2008

My name is Teresa Jesús Caterina. I am a Me'phaa.

Today I am old, but I still suffer from the rapes I endured. They were in 1993.

My daughter and I were on our way to work in the fields. We stopped by a stream to catch crabs. Some soldiers came by and ordered us in Spanish to give them some water. I answered in my native language, Me'phaa: "You have hands, get it yourselves!" Then they forced us to follow them to their camp in the hills. Two women from my community were already there.

My daughter and I were kept without food or drink and raped for two days by the soldiers.

Then we all left the camp and started walking. On the road we passed my husband, who was drunk, and who asked them to let us go. They replied, "Here we are the boss, you are nothing," before tying him to a tree and beating him.

We continued our march, taking my husband with us. The women were raped at regular intervals, about every four hours. And because I tried to defend myself, I was roped by the neck and dragged along.

We arrived in our village, where they tied up and beat my husband again.

Then, they offered to release me and my daughter in exchange for a meal that I had to make for them. "If you don't serve us, if you don't keep quiet, we'll come back and get you, now we know where to find you!" Then they left.

It's very hard for me to tell you all this. My husband is dead. He didn't want me to tell my story because he was afraid of how the community would react.

Today, I want to bear witness.

Figure 7. *Teresa Jesús Caterina*. Photograph by Guillaume Herbaut, 2008.

Figure 8. *Detail of a Kitchen from a House in La Montaña*. Photograph by Guillaume Herbaut, 2008.

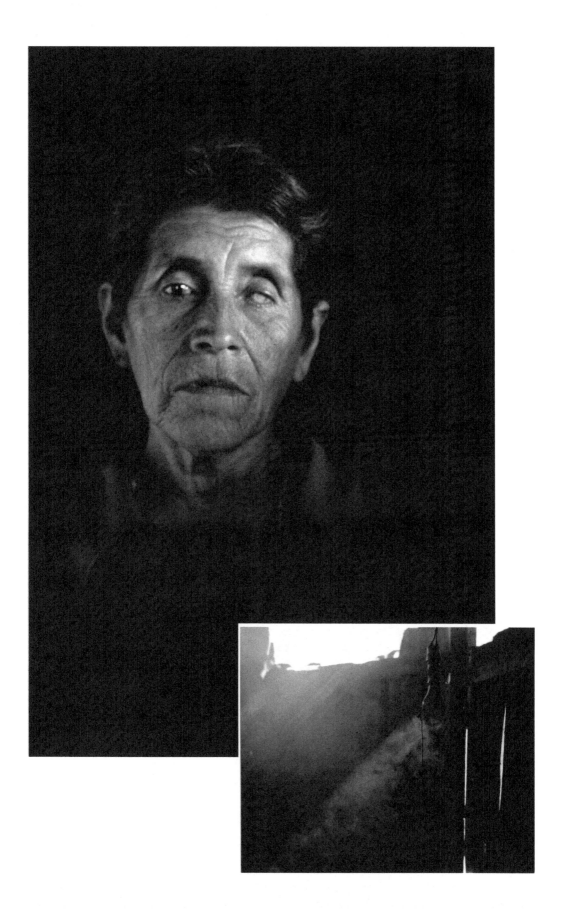

TESTIMONY OF RAÚL LUCAS LUCÍA

Raúl Lucas Lucía shows the position he was forced to hold when soldiers beat him in November 2003.

December 2008

My name is Raúl Lucas Lucía. I belong to the El Charco community.

In November 2003, soldiers came to my home. It was seven in the morning. I was having a coffee in front of my house before going to work. I heard the click of their rifles, and I could see they wanted to beat me right away. "Not in front of my family," I said.

So we went into the hills. When we were alone there, they undressed me. I was left in just my underpants, and they forced me to crouch down. Then they beat me with their rifles. "Where did you hide the weapons?" they asked me. "I haven't hidden anything, I have no weapons." They insulted me, humiliated me. At last, in the afternoon, they let me go.

There had been rumors that I belonged to the guerrillas. Each year I would gather with others at the site of the El Charco massacre, as it is called. My brother-in-law was in fact one of the eleven people killed by the Mexican army on June 7, 1998, during a break after a meeting of indigenous communities in the village schoolhouse.

When the soldiers left, they threatened to kill me and my family if I told anyone what had happened. They were from the 48th regiment of Cruz Grande. I later denounced the soldiers at the Human Rights Commission, but the law didn't do anything.

On February 22, 2009, the body of Raúl Lucas Lucía was found at Ayutla de los Libres, together with the body of another human rights defender, Manuel Ponce Rosas. They were, respectively, president and secretary of the Organization for the Future of the Mixtec People (OFPM). The two activists had been abducted by armed men posing as policemen during a public demonstration on February 13. A short time before, Raúl Lucas Lucía had met a delegation from Amnesty International.

Figure 9. *Raúl Lucas Lucía.* Photograph by Guillaume Herbaut, 2008.

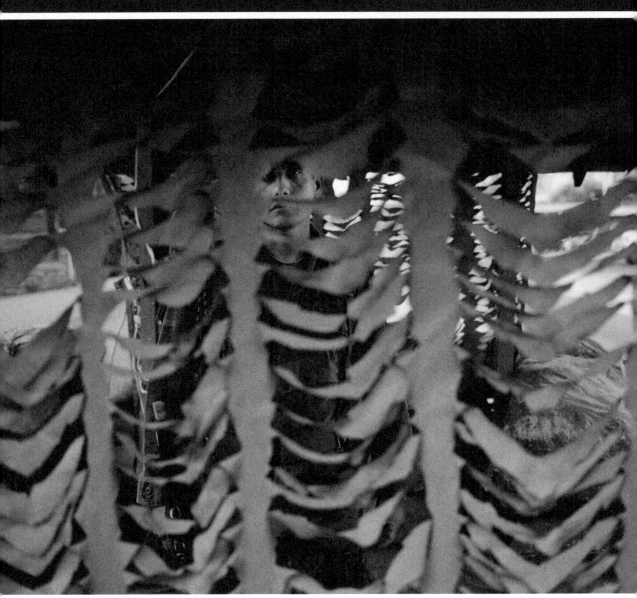

Figure 10. *A Soldier from the 48th Battalion of the Mexican Army at a Roadblock in Guerrero.*
Photograph by Guillaume Herbaut, 2008.

Modesta Cruz Victoriano, forty-two, is the widow of Lorenzo Fernández Ortega. An activist with OPIM, Lorenzo was campaigning on behalf of fourteen male members of the Me'phaa indigenous community who claimed to have been forcibly sterilized in 1998. He also sought justice for his sister, Inés, who had been raped by soldiers in 2002. He was assassinated on February 9, 2008, at the age of thirty-nine. He was taken and tortured before being killed. Modesta Cruz Victoriano is holding a photograph of her husband's body. Village of El Camalote, La Montaña, Guerrero.

Figure 11. *Modesta Cruz Victoriano*. Photograph by Guillaume Herbaut, 2008.

The municipal police force at Ayutla de los Libres is widely suspected of corruption.

Figure 12. *A Police Checkpoint at Ayutla de los Libres*. Photograph by Guillaume Herbaut, 2008.

At the municipal prison at Ayutla de los Libres, five activists with OPIM—Natalio Ortega Cruz, Romualdo Santiago Enedina, Raúl Hernández Abundio, Orlando Manzanarez Lorenzo, and Manuel Cruz Victoriano—are accused of murder. They were arrested on April 18, 2008. They are part of a group of fifteen members of OPIM whose arrests were ordered April 11, 2008. This group has been defending the rights of the indigenous communities of Ayutla de los Libres and Acatepec since its creation in 2002.

Figure 13. *The Municipal Prison at Ayutla de los Libres.* Photograph by Guillaume Herbaut, 2008.

TESTIMONY OF INÉS FERNÁNDEZ ORTEGA

December 2008

On March 22, 2002, the soldiers arrived here at my house.

I try not to remember the rape, it's too hard.

The soldiers came in through the back of the house. It was between noon and two in the afternoon. They greeted me. Then three of them grabbed me and took me into the kitchen. I had meat drying there. They took it and said: "Where did you steal this meat?" I told them: "It's my cow." Then one of the soldiers pointed his gun at me. "You must stop stealing." Then they seized me, and my children ran to their grandparents' house 275 yards away.

I was raped by three soldiers. Nine others stood guard around the kitchen. It all seemed very organized.

Ever since I denounced this crime, the community has looked at me differently. So has my husband. He has become violent. I don't trust him anymore. He doesn't want me to tell my story. Every day I argue with him and he keeps saying: "You were touched by soldiers, you might as well go off with them!" He insults me in front of our five children, kicks me in the stomach, slaps my face, and pulls my hair.

Then I run off and hide in the hills, standing behind the trees. At night, I would like to be able to dream, but every time I fall asleep I relive the rape in nightmares. Today I'm constantly afraid for my children, afraid something will happen to them. I'm afraid to go out and be raped again.

The government and the local authorities have never helped me find the men who did that to me. In any case, they have never done anything for us, for the indigenous people.

My brother, Lorenzo Fernández Ortega, was assassinated in February 1998. He was abducted and tortured by the paramilitary so that I would keep quiet and withdraw my complaints.

My name is Inés Fernández Ortega. I am a Me'phaa from the Tecuani community.

Figure 14. *Inés Fernández Ortega in Her Kitchen*.
Photograph by Guillaume Herbaut, 2008.

CHAPTER 13

India

JOHANN ROUSSELOT
Translated by Julia V. Douthwaite

While India's economic boom has been fostered by new technologies, the central-eastern state of Odisha, formerly named Orissa, is experiencing an industrial revolution based on the exploitation of its rich mining resources by Indian and foreign companies. Since 2000, the Odisha state government has signed fifty-some agreements with industrial and mining outfits to allow for new factories and drilling operations to be built. The priority given to investors has unforeseen consequences.

The lives and rights of thousands of people have been and continue to be seriously affected by these changes. Aboriginal communities are obliged to relocate—often by force—from land that they have occupied for years and that they consider sacred. The populations suddenly find themselves deprived of their means of subsistence. Promises of employment and rehousing linked to the setting up of new factories are slow to materialize. Excluded from the decisions that are turning their lives upside-down, these men and women have abruptly seen their status reduced to long-term poverty and marginalization.

Future generations are also being affected by this race for profit. Although it contains remarkable biodiversity, the remote province is already being scarred by evidence of industrial over-exploitation. Looking ahead, the scenario seems to promise a smooth and immutable order of things: the inhabitants will helplessly stand by while the region is devastated through pollution and deforestation; they will lose their homes and their lands while new industrial projects flourish.

However, resistance is in the air. The inhabitants have learned lessons the hard way, from earlier scenes of devastation, and they are increasingly speaking up to demand justice and transparency. They want to teach others about their rights, and to ensure that no new projects will be allowed to infringe on those rights. These movements, which are sometimes violently repressed by the authorities, find vital support from international groups. The international community can play a major role by demanding that Indian authorities and multinational corporations provide fair compensation, and by requiring that statutes be enforced to protect the people from any new project that might infringe on their rights. Respect for the law is the best means to ensure sustainable economic development.

THE WAR OVER THE EARTH

The state of Odisha is the motherlode of India. This chapter addresses six individual contexts in detail. A system of cross-referencing inscribed in the photo captions allows readers to place each image in its context.

KEONJHAR. The wooded Keonjhar district is primarily inhabited by aboriginal peoples and those belonging to the lower castes. The land contains colossal stretches of metallic mineral deposits which are attracting interest among numerous mining and industrial companies. KIRDTI, a local NGO, has undertaken a campaign to raise awareness and to promote education among the local indigenous peoples who were, until recently, completely unaware of their most basic rights and the destructive consequences of the mining industry. KIRDTI has been especially focused on teaching the locals to see for themselves the damages that have already been caused by over-exploitation in the Joda region. Since Keonjhar is near Joda, this should warn them to what may lie ahead.

KASHIPUR. Three people from an indigenous group were killed here in December 2000. They were part of a demonstration protesting plans by UAIL (Utkal Alumina International Ltd.) to install a bauxite industry on-site. Since then, the situation has been labeled "the social conflict of Kashipur." UAIL's plans are still advancing, thanks to sporadic waves of police brutality to keep the population calm. The village of Kucheipadar remains undaunted, however. They exemplify the force of resistance.

VEDANTA. Vedanta, a British company, plans to develop the mining of bauxite deposits that are buried under the Niyamgiri mountain range. This area is a haven of biodiversity and is sacred for the Dongria Kondh tribe that lives there and subsists on hunting, gathering, and slash-and-burn cultivation. They worship Mother Earth and Niyam Raja, the patron god of these hills. The development of bauxite mining will bring an end to this unique community. At Lanjigarh, a village in the foothills, Vedanta built a large aluminum refinery before receiving authorization for its mining enterprise. Vedanta took this measure in complete disregard for the law, but with

Figure 15. *Two Men in a Village of the Juang Tribe*. Keonjhar district, Odisha. KEONJHAR.
Photograph by Johann Rousselot, 2008.

implicit support by the powers that be, and has confronted the population with a *fait accompli*. According to D. Sarangi, an anti-mining organizer, this is the latest example of the impunity with which mining companies work in the state of Odisha.

POSCO. Thousands of peasants living in ten different villages are opposed to the construction of an ironworks proposed by the Korean company POSCO (Pohang Iron and Steel Company), which is the third leading iron producer in the world. POSCO's project would bring $12 million to India: this would make it the largest foreign investment in India's history. Like many other industrial corporations (such as Tata Steel and Arcelor Mittal), POSCO is drawn by the presence of enormous iron deposits that lie in the district of Keonjhar. Fearing the loss of their lands, the peasants and fishermen of the coastal region have successfully blocked access to the site for more than two years. It is one of the rare sites in the state of Odisha where agriculture flourishes, thanks to the farming of betel leaf. Confrontations between pro-POSCO and anti-POSCO forces have already broken out on several occasions, and many people have been wounded as a result. Suspicions surround those peasants who are in favor of the project; people fear they have been bought out by POSCO. By exploiting individual lust for profit, the industrialists' divide-and-conquer method seems to be stirring up ill-feeling in the resistance.

KALINGA NAGAR. The Indian industrial giant Tata Steel wants to build a factory for iron and steel metallurgy in Kalinga Nagar. The site is envisioned as a vast center for expanding the industry and transforming metallurgical processes. On January 2, 2006, the police opened fire on a group of peasants who were demonstrating against this project and killed fourteen people, all of whom were *adivasi* (indigenous peoples). Hundreds of *adivasi* had risen up in protest that day to denounce Tata Steel for the insufficient indemnities it offers to displaced peoples, or simply to voice their refusal to leave. Since that day and the national media attention brought to the massacre, a battle continues to pit small-scale indigenous farmers against the monolithic forces of Tata Steel. The violence continues.

JODA. The region of Joda is in the heart of the iron-mining region of Odisha. It is part of a geological deposit that contains the biggest iron ore reserves in Asia. Fifty-some companies are situated here alongside local mafias, and several multinational metallurgy corporations are campaigning the local government to get their slice of the pie. The vast majority of workers in the mine are members of the lower castes and indigenous communities. They constitute a mass of laborers who may be exploited at will, for whom employment is extremely precarious, education is virtually non-existent, and whose housing and sanitation conditions are deplorable. The pollution in this area is everywhere: air, rivers, and arable lands. The region is regularly bathed in a cloud of red, poisonous dust, except during the two months of the monsoon season, which partly transforms that dust into thick mud.

Figure 16. *Kucheipadar Water Carrier*. Rayagada district, Odisha. KASHIPUR. Photograph by Johann Rousselot, 2008.

Figure 17. *Village Scene, Kucheipadar*. KASHIPUR. Photograph by Johann Rousselot, 2008.

This forest path leads to the home of the Dongria Kondh tribe.

Figure 18. *Forest Path*. Kalahandi district, Odisha. VEDANTA. Photograph by Johann Rousselot, 2008.

Living in traditionally cooperative, self-sufficient, and effectively ecological so-cieties, the *adivasi* are indigenous Indian peoples and account for about 8 percent of the country's population. They represent an India that is simple, endearing, and peaceful. To ensure the preservation of their cultures and their socioeconomic well-being, appendix 5 of the Indian Constitution declares as illegal the transfer of lands

Figure 19. *A Working Man in Juruli*. Keonjhar district, Odisha. JODA. Photograph by Johann Rousselot, 2008.

classified as tribal to a nontribal entity. By doing so, it grants these communities special rights to ensure that they are not dispossessed of their only wealth: their land. Most of these people, however, are unaware that these rights exist, and their lack of access to education makes recourse to the law very difficult. Deprived of land for farming and without the means to retrain for other kinds of work, they often fall prey to poverty and alcoholism, and join the ranks of the disadvantaged.

Figure 20. *Open-case Mine in the Keonjhar District*. JODA. Photograph by Johann Rousselot, 2008.

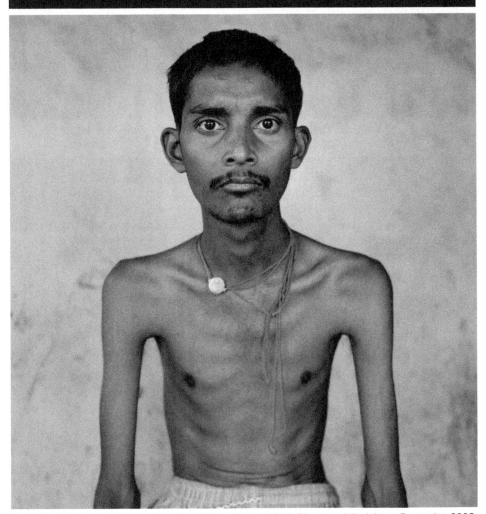

Trilachan Mohanta, age thirty, was born in the hamlet of Juruli. At the time this picture was taken, he had had tuberculosis for a year and a half. He is fortunate to be in a doctor's care, thanks to the collective efforts of his fellow villagers in Juruli, but he has not been able to find work since his disease broke out. He is a member of an "OBC" (Other Backward Classes), a label that covers the lower castes who are habitually neglected and held in contempt.

Figure 21. *Trilachan Mohanta*. Keonjhar district, Odisha. JODA. Photograph by Johann Rousselot, 2008.

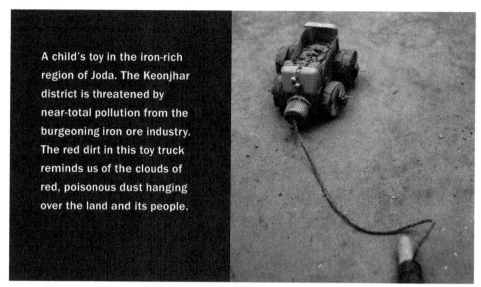

A child's toy in the iron-rich region of Joda. The Keonjhar district is threatened by near-total pollution from the burgeoning iron ore industry. The red dirt in this toy truck reminds us of the clouds of red, poisonous dust hanging over the land and its people.

Figure 22. *Child's Toy*. Keonjhar district, Odisha. JODA. Photograph by Johann Rousselot, 2008.

This is a memorial in honor of the fourteen farmers killed by police during a demonstration against the Tata Steel project in Kalinga Nagar.

Figure 23. *Memorial*. Jajpur district, Odisha. KALINGA NAGAR. Photograph by Johann Rousselot, 2008.

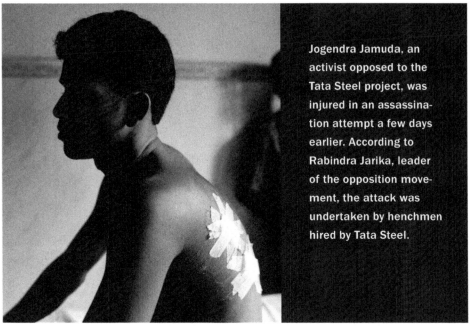

Jogendra Jamuda, an activist opposed to the Tata Steel project, was injured in an assassination attempt a few days earlier. According to Rabindra Jarika, leader of the opposition movement, the attack was undertaken by henchmen hired by Tata Steel.

Figure 24. *Jogendra Jamuda*. Jajpur district, Odisha. KALINGA NAGAR. Photograph by Johann Rousselot, 2008.

Denial of the most elementary rights has persisted for decades without meeting any real resistance or protest. Unaware of the social and economic consequences, people have seen the big industrial projects as emblems of progress and patriotic pride. In addition, the caste system naturally precludes the idea of rebellion and legitimizes a "natural" contempt for tribal communities and lower castes. An activist movement supported by various NGOs, however, has been growing in strength over the past few years and is making itself heard. The inhabitants of Odisha are learning more and more from the past and from the social disasters generated by this type of industrialization. The task of activists today is to build awareness and mobilize these fragile, ill-informed populations, give them legal assistance, unite them in their struggle, and hopefully win new battles. It is a combat between David and Goliath. And a race against time.

Abhay Sahoo, an activist and member of the Indian Communist Party, coordinates village resistance activities against the POSCO project. Fearing an escalation of violence, the authorities have restrained access to the region and declared it a "special security zone." On this day, the demonstration went off without incident. Jagatsinghpur district, Odisha. POSCO.

Figure 25. *Abhay Sahoo*. Jagatsinghpur district, Odisha. POSCO. Photograph by Johann Rousselot, 2008.

Villagers opposed to the Tata Steel project meet to discuss plans.

Figure 26. *Jajpur District Villagers*. Jajpur district, Odisha. KALINGA NAGAR. Photograph by Johann Rousselot, 2008.

CHAPTER 14

Egypt

PHILIPPE BRAULT

Translated by Lea Malewitz

The question of housing is explosive in the Egyptian capital, which continues to attract new residents every year. It is estimated that around half of the city's 18 million residents live in so-called informal settlements. Cairo today is an aggregate of districts, remnants of successive policies of urban planning. The inhabitants of these more or less peripheral zones generally exist outside of any legal framework. Most of them do not have deeds to their property and many do not even exist in the eyes of the law, since their parents could not afford a birth certificate when they were born. They are reduced to a life of uncertainty.

Generally subsisting without water and electricity, they have very limited access to health care, education, or jobs outside the shantytowns. The land on which they live is unhealthy and dangerous. In September 2008, the landslide in Al-Duwayqa demonstrated one of the dangers of this area and revealed the authorities' lack of consideration for its inhabitants.

Regularly called to order—particularly by the United Nations—since 1990, the Egyptian authorities have launched many initiatives to tackle housing problems. The political motivation for this is not surprising, since the shantytowns are considered the breeding ground for radical Islamists. In 2008 the Minister of Housing, Utilities, and Urban Development unveiled the major points of an urban development called "Cairo 2050," which consists of the demolition of many informal settlements and the relocation of their inhabitants. Bolstered by reports drawn up year after year, national and international NGOs have identified the real risk: that these men and women without a legal identity or the right to vote, who have no voice on the issue, will continue to have their rights abused. Putting this population further at risk, urban development plans rarely include adequate thought to relocation for those who are unaware of their rights. Local and international pressure is essential in reminding the authorities of their obligations. It is not a matter of questioning the need to manage the demographic pressure in Cairo, but of emphasizing that any sustainable plan must keep the rights of each person at its heart.

CAIRO'S FORGOTTEN PEOPLE

December 2008

The buildings tower up from the sand on the outskirts of the Sinai Peninsula. Ezbet Al-Haggana was previously a military camp installed on the border. Today it is one of the biggest shantytowns just northeast of Cairo, with supposedly one million inhabitants. I saw hallways leading towards tiny rooms of bare brick with plastic tarps for ceilings. Despite the high-voltage cables that run above the roofs, Ezbet Al-Haggana does not have electricity. At night, one can see almost nothing. One walks blindly, bumps into things, and listens. And when it is time to light up Ihaab, the young bride, the men climb the length of the massive pylons to tap a bit of current for electricity.

Dominating the city-center, at the top of the Mokattam Hill, are lines of bare concrete, empty lots as far as the eye can see: a settlement that people just call Mokattam. During the earthquake of 1993 it was the hope and refuge of thousands of displaced persons. Today these hastily constructed buildings have become concrete hovels. Now they are permanent. Mokattam is crammed with outcasts, the unemployed, and victims of the September 2008 landslide.

At the foot of the same hill lies another group of hovels: Manchiet Nasser. Jumbled alleys and buildings squeeze against each other. Piles of garbage lie on the porches, on the terraces, and even on the roofs. In the middle of congested alleys, children play barefoot among the debris.

Since the 1940s Coptic migrants originally from provinces in the south of Egypt have settled in the neighborhood situated along Mokattam Hill. The *Zabbaleens* (garbage collectors) have taken care of the city's refuse for decades; Cairo does not have a garbage disposal system. Nevertheless, over the last several years, the Egyptian government has contracted foreign and local companies to undertake the collection of garbage produced by Cairo's residents.

In 2003 the establishment of these contracts brought about a crisis. Threatened by the loss of their only source of income, the *Zabbaleens* mobilized against privatization and began negotiations with the government.

The settlement is also jeopardized by Mokattam Hill. On September 6, 2008, sixty-ton blocks of rock fell on the Duwayqa settlement, which is next to Manchiet Nasser, killing over one hundred people. Many landslides of this type had already

This image shows the results of landslides that have destroyed homes and killed more than a hundred people over the past decade. This decrepit, garbage-strewn slum is home to thousands. Faced with an indifferent government, the inhabitants live in constant fear of catastrophe.

Figure 27. *The Manchiet Nasser District of Cairo.* Photograph by Philippe Brault, 2008.

taken place, notably in 1993. Faced with the inaction of the Egyptian government, the inhabitants still live with the threat of catastrophe.

The *Zabbaleens* of Manchiet Nasser salvage, sort, treat, and recycle the city's garbage. This has been their life for decades. War does not mark the landscape of

Figure 28. *Empty Plastic Bottles: The Livelihood of the "Zabbaleens."* Photograph by Philippe Brault, 2008.

Manchiet Nasser, rather, years of survival and labor. As it is said, one man's garbage is another man's treasure.

A stone's throw away is the City of the Dead, a gorge of ochre streets and walls devoured by dust. Coming from Upper Egypt or the Suez region, chased out by the advance of the desert or by wars, thousands of people "cohabit" with the dead of ancient noble families, sometimes for many generations. Certain occupants are given responsibility for upkeep of the place. It is a sort of agreement between them and the families of the dead: they can settle here on the condition that they maintain the tomb. Others have found refuge in caves or in adjacent small, basic constructions. Sometimes a simple straw mat serves as bed and table. Here, the living have colonized the cemetery; without a doubt, this is the most spectacular consequence of the crisis that is eating away at the country.

In Cairo, 40 percent of the population lives in hovels. Ezbet Al-Haggana, Manchiet Nasser, Mokattam, and the City are what they call "informal zones" where the poorest of the poor have found refuge. Of the million or more residents of Al-Haggana, only 1,200 people have a voting card because in Egypt a birth certificate is not free; most of the residents in these hovels have neither papers nor the right to vote.

Mokattam Area

The victims of the earthquake of 1993—along with some victims of the landslide of Mokattam (or Moqattam) Hill in 2008—have been relocated to this area. It is perched on the same Mokattam Hill. Today, these hastily constructed buildings have become concrete hovels.

Figure 29. *The Mokattam District of Cairo*. Photograph by Philippe Brault, 2008.

This photo reveals the shoddy construction of the tenements perched precariously on Mokattam Hill.

Figure 30. *Home Interior, Mokattam District*. Photograph by Philippe Brault, 2008.

Ezbet Al-Haggana

The hum of high voltage cables, the dust, the desert wind, and the sand that rushes everywhere. A woman sitting on a bed who hides her face. Two men planted at the foot of a half-collapsed building. Houses without roofs. One lone room for a family of seven as well as their chickens, goat, and dog.

November is not the worst part of the year, far from it. It is neither hot nor cold. Visiting in this season, one can only imagine what life must be like in the summer: living under the burning sun without running water. Looking for water is a primary, daily concern for most people in this northeastern shantytown of close to a million inhabitants. Many suffer from nervous disorders provoked by the high-voltage cables that run above the roofs.

Figure 31. *The Ezbet Al-Haggana District*. Photograph by Philippe Brault, 2008.

Figure 32. *A Woman of the Ezbet Al-Haggana District Sitting on Her Bed*. Photograph by Philippe Brault, 2008.

It was dark, completely dark, in the alleys of Al-Haggana. The men set up the light. Ihaab, the bride, was at the hairdresser. I could not take any pictures. I only brought a 4x5 inch view camera. It was like a flashback to the early days of photography. I posed the tripod while shaking the dozens of hands held out to me. I took in the groom's eyes, proud and full of emotion. They posed for four seconds. Click. I savored the privilege to be there among them.

Ihaab and her husband were both born in Al-Haggana. Like most of the young people here, they do not intend to leave after getting married because one does not leave one's own like that. In Al-Haggana, people stick together in order to survive. That night, Ihaab's father used all of his savings to rent the garlands. The young men risked their lives to climb the massive pylons to light the party. The women filled the jerry-cans with water.

Figure 33. *Ihaab on Her Wedding Day*. Photograph by Philippe Brault, 2008.

The City of the Dead

The City of the Dead is a vast "district" in the center of Cairo. It is one of the oldest Muslim cemeteries in the city. Over the centuries, settlements have grown up among sepulchers. The tombs shelter the poorest city dwellers and new arrivals from the country.

Originally from the south of the country, Ahmed Ali Abdou lives in the City of the Dead with his wife and their four children. For the last four years, Ahmed has maintained the tombs of a Cairo family in exchange for a small single room in which

In exchange for his surveillance of their ancestral tomb, the family lends him a fifteen-square-meter room, which he shares with his wife and four children.

Figure 34. *Ahmed Ali Abdou, Tomb Keeper in the City of the Dead.* Photograph by Philippe Brault, 2008.

the family lives. Ahmed talks about the insecurity of his situation: the other family can at any time change its mind and demand that they leave. Housing outside the City would cost 300 Egyptian pounds (about $50), which he and his family cannot afford.

Ramadan is a worker in marble. He shares his earnings with his family to pay for electricity and food.

Figure 35. *Ramadan, Son of Ahmed Ali Abdou*. Photograph by Philippe Brault, 2008.

Arab Abu Saeda

About twenty-five miles from the city-center lies Arab Abu Saeda and its dozens of brick factories where 5,200 children work twelve-hour days. They come mostly from Cairo's shantytowns, and sometimes from the countryside. The majority of them are barely ten years old. At night, they sleep in dormitories among the adult workers. It is just a few steps from the City of the Dead.

Abdel, age twelve, is one of the thousands of children from Cairo's shanty-towns who put in twelve-hour days as workers in the brick factories of Arab Abu Saeda. He earns $14 a week to provide for his family who lives in one of Cairo's shantytowns.

Figure 36. *Abdel*. Photograph by Philippe Brault, 2008.

CHAPTER 15

Nigeria

MICHAËL ZUMSTEIN
Translated by Lauren Wester

Nigeria is one of the main oil producers in Africa. This fossil fuel attracts a number of foreign investors—petroleum companies, banks, and telecommunication firms—whose presence in the country, and in particular in Lagos, has heightened tensions and increased real estate speculation. Today the megalopolis has more than ten million inhabitants, and its population increases each year as people come from the rest of the country or from bordering countries in the hope of finding work. They pack themselves in, mainly in the shantytowns, condemned to live in terrible conditions and to be permanently marginalized.

As the greed of the real estate developers leads to a constant search for even the tiniest piece of land or house to seize, the shantytowns have become the prime target of speculators who evict the inhabitants and then renovate and resell the buildings to businesses that open in Lagos. They exploit the inefficient legislation and policies as well as the people's ignorance of their rights. In the last few years, several large-scale operations, sometimes presented as "clean-up operations," have led to massive evictions. In 2005, a three-day operation led to the eviction of nearly three thousand residents of Makoko, one of the largest slums in Lagos. To this day, no plan for relocation has been proposed to those who have left and who are overwhelming the surrounding neighborhoods. These large-scale evictions are frequent; in one estimate, around 1.2 million people have been subjected to this type of operation in Nigeria in the last century.

Most of these undertakings occur without regard for the law and are accompanied by excessive force. In particular, the victimized populations are rarely offered fair compensation or housing, both of which they have the right to demand from the authorities. Trapped in this vicious cycle, the populations of some slums are expelled, relocated, and expelled again. However, the mobilization of NGOs in the area can be effective. Organizations such as SERAC (Social and Economic Rights Action Center) allow people access to the law. Supported by the international community, NGOs are the people's only possible recourse and defense today. Requiring authorities to respect national and international responsibilities is a priority in fighting these evictions and in ensuring compensation. It is essential for the authorities to take sustainable, long-term measures to protect and guarantee the people's right to housing.

THE EVICTED PEOPLE OF LAGOS: "THIS HOUSE IS NOT FOR SALE!"

The alley is vile. The odor is unbearable. The spongy ground is made of feces and trash that have washed up from everyone living in the lagoon. Thousands of families cram in and live on their own waste, between chronic illness and unemployment.

We're in Makoko, the largest slum in Lagos, constructed between land and sea on one of the capital's peninsulas. This daily violence, sometimes more difficult to accept than that of an open conflict, is the consequence of a harsh economic reality, corruption, and indifference.

And yet this hell on earth is worth gold: twenty years ago, a couple miles away, a similar shantytown, Maroko, was destroyed and evacuated, forcing thousands of people to flee without anywhere to go. Today at the site of that former slum, there is a mall, some banks, a go-kart track, the headquarters of several foreign companies attracted by Nigerian oil, and the frameworks of the many luxury hotels being constructed for businessmen.

In this big city where demographic tensions run high, the presence of a shantytown like Makoko that covers dozens of square miles represents economic nonsense for real estate developers. The double digit economic growth of these past few years thinly veils a social disaster. The millions of people who dwell in the slums are outcasts from developmental policies, and harbor resentment against the state. Their anger explodes when the state evicts them from their makeshift lodgings in order to seize the land.

For many years, Maroko was one of the biggest slums of Lagos. In the 1990s the authorities allowed a massive expulsion of the majority of its inhabitants, disregarding their rights, in order to make room for enormous construction projects. Today it's one of the most elite areas for realtors and a symbol of the city's expansion that only benefits a few.

The Ocean Wind Project is being built on the land of a shantytown which was evacuated in order to make room for the luxury hotel complex that the city needs to accommodate foreigners who work in the oil sector.

This luxury hotel, being constructed in Maroko, will accommodate foreigners working in the thriving oil sector.

Figure 37. *Maroko, Lagos*. Photograph by Michaël Zumstein, 2008.

Souleyman Ades is a workman on the Ocean Wind Project in Maroko, Lagos.

Figure 38. *Souleyman Ades*. Photograph by Michaël Zumstein, 2008.

Without offering alternate housing, without considering the people living in poverty, and by disregarding the most basic rights of the shantytown residents, the Nigerian government is endangering the country's future. Living in Lagos today is to witness the beginning and the end of a civilization. One comes across vestiges of a once utopian place where freedoms have been replaced by inequalities. One is sickened by the economic turmoil of a society that becomes more selfish and hostile with each passing day.

Driving in Lagos, one passes by slums like Makoko and then ends up at FESTAC Town. It's hardly six miles from the city-center, but three hours by public transportation. This model city, constructed in the beginning of the 1970s during the height of a dramatic Pan-African movement, has not had electricity or running water for a long time. The city has been allowed to fall into disrepair. While the state tries to collect the rent that the inhabitants refuse to pay, the inhabitants criticize the state for its lack of involvement and the lack of upkeep. Isolated from the city-center, without help, the denizens of FESTAC Town are forced to be self-sufficient.

Surviving in Lagos could also mean living in Jakonde. There is water everywhere. The water is stagnant, green, and foul smelling. It inundates the city every rainy season, making the latrines overflow and forcing the residents to wear plastic boots or to construct footbridges. Jakonde is where the inhabitants of Maroko ended up twenty years ago, after having been evicted from their own shantytown.

On this nonviable land that was abandoned by a real estate developer who went bankrupt, the former residents of Maroko formed an association through which they continued in vain their battle for decent housing. But today, Jakonde is surrounded by guarded housing developments that are reserved for the Nigerian middle class. The land went up in value.

Soon, they will have to construct a mall, some banks, and a go-kart track.

Makoko

Makoko is one of the largest shantytowns in West Africa. Each year the number of inhabitants grows and the people cram themselves into unsanitary housing. However, because of its location and its condition, this land is coveted by realtors. Evictions are beginning, without guarantees of relocation.

Figure 39. *Residential Neighborhood, Makoko, Lagos*. Photograph by Michaël Zumstein, 2008.

Figure 40. *Laundry on a Clothesline*. Photograph by Michaël Zumstein, 2008.

FESTAC Town

Built in 1977 for the FESTAC (Festival for Black Arts and Culture), this area was at the time supposed to be a symbol of modernity. Today it's a peripheral neighborhood—situated two hours from the city—that is crumbling before our eyes. The infrastructure is falling apart. Its many inhabitants—cast out of society—have had to resort to an economy of survival. Garbage is no longer picked up, a sign of the neighborhood's deterioration and the neglect that the residents live in. The authorities are doing nothing to remedy the situation.

Everywhere in Lagos new real estate projects are flourishing on the sites of former shantytowns. Only the wealthy have access to these lodgings. The overwhelming majority of the people are subjected to real estate speculation and are regularly evicted from the slums without compensation. Oil is the country's wealth, but only a small part of the population profits from it. Everywhere, visitors see developers destroying hovels to build up wealth, thereby forcing people to move into already overpopulated slums.

Figure 41. *Street Scene, FESTAC Town*. Photograph by Michaël Zumstein, 2008.

Ahmed sells water to the citizens of FESTAC Town. This once modern neighborhood no longer has electricity or running water.

Figure 42. *Ahmed, Water-Carrier of FESTAC Town*. Photograph by Michaël Zumstein, 2008.

In order to avoid illegal—but nevertheless frequent—re-sales by their tenants, landlords write on the houses: This house is not for sale. This measure is meant to deter real estate developers.

Figure 43. *This House Is Not for Sale*. Photograph by Michaël Zumstein, 2008.

A workman repairs the road in front of the headquarters of Mike Adenuga, a giant in the telecommunications and real estate business—a vital sector whose success is directly linked to the oil business.

Figure 44. *Workman in Front of the Headquarters of Mike Adenuga.* Photograph by Michaël Zumstein, 2008.

Jakonde

This neighborhood houses some of the former inhabitants of Maroko who found refuge here after the wave of evictions in the 1990s. Regardless of the frequent floods that make Jakonde uninhabitable, real estate development continues apace. Thousands of families cram in and live on their own waste in this slum, surviving as best they can between chronic illness and unemployment.

Figure 45. *Rasheed Ajaï, Baker*. Photograph by Michaël Zumstein, 2008.

Figure 46. *Boy with Soccer Ball in Jakonde*. Photograph by Michaël Zumstein, 2008.

CHAPTER 16

Macedonia

JEAN-FRANÇOIS JOLY
Translated by Lea Malewitz

Today, the Roma make up between 2 and 10 percent of the population of Macedonia, where they've been present since the sixteenth century. The obstacles that this minority faces in obtaining legal and administrative recognition make it difficult to estimate their numbers with precision. The Roma community has forever been stigmatized by the rest of society because of its lifestyle. Lacking legal status has in turn made the Roma vulnerable to violations of their fundamental rights. Until the authorities take adequate measures in their defense and popular sentiments change, the Roma are condemned to remain second-class citizens.

Even if they seem to be better off than those who live in other countries of the former Yugoslavia, the Roma of Macedonia continue to be ostracized by society and the state. The attitude of the authorities, who do nothing to fight this discrimination, strongly reinforces their marginalization. The Roma today are among the poorest in the country, and their economic uncertainty is reinforced by their absence of legal recognition. Obtaining nationality resembles an assault course. Most of the Roma struggle to get the birth certificates they need to get identity papers because they cost money. These papers, however, are essential for accessing numerous fundamental rights. Thus it is particularly difficult for the Roma to send their children to school even though education is a key element of integration. Those who do manage to go to school often have a hard time getting diplomas because they do not have identity papers. Further, quitting after primary school is common: the children's labor allows their families to survive.

Because the Roma community has a hard time organizing to assert its rights, international pressure is crucial. As a candidate for European integration, Macedonia

Mefail Asanovski, age 42. Radaxiski Pat District in Chtip. May 2, 2008.
In 1998, Mefail was in a bar where a wedding was taking place when a confrontation exploded outside between some guests and the authorities. A policeman accompanied by plain-clothes men appeared suddenly and beat up all of the guests. "I wanted to call the police, but I got hit really hard on the head. They kicked me, handcuffed me, and then took me to the police station in a police car. Next, they beat me until I lost consciousness. They sprayed me with water so that I came to, then beat me again, more than fifteen times in a row. When they thought I was dead, they called for a doctor. I heard him say, 'This guy's not for me, but for the hospital.' I didn't have any reflexes left. When the policeman who was hit at the bar arrived, he recognized that I wasn't the one who hit him. He offered me a cup of coffee! Chtip's hospital did not want to do an official medical exam for me. I had to go to Skopje to get one."

Mefail continues, "To this day, my back aches and, often, so does my head. I received 3,000 Euros (about $4,250) from the European Court of Justice. This money is nothing compared to what I went through."

Figure 47. *Mefail Asanovski*. Photograph by Jean-François Joly, 2008.

has been criticized many times for its treatment of the Roma, as in the judgments of the European Court of Human Rights and in several United Nations reports.

The few Macedonian initiatives taken in return, such as those which constitute the "Decade of Roma Inclusion"—an official campaign launched in 2005 that was supposed to attract attention to the problems of the Roma and their community—are of little consequence. Increasing mobilization in order to make people recognize the rights of this group to be full citizens remains imperative.

SOMEWHERE IN THE OUTSKIRTS OF SKOPJE

Like every day since my arrival, I pick up Sarita at his house. Of Roma origin, Sarita directs a small local NGO, LIL, which provides aid to many needy Roma. Sitting in the back of a taxi, we travel three-quarters of an hour under relentless rain.

The car finally stops. We are in the middle of a vegetable field. Up ahead, a path potholed by agricultural machinery. A little worse for the wear, we bump along through water-filled ruts.

Several hundred yards from us, I can make out through the curtain of rain a very small house next to the path. In another time and place, this could have seemed bucolic. Today, it is anything but.

After a few minutes' walk under the torrential rain, we arrive drenched. Despite the mud covering our pants, Albert welcomes us with kindness and strong coffee. He lives in this little cinderblock house with a sheet metal roof with his wife Lola and their four young children. Although his wife considers them blessed because they live in what she calls "a real house built by my husband," their daily life is not really better than that of other families I have met since my arrival. Like many other Roma, they share with me their struggles to live in a society that rejects them.

After the Roma coffee ritual is shared and the interview and portrait are done, Sarita leaves me alone and launches into a lively chat with Lola. The rain is banging on the sheet metal above our heads. While left to myself, I think back over some of the testimonies I've heard since my arrival.

"Sometimes I would rather not open my eyes, so I could avoid seeing all the problems that I face day after day."

"I am sad because I don't see any possible future. I only think about buying food for my kids."

"Too often, I go to bed on an empty stomach."

"My husband is in prison. I am raising my four kids alone. They are not 'registered.'"

"I can't get any help. My life is a true catastrophe."

"I am so afraid to return to Kosovo. Everybody took their families and ran away. I don't know what became of my brother and sister."

Idzabi Dzeladin, 22, and Eldijana Dzeladin, age 24. Dame Gruev District in Skopje.
April 29, 2008.

They are both Macedonians. Idzabi was born in this courtyard. Officially married for two years, they have three children. They receive 80 Euros (about $113) each month in social aid. By picking up plastic bottles and trash, Idzabi earns around 40 Euros (about $56) per month. They don't want any more children because they are too poor to support them. Plastic, collected and resold, has become the primary financial resource of many Roma families in Macedonia. These families are worried at the prospect that the government might demand a garbage sorting system for ecological reasons. If the system is put in place, what will they do to survive?

Figure 48. *Idzabi Dzeladin and Eldijana Dzeladin with Their Three Children in Front of Their Home in Skopje*. Photograph by Jean-François Joly, 2008.

"The police beat me like a dog. I don't want to stay in this country anymore. I only think of getting away from this hell. Every day, we are humiliated."

"Our children don't go to school. They need clothes and food to be like the others. We can't afford that, so they don't go."

"Our husbands drink because they can't dream of having a better life. It is true that alcohol makes them violent, but it's this apartheid society that makes it that way!"

"We don't have water or electricity. We live like animals. What good is it to live in these conditions?"

Facing me, there is a small, white-curtained sideboard next to a Formica cupboard. A mute TV is set on a small table covered with a large, light veil. Above the cupboard, beside a vase of yellow plastic flowers, there is a little red Formula 1 race car with a missing back wheel. To my left, the mother nurses her youngest child. Her oldest son plays on a rug on the floor. To my right, her husband and another man are sitting on a couch, chatting and sharing a beer from the same bottle. On the back of the couch I'm sitting on, there are three pairs of new, clear plastic sandals and dark-colored children's clothes. Behind me there are new children's clothes hanging from the wall. Above the TV, there is a big calendar with some scantily clad women, and some framed landscape pictures. Everything is very clean.

The man who is talking to Albert stares at me. His gaze is clear and intense. Unable to talk, we look at each other. Time is suspended. He smiles at me, turns to Albert, and resumes his conversation.

Brenda Gjevrije, age 14. Shutka district in Skopje. May 3, 2008.
The oldest of six siblings, Brenda was raped by a family friend. He is in prison. She fears that he will get out quickly and return for revenge. Originally from Kosovo, her family fled the country during the war of 1998 without a single document. As refugees they benefit from the aid of the UNHCR (United Nations High Commission for Refugees). "We are illiterate. We only speak Romani. It's an obstacle to leaving this place. We will never return to Kosovo. We suffered too much there." Her mother spends all of her time at the house with the children; they don't go to school. Her father sometimes finds work in manual labor. Their living situation is extremely precarious. There is just a television and some floor rugs in this hovel; some of the windows don't even have any glass. They live in Shutka, the biggest Roma district in Europe.

Figure 49. *Brenda Gjevrije, Shutka District, Skopje*. Photograph by Jean-François Joly, 2008.

Subihan Nazirov, age 17. Radaxiski Pat District in Chtip. May 2, 2008.
Following an identity check, Subihan, who didn't have his papers on him, was brought to the police station. "Beaten for twenty-four hours by five cops, I couldn't think anymore, I was in such pain." His father Bajlam continues: "From the police chief's office, I heard my son yelling in the next room but I couldn't do anything. Even dogs are treated better than that. Here we are nothing. Unlike Skopje, in this city there is only one Roma representative on the municipal council. What can we do? Nothing, absolutely nothing! I couldn't even afford to pay a doctor to do a medical report." For ten years, Bajlam has raised his four children alone. He receives around 25 Euros (about $35) per month from the social center, and he does odd jobs in order to buy food for his family.

Figure 50. *Subihan Nazirov*. Photograph by Jean-François Joly, 2008.

Mejrem Zitkova, age 33. Momin Potok District, Skopje. May 5, 2008.

Mejrem lives alone with her two children. "I have been separated for a long time. I had problems with my husband (of an unregistered marriage). He was violent and went with other women. I left him." She doesn't receive any social aid. "My two children are in the process of getting registered. I'm waiting for their birth certificates; with them, I will be able to obtain social aid for the first time." To survive, she collects and resells plastic.

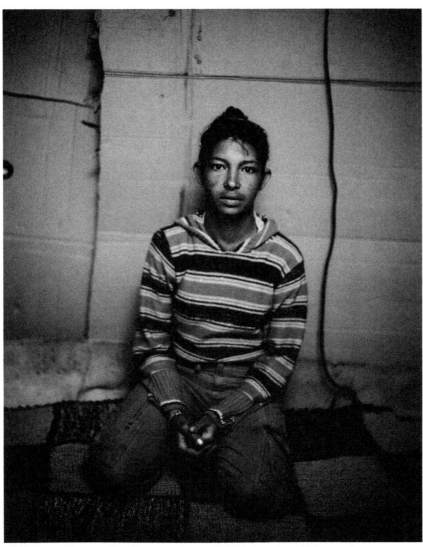

Figure 51. *Mejrem Zitkova, Momin Potok District, Skopje*. Photograph by Jean-François Joly, 2008.

Imerovska Firdez, age 58. Bitola. May 9, 2008.

Imerovska was born in Bitola. Her house burned down in December 2007. "Everything was destroyed. In a few hours, I had nothing left. Nothing remained but ashes. For six months, without a roof, I slept every night from pillar to post, with family." Today, with the help of a Roma association and the support of the city council, she will be allowed to squat in an apartment, or at least what is left of it, for one year.

Figure 52. *Imerovska Firdez*. Photograph by Jean-François Joly, 2008.

Vejsel Salihi, age 20. Zlokucani District in Skopje. April 25, 2008.
Not yet married, Vejsel lives alone, not far from his two brothers, and survives by picking up plastic, old papers, and boxes. "Here, everyone fends for himself. I earn about 60 Euros (about $85) per month. Sometimes, I go to bed on an empty stomach hoping that the next day, I will be able to earn enough to eat."

Figure 53. *Vejsel Salihi*. Photograph by Jean-François Joly, 2008.

Makber Ibraimi, age 42. Dame Gruev District in Skopje. April 29, 2008.
Makber is the mother of seven children, ages four to twenty-one. Not one of them was able to finish school. The oldest works illegally for a metal recycling company. Her husband and other sons pick up plastic. Her family lives in a difficult social situation, with 120 Euros (about $170) per month.

Figure 54. *Makber Ibraimi, Mother of Seven, in the Dame Gruev District, Skopje*. Photograph by Jean-François Joly, 2008.

Purmiseva Remzijc, age 31, and her son Abdi Durmishev, age 10. Radaxiski Pat District in Chtip. May 2, 2008.

Like Mefail Asanovski, Purmiseva endured violence from the Chtip police. "The police entered the bar. I had my oldest son in my arms. They took me by the hair and hit me with a club. They hit me in the stomach even though I was seven months pregnant. I feared for my baby. My water broke. Abdi was born with only two phalanges on three of his fingers. I'm convinced that it is a result of the beating. I am afraid to remember all of that violence." Purmiseva is one of five people who obtained 3,000 Euros (about $4,250) from bringing their issue to the European Court of Justice.

Figure 55. *Purmiseva Remzijc and Her Son Abdi Durmishev*. Photograph by Jean-François Joly, 2008.

Kes, age 16. City-center of Skopje. April 29, 2008.

Born in Italy, Kes arrived in Macedonia at age ten without a birth certificate. Since he has no nationality and no home, he sleeps in a tent with six members of his family in downtown Skopje. In the city-center of the Macedonian capital, he cleans windshields to survive.

Figure 56. *Kes*. Photograph by Jean-François Joly, 2008.

Part Four

_____

TEACH THIS!

CHAPTER 17

Audience Responses to Rousseau 2012/DIGNITY

PRESENTED BY JULIA V. DOUTHWAITE

Three groups of people speak out in this section: (1) members of a photography class for children who met photographer Johann Rousselot during his visit to South Bend, Indiana, and attended a workshop on DIGNITY at the Snite Museum, (2) teens and children from the South Bend area who attended three similar workshops at the Snite, and (3) college students and teachers who participated in events as part of their coursework. Their texts and images are presented in order of the participants' ages.

THE PHOTOGRAPHY CLASS

Thanks to Jacqueline Dickey, teacher of the photography class at the Robinson Community Learning Center, for joining events and for securing the children's materials for this volume.

Damaris Buendio Escobedo, age 10, South Bend, Indiana. Figure 46, *Boy with Soccer Ball in Jakonde*, impressed Damaris to say, "When I see this, it makes me feel sad because the boy looks sad and there is no color. It is black."

Daniela Buendio Escobedo, age 10, South Bend, Indiana. Looking at *The Manchiet Nasser District of Cairo* (fig. 27), Daniela wrote: "I think this picture is about how some houses don't have roofs. The city has a lot of trash; you cannot walk because there is trash in the streets and driveways. There are not a lot of people outside. I think I am lucky because where I live there is not a lot of trash in the streets. People can play outside."

Figure 57. *Portrait of Trilachan Mohanta.* Drawing by Kasey Bridges, 2012.

Kasey Bridges, fifth grade, Granger, Indiana. In her portrait (fig. 57) and words, Kasey Bridges expressed compassion for Trilachan Mohanta (fig. 21): "I feel bad for this young man and probably he can't even pay his medical bills. He is very skinny."

Joseph Habimana, age eleven, Mishawaka, Indiana. Joseph picked the portrait of *Souleyman Ades* (fig. 38), and explained: "The reason I picked this picture is because of his face. His face tells me that he hates his job, because his face has four scars and his hands are bleeding. It looks like it is windy. It looks like he has to do everything by himself."

Tamera Bruce, age twelve, South Bend, Indiana. "Let's make a change in our world!" exclaimed Tamera. Studying *Ihaab on Her Wedding Day* (fig. 33), she wrote: "Let's face it. How many people do we know or hear about in that city [Cairo] with no lights who are able to have a beautiful dress, jewelry, and light? When I look at this lady, I always smile because that's how I want other people to feel. Every day. I know for one thing that if everybody worked together, we can make our last years worth it . . . we can change our world."

Raini Fleming, age thirteen, South Bend, Indiana. "In order to keep their houses," Raini explained, "people in Nigeria have to put up a sign that says THIS HOUSE IS NOT FOR SALE BEWARE OF 419" (fig. 43). "Just imagine seeing that, every time you come home. Just think how you would feel and act. I would feel mad, but good, because I would know I could keep my house."

TEENS AND CHILDREN FROM THE SOUTH BEND AREA

Thanks to the student volunteers who assisted with these events: Savannah Hayes, Lea Malewitz, Michelle Mowry, Amie Wei, and teacher Claire Fyrqvist.

Mateo Graubart, age seven, South Bend, Indiana. Mateo took in the whole DIGNITY exhibit and noted how poverty and substandard housing cannot kill the human spirit. In his drawing (fig. 58), he wrote: "Some people who barely have a place to live still stand strong."

Figure 58. *Still Standing Strong*. Drawing by Mateo Graubart, 2012.

Ruben Velazquez, age ten, South Bend, Indiana. Ruben focused on the Macedonia section (figs. 47–56), and suggested a lesson to take away from them: "I feel that these pictures are saying: live with what you have. Sure, they might not have TV or even electricity. Some people may look at a test they did and they got a 60/100 and be sad, but some of these people can't even go to school. You don't need to cry over your test. If you were them, you wouldn't be reading this."

Maximiliana M. Heller, age ten, Mishawaka, Indiana. After contemplating the portrait of *Rasheed Ajaï, Baker* (fig. 45), Maximiliana wrote with great feeling:

> The way he had risen above the water almost seemed to represent his ability to overcome his problems: he had risen above his poorness and he had still been proud and had not seemed defeated. It's a very empowering picture. It makes you feel lucky for how privileged you are and that you are able to come home to a nice house and not worry about whether or not you'll still have a home tomorrow, and that you have those opportunities. The way the picture was taken makes him look almost holy, like he is walking on the water, and in a way he is walking on top of his problems and being able to still be proud of who he is. It makes you wonder if you were in a situation like this, would you be able to rise above it and persevere and still be yourself? I believe that it represents the true meaning of dignity, to rise above one's problems and troubles.

Sofia Lora, age eleven, South Bend, Indiana. Sofia took an optimistic view on the picture of *Ahmed, Water Carrier of FESTAC Town* (fig. 42), declaring that: "There is still hope for people regardless of what they have. Ahmed is really trying to help people get water and make a little money for himself. I think it helps me understand that I should be thankful for what I have and my life could be a whole lot worse than what it is today. You can tell that he won't give up and he is trying to look at the bright side of everything. A gift like dignity is one you can only see or have with a kind heart."

Kieran McKenna, age twelve, South Bend, Indiana. Indignation fueled the reflection written by Kieran, who exclaimed: "It is incredible to me, the way that the Nigeria and India exhibits display the awful capacity people have not to care for others. The fact that an effort has not been made to clean streets full of feces and contaminated water, or to stop companies from invading rural, peaceful areas is terribly depressing. The industrial issue of companies developing themselves in rural areas also perpetuates and fulfills the 'expectation' that the rich get richer."

Alice Goulding, age twelve, South Bend, Indiana. Responding to *Ihaab on Her Wedding Day* (fig. 33), Alice wrote: "It is the woman's wedding day. She looks happy and excited. For me, it provokes a feeling of hope. That even though where she lives is not nice, and how much she earns is not a lot, she is content. She has a beautiful dress and jewelry and a family who risks their lives to get a little electricity for one night, and that is enough. She will not have a honeymoon or a new place to live. Her life will stay the same, but this one day of pure happiness and love is enough to give her something to smile about. Though I have never heard a word from her mouth or seen her, I feel that she is the person that we should all strive to be. Someone who is happy with the way things are."

Jack Griffin, age thirteen, South Bend, Indiana. "Figure 45 really struck me as special," noted Jack. "It is a photo of a baker in Nigeria named Rasheed Ajaï who is standing on a rock in a flood of feces, trash, and water next to his shantytown bakery. This picture struck me because this man, despite all that he's gone through, seems so calm and collected. He is literally and figuratively on top of his sorrows and problems. This photo by Michaël Zumstein is my favorite in the exhibit. I love how his photos make you see an image of light and hope in the ever-increasing darkness."

Michael Kirbie, age thirteen, South Bend, Indiana. Writing on the Nigeria exhibit and especially *Boy with Soccer Ball in Jakonde* (fig. 46), Michael commented, "These people do not live life. Rather, one would say, they endure it. The idea of a child growing up in these conditions breaks our hearts. . . . Soccer is such a simple idea. Playing with a ball by itself is even simpler. But to think of a place where kids grow up in grotesque streets is just wrong."

John "Jack" Driscoll, age thirteen, South Bend, Indiana. Commenting on *A Working Man in Juruli* (fig. 19), Jack noted, "The man seems to be in a hurry, with a somewhat surprised look on his face, eyes wide open looking away from the camera into the distance. . . . The man's face tells of the horrors and depression of poverty in India. The strength and pain that it takes to roll a tire down a muddy road might equal the pain this man is going through, living in distress."

Sophia Zovich, age sixteen, South Bend, Indiana. Responding to *Modesta Cruz Victoriano* (fig. 11), Sophia pondered, "Every time I look at this picture of the woman, there is something else I see. The colors are quite vibrant, but the woman still seems to be sad. The sun shines through the blue and brown curtains. She sits on a ledge of rock. She seems to think that life is dead without the one she loves. The woman is so beautiful but she seems so sad that it almost hurts to look at the picture. She has respect for herself, and those around her, even if she seems trapped behind bars of steel like a bird."

Sydney Weber, age sixteen, South Bend, Indiana. Looking at the pictures in the Macedonia section (figs. 47–56), Sydney wrote: "I see these people who look straight into the camera saying: 'I challenge you to see ME,' for they live in a place where it's hard to ask for anything, but they should be able to ask for this."

Patrick Kline, age seventeen, South Bend, Indiana. That Patrick was moved by the whole DIGNITY exhibit is evident in this stunning poem, which incorporates echoes of numerous images. Readers will note allusions to the portrait of Rasheed Ajaï (the "Floating Baker," fig. 45), the toxic red dust of India that cloaks the child's toy in figure 22, the working man of Juruli (fig. 19), and the decrepit housing of Lagos, Nigeria (figs. 39–40). His message draws on the quiet air of desperation emanating from the Macedonian portraits (figs. 47–56), the pride of young *Abdel* (fig. 36), and the sorrow of *Maria* (fig. 5).

DIGNIFIED

I fly like a baker, and hide like a dog
I brave the dangers of my house and the law
I have no identity
> No education
> No hope
As a child I played in red poison
As a child I worked in the factory
As a child I watched my dad die
> Die of red lung
> Die from red poison
I have no life
I have no worth
I have no hope
> No possessions
> No being
I have only this picture
> Dignity
> And a plea

Riham Abu-Gdairi, age eighteen, South Bend, Indiana. Riham contemplated the Egyptian exhibit with interest, and noted, "This woman (fig. 32) may be staring at the only supply of water that she—and maybe her entire family—has for a while. She is sitting on a bed, fully dressed in her hijab and abaya. This probably means that she is not free to dress how she pleases. It seems like her house may not have a roof. That would explain why she cannot dress without her hijab, even though she is with family."

COLLEGE STUDENTS AND TEACHER RESPONSES

The people gathered here studied Rousseau's works in courses taken during the DIG-NITY exhibit and the Rousseau 2012 lecture series. We asked them to submit short essays that bring quotes by Rousseau to bear on the work of the DIGNITY team. The students' essays are presented in alphabetical order; Professor Alison Rice's contribution elegantly closes the section.

Alexa Craig, age twenty-two, "On the Portrait of Souleyman Ades"

> But from the moment one man needed the help of another, as soon as they observed that it was useful for a single person to have provisions for two, equality disappeared, property was introduced, labor became necessary; and vast forests were changed into smiling fields which had to be watered with the sweat of men, and in which slavery and misery were soon seen to germinate and grow with the crops. (Rousseau, *DOI*, CW, 3:49)

This quote from Rousseau relates to the photograph of Souleyman Ades, a laborer on the Ocean Wind Project (fig. 38). Since Nigeria is a big producer of petroleum, it is necessary for managers to depend on the work of laborers. The 10 million inhabitants of Nigeria need the security offered by companies like the Ocean Wind Project because they have no other way of making a living. At the same time, however, the investors desire to make a profit, possibly to provide for their families, so all of this misery has its origin in human codependence. The final part of the quote demonstrates that equality ends with the rise of private property and mutual dependence, because the disparities of wealth that follow require one man to do the work of two. And workers like Souleyman Ades end up worse off than they were.

Kathleen Ginty, age twenty-two, "The Limits of Unity"

> "Let us unite," he says to them, "to protect the weak from oppression, restrain the ambitious, and secure for everyone the possession of what belongs to him. . . . In a word, instead of turning our forces against ourselves, let us gather them into one supreme power which governs us according to wise laws, protects and defends all the members of the association, repulses common enemies, and maintains us in an eternal concord." . . . [E]ven the wise saw the necessity of resolving to sacrifice one part of their freedom for the preservation of the other, just as a wounded man has his arm cut off to save the rest of his Body. (Rousseau, *DOI*, CW, 3:53–54)

This citation makes me think back to the photos taken of Mexico by Guillaume Herbaut. In chapter 12 above, Herbaut notes: "Here, everybody distrusts everybody. Everybody is afraid of dying." These people live in fear: fear for themselves, for their family, for their security. Homicide is the principal cause of mortality. Further, they are men from the same country, fighting against each other (as in the soldier of figure 10). This soldier's battalion is suspected of having committed rape, torture, and arbitrary executions upon the indigenous communities. . . . To have a government or an army that will protect, rather than threaten, the rights and the lives of its citizens should not be a far-fetched or outlandish concept.

Ryan Koter, age twenty-one, "Rousseau and DIGNITY: An Unworking of the Real"

There are profound similarities between the way that Joly illustrates the lives of the Macedonians (figs. 47–56) and the way that Rousseau presents his own life in writing. The preamble to *The Confessions* demonstrates how Rousseau saw his work: "Let the trumpet of the last judgment sound when it will; I shall come with this book in my hands to present myself before the Sovereign Judge. I shall say loudly, 'Behold what I have done, what I have thought, what I have been'" (*Conf*, CW, 5:5). As if he were giving a speech in front of a crowd of thousands, Rousseau proclaims stridently, without restriction, his actions and thoughts. It is with this in mind that he begins analyzing his life through the process of *désœuvrement* or "unworking."

The process of unworking begins initially with a split, dividing himself into two people. Because of this radical separation, there is no longer just Rousseau, but two men: the author and a man who is the subject of writing, a fictional character. The images displayed in the DIGNITY exhibit resemble Rousseau's approach, but they use photographs instead of memories.

There are several ways in which Joly's tactics, in the portraits of the Roma of Macedonia (figs. 47–56), mirror Rousseau's tactics in the autobiographical works. First, the Romani people are seen in their natural environment: in rundown homes or the middle of the street. Second, each person is shown in ordinary clothing and looking somber; no one put on an artificial smile for the picture. Third, the view is unobstructed and seems unadulterated: an observer can gaze directly into the eyes of the sitters and get a sense of the arduous lives they endure. The observer can develop an understanding of who they are through a single black-and-white photograph. Just as Rousseau does in his works, each person stands in front of the camera and stops for a moment to state, "Voilà, this is who I am."

Lea Malewitz, age twenty-two, "The Frailty of Force"

After all, the pistol he holds is also a power. Let us agree, therefore, that force does not make right, and that one is only obligated to obey legitimate powers. (*SC*, CW, 4:134).

Guillaume Herbaut's photo *A Police Checkpoint at Ayutla de los Libres* (fig. 12) reminds me of the right of the strongest in the *Social Contract*. The focal point is the weapon, which emphasizes violent force. However, because the man holding it does not have a face, he has lost his dignity. Unlike *Trilachan Mohanta* (fig. 21), this man cannot look at the world with pride. Rousseau explains why: even though we have to obey the strongest sometimes in order to survive, that kind of power is not legitimate. Rousseau teaches us that while one person confronted with force is powerless, together, we can force illegitimate regimes to change. I also appreciate the contrast between the technology of the man's weapon and the natural background of the photo. The juxtaposition underlines the unnaturalness of the force wrought by the man-made weapon.

Darsie Malynn, age twenty-two, "Child's Play and the Pursuit of Happiness"

> Being deprived [of those commodities] became much more cruel than possessing them was sweet; and people were unhappy to lose them without being happy to possess them. (*DOI*, CW, 3:46)

This quotation makes me think of the photograph of the Odishan child's toy truck (fig. 22). The photo is supposed to be shocking, but aside from being dirty, I do not think that the image should provoke sadness and pity. I remember when I was young and my brother and I were content to play with a cardboard box for hours upon hours, imagining that it was a train or a time machine. The fact that we become sad in seeing this photo, thinking about the poor children who do not have Wiis or X-boxes, reveals the real problem. We Westerners should not project our ideas of happiness on other cultures. We may think that it is impossible to live without technology or so-called advancement, but in these cultures, the introduction of more technology and business would probably create more problems than solutions.

Amie Wei, age twenty, "Identity and Dignity as Observed by Little Kids"

At the children's event where I volunteered, the children chose their favorite photo and drew or wrote about their reasons for choosing it. The majority of the children were very young, so the word "dignity" was a foreign concept for them. It was surprising to me that most of them realized that some of the people in the photos are not exhibiting negative emotions such as sorrow or anger despite the fact that they live in harsh conditions. On the contrary, although these people are not wearing new clothes or living in houses as comfortable as ours, they seem content with what they have and look proud of their families. It was incredible that these young children already identified the concept of dignity without realizing it! Their reaction exemplifies the significance of being dignified. It seems to me that dignity is like a halo that illuminates the inner radiance of a person. As long as the person has self-respect and appreciates those nearby, he or she is dignified.

Alison Rice, "Dignified Detachment: Rousseau and the Solitary Self-Portrait"

"I am now alone on earth, no longer having any brother, neighbor, friend, or society other than myself" (*Reveries*, CW, 8:3). This oft-cited opening line from Rousseau's *Reveries of the Solitary Walker* could justifiably serve as a caption for many of the striking photographs that make up DIGNITY. While significant images from the exhibit show people in relation to others, whether standing alongside other prisoners or sitting next to family members, or even gazing at pictures of deceased loved ones, a remarkable number are solo shots. The penetrating gazes of the individuals who look directly at the camera recall another of Rousseau's celebrated sentences, this one from *The Confessions*: "I wish to show to my fellows a man in all the truth of nature; and this man will be myself" (*Conf*, CW, 5:5). The exclamation that follows, "Myself alone," emphasizes the solitude that Rousseau thought was unique to his situation and indicates his desire to unveil himself in an unprecedented—and, he believed, inimitable—manner. Recent French texts often contain personal details of a heartrending nature, and make it clear that the sentiments of exclusion and injustice that Rousseau explored three hundred years ago live on today.

Intimate and revealing passages from contemporary French writings that draw inspiration from Rousseau take on special relevance when they are studied alongside the DIGNITY images. In a short story titled "Family Portrait," Guadeloupean writer Maryse Condé describes the racism she and her family regularly encountered during her childhood when they went on vacation to France.[1] Sitting at a Parisian café, they stood out from the other patrons because of their skin color, and they were treated differently. She remembers that her older brother alerted her to their parents' precarious identity, referring to their attempts to belong to a far-removed French society that continually rejected them. The writer contemplates in these pages whether or not her mother and father were truly "alienated" from their African heritage and Creole civilization, and she revisits the isolation that characterized her upbringing.

In his written work, Magyd Cherfi describes the difficulty of growing up as the French-born son of Algerian immigrants. The discrimination he encountered was so great that he claims it would have been preferable to be an animal in French society than a human being from a racial minority. Like Rousseau, Cherfi took up the pen to express the deep isolation, the unthinkable ghettoization, that he knew, even if this gesture brings with it a certain separation from those whose plight is similar to his: "this is the price to pay . . . to be distanced from everything, from everyone."[2] In the *Reveries*, Rousseau refers to his own distance as detachment: "Thus, everything contributed to detach my affections from this world, even before the misfortunes which were destined to alienate me from it completely" (*Reveries*, CW, 8:19). The challenge is therefore that of finding out who he is, now that he is apart from all that previously surrounded him, of all that helped to define him: "But I, detached from them and from everything, what am I?" (*Reveries*, CW, 8:3). This is the question that we could pose to the individuals featured in DIGNITY.

Abdel, a twelve-year-old boy from a Cairo shantytown (fig. 36), possesses a solemn face that speaks volumes. The twist in his lips indicates his resignation to the long hours he is forced to work at the brick factory. The intensity of his eyes indicates that his spirit has not yet been crushed, but his slightly slumped shoulders hint that he is tired. Souleyman Ades, a workman on the Ocean Wind Project in Lagos, adopts a powerful pose (fig. 38), consisting of crossed arms and a back that is partially turned toward the photographer. His face is clearly visible and his eyes glare with severity, while his jaw is clenched and the scars on his cheek stand out. One cannot help but feel he is sending a message of reproach to all who can read it.

The women and girls who have suffered from rape show special bravery in their frank self-portrayals before the camera. Teresa Jesús Caterina (fig. 7) appears to be blind in one eye, but this doesn't stop her from looking straight ahead, with a gaze that reveals her suffering. Inés Fernández Ortega (fig. 14) has experienced rejection from her entire community, including her husband, in the aftermath of rape by soldiers; she stands solidly but with a shrug, and her face breathes the intense pain of her status as an outcast with no place to turn for justice. Fourteen-year-old Brenda Gjevrije (fig. 49) kneels with her hands slightly clasped in front of her; her slim figure, short hair, and androgynous clothing make a statement, while her wide eyes communicate her inner struggles and ongoing fear, as well as a paradoxical strength.

While these images do not constitute "self-portraits" in the traditional sense of the term, they focus on individuals who have chosen their stances and expressions in ways that allow them to speak convincingly of their lives through the medium of photography. Just as contemporary writers have sought the appropriate articulation of their personal experience, so these figures have aimed to tell their story, however difficult, while retaining a sense of self that is made possible through detachment. They are not detached emotionally—their feelings are evident—but physically, for courage has given them independence. They have withdrawn just enough to be able to stand on their own. And they have risen above just enough so that they can withstand the pain of being alone in a hostile society. Though their circumstances may be dissimilar to Rousseau's, they have adopted his understanding of soul-searching: "No, nothing personal, nothing which concerns my body can truly occupy my soul" (*Reveries*, CW, 8:61).

NOTES

1. See Maryse Condé, *Tales from the Heart: True Stories from My Childhood*, trans. Richard Philcox (New York: Soho Press, 2001).
2. Magyd Cherfi, *Livret de famille* (Arles: Actes Sud, 2004), 8.

CHAPTER 18

The Video Letters of *Entre nous Jean-Jacques*

PRESENTED BY DELPHINE MOREAU

Translated by Julia V. Douthwaite

This chapter illustrates how Rousseau's writings allowed people to think about what it means to live with dignity. It includes key scenes from the film *Entre nous Jean-Jacques*, presented by the director.[1]

THE LITERACY CLASS

In French, the word dignity (*dignité*) immediately calls to mind a revolutionary mind-set. It conjures up the famous "Declaration of the Rights of Man and Citizen" (1789), which laid the groundwork for the constitution of the first French Republic. This was the first text in French to articulate explicitly that all people have natural rights and, implicitly, that these rights should allow them to live with dignity. Its influence undergirds the present constitution of the Fifth Republic as well.

For adults in a literacy class, such ideals can seem unattainable. When you cannot express yourself in speaking, or read and write adequately, it is hard to feel included and "dignified." You're more likely to feel ashamed and excluded. Some of the people we worked with fell into illiteracy early on because their family's financial difficulties blocked their access to education while they were growing up. Others discovered the humiliation of being considered illiterate more recently, after arriving in France as a refugee from political or ethnic persecution or as an immigrant in search of work. All of them know what it is like to live on the margins of society; all of them have experienced injustice.

Thanks to the Association Française pour la Lecture (a literacy nonprofit) and its policy of providing long-term support and guidance to adults in need, a sense of complicity and friendly dialogue had already been created in the group before our team arrived, and it allowed participants to rise to the challenge of contributing to *Entre nous Jean-Jacques* with confidence.[2] What follows are a few notes on the authors and the video letters that they wrote to Rousseau.

Fly, Pigeon, by Arnaud

At age nineteen, Arnaud had already lived through some tough times growing up in France. He was not too keen on the idea of a philosophical discussion. Nevertheless he joined the project with great gusto once he found a way to connect with it. He feels no small pride in his film, *Fly, Pigeon,* where he relates the love of rural life and animals: an important theme in the life and work of Jean-Jacques Rousseau.

> Letter to Rousseau. I also love the peace of the countryside. I don't like cities; city people are nervous and aggressive. I prefer the company of animals. My foster family had two dogs when I was growing up. Now I have a roe deer, nine chickens, and twenty-six pigeons. How do you tame a pigeon? Rousseau got it right in *The Confessions.*[3] Like him, I think that the animals you tame have to want to come to you, of their own free will and in friendship.

Get Lost! by Maïmouna and Fatimata

Like Arnaud, Maïmouna underwent a huge change during the course of this project. When we first met her she seemed bored and distant, but she gradually came out of her shell as we studied the political themes in Rousseau together. Although she left her native Senegal long ago, she still bears the traces of a violent past. Her present situation as an undocumented immigrant in a foreign land, barely able to converse in its language, is not much of an improvement. For our project, however, she was able to collaborate with another Senegalese woman, and Rousseau's *Social Contract* became a springboard for a lively conversation on the importance of democratic institutions in Senegal. This was particularly relevant for them, given the corruption surrounding recent elections there.

Their video letter begins with Fatimata speaking Soninke and explaining the relevance of this excerpt for the situation in Senegal: "The strongest is never strong enough to be the master forever unless he transforms his force into right and obedience into duty" (*SC*, CW, 4:133). A chessboard then flashes onto the screen and the two women demonstrate—by moving chess pieces across the squares—how the Senegalese people demonstrated against the two candidates up for election. Maïmouna wraps up the sequence by reciting the same phrase as above, but this time in a veritable "slam." Viewers can tell that she is in total mastery of the concept and knows exactly what she is talking about. The meaning of *Get Lost!* is very clear in French, Soninke, and as demonstrated on the pieces being thrown off the chessboard!

The Earth Belongs to No One, by Esma

A nurse by training, Esma came to France as a political refugee from her native Yugoslavia. At first she refused to talk about her past, yet she was always very attentive during our workshops on the *Discourse on the Origins of Inequality* and the *Social Contract.* (These were the same sessions that Arnaud, for example, found incomprehensible!) She seemed to enjoy an intellectual activity that allowed for more engagement than the usual French grammar lessons. As time went by, our study of political theory enabled Esma to revisit her experience of war. This was not an easy process. During a screening of Marjane Satrapi's animated film, *Persepolis,* which shows a young Iranian girl learning about war and exile, Esma became very upset and left the room. It is telling that in her video letter, she turned her back to the camera. But the message she conveys through her voice and words is powerful. As she says in the opening sequence: "This is the Yugoslavian flag. The ex-Yugoslavia. After the war, it became Macedonia. This is the flag of Croatia. This is the flag of Serbia. This is the flag of Slovenia. They all got their independence without a war. But in Bosnia, there were a lot of massacres. Now it is a new country called Kosovo but it is not yet recognized. That's how it is."

Then she launches into her video letter while standing in front of a globe: "We are all born on the earth and we are all living beings. We all have the right to live on this planet. We have no say over when we're born or when we'll die, but we'll all end up the same, back in the earth. Rich or poor, tyrant or slave, we all wonder, 'What are we doing here?' You can compose beautiful music like Beethoven or write plays like Shakespeare or philosophy like Jean-Jacques Rousseau. Are we really here to massacre each other, to fight wars, and destroy the earth? To deprive other people of their right to live? To take away their land? We can all be free, equal, and respect each other. I am going to tell you what I think: 'You are lost if you forget that the fruits belong to all and the Earth to no one!'" (*DOI,* CW, 3:43). *Then she destroys the globe.*

A False Contract, by Sulasemi

> Dear Rousseau. Sometimes people *do* have to renounce their freedom and their rights in order to work. I am going to tell you my story. I was born in Indonesia, in a little mountain village in the middle of a forest. Life was hard but the people in my village were happy; they often smiled and were very open with each other. Every morning, I would get up at 3:00 am to go sell coconuts before going to

school. But I had a dream. I wanted to live in a developed country, to get a better life, and to make more money. When I turned eighteen I decided to go to Hong Kong to work. I had to sign a contract I did not agree with (and I still resent it). [She tells how she was sold into slavery.] Today Hong Kong is far away and I'm relieved. Rousseau, you say: "To renounce one's freedom is to renounce one's status as a man, the rights of humanity and even its duties" (*SC*, CW, 4:135). That's easy to say. But some people will always want to exploit other people and take away their freedoms.

Sulasemi's clip ends with a passage from the *Social Contract* read in Indonesian. We put the written words on the screen with her voice-over in Indonesian; this seemed the best way to commemorate Rousseau's fascination with the musicality of languages. It also captures the speaker's hope of communicating her message to others—a crucial component in a documentary.

Chakma People, by Partha

Partha is an agricultural engineer from Bangladesh who arrived in France just months before *Entre nous Jean-Jacques* was shot. During the first workshops, when the other participants brought pictures of their countries or personal snapshots, Partha brought a portrait of Gandhi and the lake that lies over his ancestral village. He chose this quote from the *Social Contract*: "War is not, therefore, a relation between man and man, but between State and State" (*SC*, CW, 4:135), and he commented:

> For my people—an indigenous people of Bangladesh—warfare means resistance. Ever since 1964, when the state built a hydroelectric dam in our region to bring electricity to the rest of the country, we have been fighting a war of resistance against a state that refuses to acknowledge our existence and our rights. [Partha explains how he grew up alongside a lake where his people—the Chakma—live and work illegally now and are considered a displaced population.] Today, the lake is a tourist attraction, but under its calm waters, our village, our land, and our history remain. They are buried there; everything has disappeared. Thanks to electric power, the rest of the country has gotten richer, but not us. Most of my people still live in darkness (*dans l'obscurité*). Two years ago, I had to leave too, because of a military threat.

There may seem to be a disconnect between Partha's words and the images he chose—some of them are old photos of his region or peaceful images of a river; they conjure up a lost world or perhaps a dream-world, whose serenity clashes with the violence he recounts. But the message is clear. Rousseau is wrong, Partha declares, to assume that wars are only waged between states. Sometimes a country wages war against its own people. With his video letter, the Chakmas' story will be told and their injustices will be known.

Feathers of Exile, by Zeliha

> I left in 1989 to move to Turkey. I was nine years old and had always lived in Bulgaria. I was very sad to leave my friends and my country. One day I found some duck feathers on the ground, and suddenly I had the idea that these feathers could fly back to my country and bring news to my friends. It was hard for me, a little nine-year-old girl; I didn't understand anything about politics. At that time the communist regime in Bulgaria did not respect the cultural and religious traditions of certain minorities. I liked living in Turkey. It was more tolerant there and I felt freer. Like everyone else, we loved Ataturk. He was a secular man. Inspired by the ideas of Jean-Jacques Rousseau, he valued freedom and thought everyone should have the right to express themselves.

A poetic sequence follows where Zeliha blows feathers through the air, then she puts on a series of colored head scarves—symbols of her new sense of religious freedom. Finally, a line of portraits fills the screen and reveals a striking resemblance between Ataturk and Rousseau.

I believe that this group of men and women who have experienced devastating loss and hardship makes a fitting homage to Rousseau. The goals we had for *Entre nous Jean-Jacques* are beautifully captured by the combination of autobiography, analysis, and documentary evidence. What is more important, I am convinced that by participating in this project—by studying Rousseau and appropriating his ideas in their own words—they have regained a sense of pride for what they've overcome and a newfound feeling of dignity.

THE ELDERLY

When French people talk about old women they sometimes use the expression, "she is very dignified" (*elle est très digne*). This means that she carries herself with a stately air despite her advanced age and frailty. But our society is harsh toward the elderly. Once people retire, they are considered useless and are made to feel ashamed for their physical dependence on others. The worst thing is their solitude. Working among the elderly in a nursing home really made us feel that, and it made our theme even more poignant: we studied Rousseau's last work, the *Reveries of the Solitary Walker,* and the pursuit of happiness. Even though they were all elderly, every member of our group could identify with the pursuit of happiness; they were still searching for that ineffable state! The connection with Rousseau was palpable. Like the aged writer of the *Reveries*, they too enjoyed reliving the past and musing on people they'd known. I think that this experience made them happy, actually. The intellectual stimulation and the feeling of reaching out to a waiting audience seemed to do them good. If there is one thing that I have learned from this project, it is that we all owe respect to the aged and have much to learn from them about dignity.

First Promenade, by Andrée Doucet[4]

> Oh, I would not say that I am unhappy. But I'm not completely happy either, because there are some things I would love to see again and I know they are lost forever. Friends come and say, "So, you're all alone?" Well, yes, I am all alone. That doesn't bother me a whit. Paris, however, I will always miss Paris. I used to love walking along the quays of the Seine, visiting the book-sellers, and leafing through their books. Or the Luxembourg Garden. In summer I would take a book and read in the garden. One day the leaves would be all yellow and the next day there would be buds bursting into bloom. It's the cycle of nature. And the little birds . . . I love to hear them sing. I like it even better when they come up to me and eat the bread or croissant crumbs I put out for them. Then I'm really happy!

A Passion for Roses, by Lucienne Calleja

Mme Calleja reads the following quote from the *Confessions*: "One would say that my heart and my mind do not belong to the same individual. Feeling comes to fill my soul quicker than lightning, but instead of enlightening me it sets me on fire and dazzles me. I feel everything and I see nothing. I am fiery but stupid: I need to be cool in order to think" (*Conf*, CW, 5:95). Then she exclaims: "That's it exactly. That's me. Absolutely! Every word reflects my feelings."

On the Utility of Nature, by Gilberte Vidal

Mme Vidal reads aloud two passages from Rousseau: "Botany, as I have always considered it and as it began to become a passion for me, was precisely an idle study, suited to filling up the whole void of my leisure, without leaving room for the delirium of the imagination, or for the boredom of total inactivity" (*Conf*, CW, 5:537); and "No longer able to do any good which does not turn to evil, no longer able to act without harming another or myself, to abstain has become my sole duty" (*Reveries*, CW, 8:7). She sums up by noting: "What he's saying here is that, whatever century you live in, when you get to the end of your life, you have a hunch—no, you are sure—that you are not good for much of anything anymore, really." Then we see her in the nursing home garden, naming all the spring flowers. "Like Jean-Jacques Rousseau, I feel peaceful looking at nature because I know it will live on. Life still gives me moments of happiness; at least I still have that."

Memories of the Orient, by Noélie Lafon

Surrounded by photos, Mme Lafon shares her happiest moments with us, from when she lived in Egypt in the 1950s as an adolescent. Her kinship with Rousseau is palpable when she reads this passage from the *Confessions*: "As for me, I know that the remembrance of such a beautiful day touches me more, charms me more, returns more to my heart than that of any pleasures that I have tasted in my life" (*Conf,* CW, 5:116). As she comments afterwards, "It's a powerful lesson: to face our life instead of brushing it under the rug. It takes courage."

Each of these little portraits—whether it speaks directly to Rousseau, renders homage to his work, or just proffers a glance in his direction—reveals the participant's personality. After watching this series of shorts, I think that people will be less inclined to assume that the elderly have nothing to teach us. The women's letters all bespeak a certain fragility but they do so without batting an eye. They embrace their situation. That makes us feel close to them; it makes us admire them. They are *dignes*.

THE TEENAGERS

Rousseau's association with revolt and protest was our theme with the group of teenagers, who were all students in an exclusive private school. All adolescents can identify with that, I thought, and perhaps we could bring them around to seeing how being a good citizen requires a certain amount of resistance to authority. At age seventeen, everyone feels indignant about something, whether it is political—as in the Occupy Wall Street movement in the USA or *Los indignados* in Spain—or more personal, existential.[5] The project was not entirely successful, I admit, but it was interesting. One young man spent the night in the Paris metro, living (in a naïve and unrealistic kind of way) like a homeless person and filmed what he saw with a cell phone. Two others debated the relative merits of voting. They quote a different Rousseau than we have seen until now, the cynic who was pessimistic about the "political machine" of his time. As he wrote in "Fragment on Freedom": "Listen to our Politicians argue: they have nothing but the defense and advantage of peoples on view. Watch them act: they work only to oppress them."[6] A critical attitude toward Rousseau was one of the biggest surprises we found with the teens. They attacked him on his attitude toward women and his neglect of his children. Perhaps that was their way to prove their mettle, to show that they too are worthy of interest.

THE CHILDREN

The most striking lesson I took away from the work we did with the fourth graders (ages nine to ten) is simply how important it is that children be given the chance to express themselves in non-academic ways. Taking our cue from *Emile*, we designed the workshops so that the participants would feel less inhibited and more engaged in the joy of thinking and creating. We did not treat them as imperfect adults or unfinished products, but rather sought to respect each in his or her own right. What a pleasure it was to hear their stories take on a Rousseauian tone! Consider *The Rustic Life*, in which two children (and a third wearing a Jean-Jacques mask; fig. 59) discuss their dream picnic: "It is in a forest. It smells like a barbecue. The sky is very blue. The children sit around tables; there are pretty cabins nearby. All our meals would be banquets. We would eat on the grass, under the trees. . . . There will be fireworks every day, and confetti, and games. Desserts would hang from the trees. Everybody would help each other." It is through experiences like this that Rousseau's beauty and imagination live on among us today.

Figure 59. *Child Wearing a Rousseau Mask During Filming of "Entre nous Jean-Jacques."* Photograph by Delphine Moreau, 2012.

NOTES

1. Some of the scenes translated here are available on-line; contact cinespheres@gmail .com for more information.

2. Two or three volunteers from the association were always on hand during our work and helped participants correct their writing and improve their pronunciation.

3. In book 6 of the *Confessions* Rousseau describes his fondness for taming pigeons and keeping bees: "I have always taken a singular pleasure in taming animals, above all those that are fearful and wild. It appeared charming to me to inspire them with a confidence that I never abused. I wanted them to love me in freedom" (*Conf*, CW, 5:196).

4. At age ninety-two, Mme Doucet was the doyenne of the group!

5. *Les indignados* is a movement that came to life in Madrid in May 2011 and whose slogan is "Real Democracy Now." It is very influenced by the Arab Spring and the manifesto of Stéphane Hessel, *Indignez-vous!* (Paris: Indigène, 2010).

6. Jean-Jacques Rousseau, "Fragment on Freedom," in *The Collected Writings of Rousseau*, vol. 4, ed. Roger D. Masters and Christopher Kelly, trans. Judith R. Bush, Roger D. Masters, and Christopher Kelly (Hanover, NH, and London: Dartmouth College and the University Press of New England, 1994), 4:12.

Postface

CHARLES R. LOVING

The staff of the Snite Museum of Art, University of Notre Dame, was pleased to participate in the Rousseau 2012/DIGNITY project. The associated exhibitions, lectures, class sessions, and public school programs were organized to mark the tercentennial of the birth of Swiss philosopher Jean-Jacques Rousseau by assessing the twenty-first-century relevance of his groundbreaking eighteenth-century humanitarian ideals.

"A Person's Worth" was an exhibition featuring artworks selected from the Snite Museum's permanent collection to depict the poor in the eighteenth and nineteenth centuries as a counterpart to the DIGNITY exhibit of contemporary poverty and injustice, first exhibited in Paris, France, at the Hôtel de Ville (May–July 2010). Notre Dame French Professor Julia Douthwaite was so deeply moved by the Paris exhibition—"jolted," in her words—that she determined to bring it to Notre Dame.

Fortunately, when Douthwaite visited me in 2010 to suggest that the Snite Museum exhibit DIGNITY, I was sufficiently cognizant to recognize her passion for the exhibition, adequately wise to embrace her vision for sharing it with Notre Dame, and reasonably generous to invest museum resources in the project. In retrospect, Douthwaite no doubt had arrived at my office with Rousseau's words in mind, "There is no wicked man who could not be made good for something" (SC, CW, 4:151). I thank her for this opportunity to redeem my character and, more importantly, for her having involved the Snite Museum in this important undertaking. I greatly admire Douthwaite's passion for Rousseau's ideals, her unflagging compassion for people suffering worldwide, her utter devotion to the five French photographers who created DIGNITY, her tireless commitment to her students, and her steadfast industry in translating the catalog from French to English. The Rousseau 2012/DIGNITY project would not have occurred without her indefatigable spirit.

DIGNITY

The Notre Dame DIGNITY exhibition featured fifty-two color and black-and-white photographs depicting poverty and human rights. Exhibition visitors witnessed human suffering through documentary photographs portraying victims of murder, brutality, hunger, disease, squalor, and poverty. They also glimpsed moments of un-conquerable human dignity, as evidenced by indigenous lifestyles, devotion to family, enjoyment of cultural rituals, and protest against oppressive corporations and governments.

Two noteworthy photographs contrasted dignity with degradation: the *Kuchei-padar Water Carrier* by Johann Rousselot (fig. 16), and *The Ezbet Al-Haggana District* by Philippe Brault (fig. 31). Both images feature a central "towering" figure, both photographs illustrate the distribution of a critical utility (water and electricity), and both feature barren, brown earth with a skyline positioned two-thirds up in the picture plane. While the Indian figure self-reliantly conveys water for her family, Brault informs us that the Cairo residents do not access the electricity that passes directly overhead. Similarly, while the Indian figure appears to have access to local food (chickens and their eggs) and a rich social life within a community populated by other people and at least one dog, the Cairo slum is devoid of people and the surrounding desert appears unlikely to support either crops or farm animals. Ezbet Al-Haggana is a dense jumble of unfinished (or ruined) homes, automobile tires, metal cages, rags, and satellite dishes (powered by generator?).

The critical difference is that while both communities are impoverished, dignity remains available to individuals living within the indigenous Indian community. Rousselot beautifully expresses this with the central figure who elegantly balances water, and perhaps food, within three metal containers. With one arm raised above her head and the other at her side, her arms, spine and hips form a lovely S-curve emulating the *contrapposto* pose so favored when Greeks idealized the human form. Elegant bracelets on both arms suggest an awareness of her beauty—additional signs of her innate dignity. This is a powerful, elegant human moving in grace down a road that suggests opportunities for forward movement and for self-determination. Indeed, Rousselot's text informs us that for fifteen years residents of this community have successfully resisted forced relocation sought by a mining concern.

I am very grateful to Rousselot, Brault, and the three other DIGNITY artists for allowing the Snite Museum of Art staff photographer to print exhibition prints of their digital photographs. This negated the expense, paperwork, and bureaucracy that would have been associated with packing and shipping the prints from Paris, as well as the expense and time that would have been required to hire a customs agent. Special thanks to photographers Johann Rousselot and Philippe Brault for traveling to Notre Dame to share their experiences with Amnesty International and with the DIGNITY exhibition. I am also thankful to Amnesty International for allowing the Snite Museum of Art to not only present a modified version of the exhibition, but to also publish an English-version catalog. In this regard, I am also indebted to Notre Dame attorney Timothy Flanagan for guiding Prof. Douthwaite and me in obtaining necessary copyright permissions.

Notre Dame graduate graphic designer Marie Bourgeois forewent her final college Christmas break so that she could beautifully reinterpret the original catalog within the larger, English format. Prof. Douthwaite translated the French text into English with assistance from degree candidates Lea Malewitz '12 and Lauren Wester '11, MA '12.

Similarly, Notre Dame undergraduate graphic designer Elizabeth Kelly traveled to Paris to interview the five photographers and Yves Prigent of Amnesty International. Those interviews were the basis for six videos that were available to exhibition visitors bearing smartphones—and which continue to be available on YouTube.

"A PERSON'S WORTH"

Curator of European Art Cheryl Snay and former Curator of Education, Academic Programs, Diana Matthias assisted Douthwaite in selecting fifteen works on paper from the museum's permanent collection to show how little has changed for the human condition since Rousseau's time. Artists represented included Ernst Barlach, Charles-Nicolas Cochin, Francisco de Goya, Jean-François Millet, Käthe Kollwitz (fig. 2), Félix Nadar, and others. Millet's etching *The Great Shepherdess* (fig. 60) made visual and thematic connections with Rousselot's water carrier. While once again, we see a single female on a brown earthen road that is shared with a farm animal, Millet's figure is fully clothed and in repose—perhaps to enjoy a moment in the shade. Millet frequently depicted shepherdesses to ennoble the dignity of peasant work, in comparison to dangerous and dirty conditions associated with factory labor undertaken during the Industrial Revolution.

EXHIBITION DESIGN AND INSTALLATION

The Snite Museum's "exhibition team" efficiently managed framing the prints, drawings, and photographs, designing the exhibitions, installing artworks, and overseeing lighting design. Therefore, I thank Associate Director Ann Knoll, Exhibition Designer John Phegley, and Exhibition Coordinator Ramiro Rodriguez.

Figure 60. *The Great Shepherdess*. Etching by Jean-François Millet, circa 1862. Courtesy of Snite Museum of Art, University of Notre Dame.

INSTITUTIONAL ASSISTANCE

The exhibits and events in the Snite Museum were made possible in part by a grant in support for the "Rousseau 2011: On the Road to DIGNITY Project" from the Henkels Lecture Fund, Institute for Scholarship in the Liberal Arts, College of Arts and Letters, University of Notre Dame. Additional support was provided by the Department of Romance Languages and Literatures; the Kellogg Institute for International Studies; the Program in Liberal Studies; the Department of Political Science; the Department of History; the Center for Social Concerns; the Undergraduate Minor in Poverty Studies; the Program in Gender Studies; the Department of American Studies; and the Ph.D. Program in Literature.

Numerous departments utilized the exhibition to augment spring 2012 classes. These included a variety of disciplines within the College of Arts and Letters, as well as those in the Kellogg Institute for International Studies and the Law School's Center for Civil and Human Rights.

SNITE MUSEUM ACADEMIC PROGRAMS

DIGNITY and "A Person's Worth" were exhibitions of a category often described by Snite Museum staff members as "faculty-inspired exhibitions," and they are among the most successful (and most challenging) programs we offer to engage the faculty and students of Notre Dame. As with most college and university art museums, the Snite Museum of Art serves multiple audiences: (1) Notre Dame faculty and students, (2) regional adults and schoolchildren, and (3) the international community of scholars and art aficionados.

Our primary campus audience is served through a wide variety of programs, in addition to faculty-inspired exhibitions, designed to enhance teaching and research. Snite Museum curators teach university art history and anthropology classes, curators and other staff members teach individual sessions of an art history faculty member's museum studies seminar; curators routinely provide tours for single university class sessions, as requested by faculty from numerous departments; and some faculty routinely base their classes on museum collections. For example, every two years Associate Professor Robert Randolf Coleman teaches a seminar on Italian drawings based on the museum's old master drawing collection. The seminar culminates with a museum exhibition and published exhibition catalog.

The Snite Museum art collection provides primary research material for area college students and faculty. Students from Notre Dame, Saint Mary's College, Indiana University South Bend, and other area colleges regularly use artworks on view in permanent galleries as a basis for class assignments. Art history majors often select specific works on view or in storage for research papers and theses. The curatorial and education staffs of the museum assist these students by answering their questions and often suggesting additional literary or art historical references.

The museum typically funds three graduate interns: two are graduate art history students and one is a graduate graphic design student. Each receives an academic year stipend funded by donor gifts. Art history graduate intern projects include curating exhibitions, preparing exhibition catalog essays, cataloging collections, and so forth, under the direct supervision of a curator. The graphic-design intern creates exhibition posters, opening reception invitations, exhibition brochures, and modest exhibition catalogs, which promote the museum and enrich student portfolios. Recent graduate intern projects include:

- Margaretta Higgins Intern Kirsten Appleyard (1) conducted provenance research for a forthcoming exhibition and catalog of highlights of the Noah and Muriel S. Butkin Collection of Nineteenth-Century French Art (a collection recently given to the Snite Museum of Art), (2) interviewed emeritus curator Stephen Spiro regarding the Butkins' relationship with the Snite Museum and prepared an essay on this topic for the forthcoming Butkin catalog, and (3) organized an exhibition of highlights of Rouault's *Miserere* print series.
- Under the supervision of Curator Snay, former Joan and James Bock Intern Sophia Meyers, MA '10 assisted in the preparation of the French drawing exhibition "The Epic and the Intimate." Meyers also conducted substantial original research on the Italian immigrant artist Luigi Gregori and organized an exhibition featuring his preparatory drawings for the murals in the Basilica of the Sacred Heart and the Columbus murals in the Main Building.
- Bethany Montagano, a 2010–12 Ph.D. History Fellow, prepared essays for a future exhibition catalog for the O'Grady Collection of Nineteenth-Century European Photographs of Asian Women at the Snite Museum of Art.

While student art is typically shown within art department galleries at other universities, the Snite Museum of Art annually exhibits artworks created as senior and thesis projects by graduating art students. The exhibition reception typically attracts six hundred to eight hundred guests, and an award program honors artists, designers, and art history students. The Department of Art, Art History, and Design sees this opportunity for their students to learn how to professionally exhibit their artworks as an invaluable part of their education.

Notre Dame Faculty routinely conduct research on Museum collections and publish their finding in Museum publications. Two current examples include:

- *Eclectic Antiquity: The Classical Collection of the Snite Museum of Art*, compiled and edited by Prof. Robin F. Rhodes, 2010. Beginning in 2004, Associate Director Ann Knoll, Prof. Robin Rhodes, and five visiting scholars organized images and text for an illustrated catalogue of the museum's Greco-Roman collection. This joint venture of the Classics Department, the Snite Museum, and the Department of Art, Art History, and Design was published September 2010.

- Prof. Charles Rosenberg is completing a manuscript for a collection catalog of the museum's Jack and Alfrieda Fedderson Collection of Rembrandt Etchings.

In addition, the Museum routinely organizes academic symposia in association with special exhibitions organized for the benefit of ND academic departments. Two recent examples include:

- "Documenting History, Charting Progress, Exploring the World: Nineteenth-Century Photographs of Architecture," an international conference organized by an Indiana University South Bend faculty member and the Snite Museum of Art staff in association with a Snite Museum exhibition of the same title consisting of works selected from the Janos Scholz Collection of Nineteenth-Century European Photographs. Indiana University South Bend and the Snite Museum of Art, October 3–4, 2010.
- "From Vernacular to Classical: The Perpetual Modernity of Palladio," an international conference organized by the Notre Dame School of Architecture, took place in association with the *Palladio and His Legacy: A Transatlantic Journey* exhibition, June 11, 2011.

Another project connects art to the College of Science. Curator, Arts of the Americas, Africa and Oceania, Douglas Bradley continues a collaboration with Michael Wiescher, Department of Physics, to conduct PIXE (Particle Induced X-Ray Emission) research and with Michelle Joyce, Department of Chemistry and Biochemistry, to utilize MC-ICP-MS and MS-Proteomics research in an attempt to provide useful information about paint that is no longer visible to the eye and the composition of paint pigments, rubber ball chemistry, and perhaps chocolate vessel identification for the future handbook to the Mesoamerican collection.

The Snite Museum of Art staff also includes a curator of education dedicated to the campus audience. This individual custom designs tours on themes requested by faculty members; coordinates foreign language tours of the museum for Notre Dame students studying Spanish, Italian, French, German, and Russian; coordinates classroom visits to see a discrete group of museum artworks within a seminar room; coordinates the Snite Museum Essay contest for first-year students; and created the Vital Visionaries program. Vital Visionaries is a collaborative project involving Indiana University School of Medicine, South Bend, the Forever Learning Institute, and the Snite Museum of Art. The aim of the class is to encourage socialization between senior citizens and medical students to enhance the students' powers of observation (useful in patient diagnoses) and to help them to empathize with senior patients.

FACULTY-INSPIRED MUSEUM EXHIBITIONS

Returning to faculty-initiated exhibitions, the Snite Museum of Art has experimented with exhibitions curated by or requested by members of Notre Dame faculty for approximately eight years. A recent review of temporary exhibitions presented at the Snite Museum over three academic years (July 2009 to June 2012) revealed that 21, or 54 percent, were initiated or requested by faculty members. An early example is Associate Professor of Art History Robin Rhodes's *Corinth Project* exhibition that shared much of what he has learned as Principal Investigator of the Greek Stone Architecture at the Corinth Excavations of the American School of Classical Studies at Athens. The exhibition featured a model of what the building and entire site might have looked like in Antiquity; roof tiles fabricated by utilizing ancient tile-making processes; a model depicting the design and construction of the temple's wood and tile roof; cast reproductions of stone blocks with a related replica of a stone wall; computer displays; and extensive text and photo panels. Commenting on the popular exhibition, Rhodes observed: "The Corinth exhibition was a wonderful teaching tool. After six lectures in the exhibition, my students understood more about the nature of classical architecture than they would have after an entire semester of lectures in the classroom. The exhibition was architecture, not images of architecture; it transformed the Snite's Mestrovic Studio Gallery into a multimedia installation that lifted the material presented beyond the merely didactic and into a more visceral experience of mass, materials, textures, marks, processes, and landscapes."

While I was delighted that this art museum exhibition featuring no original artworks received a strong public response, some of my colleagues were less enthusiastic not only about my having endorsed the display of facsimiles within the museum, but also for my having given a faculty member so much discretion regarding the organization and installation of the exhibition. Some colleagues were concerned that the exhibition reflected a lapse of professional standards, a dangerous abdication of curatorial control, and a confusing mixing of art and archaeology. These feelings were intensified for this exhibition because Professor Rhodes, like so many who supervise archeological digs, has very strong beliefs about the legal ownership and ethical display of cultural patrimony—one of the art museum profession's most difficult current policy challenges.

My response to the clash between art museum curators (and directors) and anthropologists regarding the acquisition and display of antiquities was to invite Professor Rhodes to join me in organizing a symposium on the topic entitled "The Acquisition and Exhibition of Classical Antiquities: Professional, Legal, and Ethical

Perspectives" in 2007. Rhodes and I were both pleased by the civility of discourse and by the recognition that archaeologists and art museum professionals actually agree on more than they disagree. In other words, I embraced a concept modeled by the former chair of the Department of Art, Art History, and Design, Professor Dennis Doordan: "teach the conflict."

Providing Professor Rhodes with a curatorial voice in organizing his exhibition was, to my mind, an extension of the curatorial freedom I try to give museum curators when they organize both permanent and temporary exhibitions for the Snite Museum. Astute visitors to the Snite Museum will note a wide variety of exhibition strategies and designs within our galleries. For example, permanent exhibitions organized by scholars trained as anthropologists present artworks within display cases similar to those found within natural history museums, and feature wall maps and photographs describing the historical and cultural locations where displayed artworks were excavated or fabricated. An example is the Native American Art Gallery. Other Snite galleries privilege artworks by limiting the number of artworks on display, by lighting artworks to maximize drama, and by minimizing competing visual noise produced by maps, photographs, text panels, long labels, and so forth. In short, it is important for some Snite Museum exhibitions to reflect the academic training, specialization, and unique point of view of the organizing curator. This underscores for our audience a simple, important truth about art—we all bring unique perspectives to the understanding of any artwork and, therefore, there is no single correct interpretation of any artwork. This is the reason we like to include a curator "byline" within introductory text panels for exhibits organized by faculty and other guest curators.

Clearly, faculty-inspired exhibitions are fraught with challenges. Most faculty members are not familiar with the inner workings of an art museum and the associated processes and professional practices required to organize a temporary exhibition. A smaller subset does not understand the necessity for meeting production and writing deadlines, and an even smaller group does not understand that their exhibition and catalog represent only one of a group of temporary exhibitions and publications that a museum staff must concurrently produce. For our part, many directors and curators are reluctant to give up control over exhibition content, exhibition interpretation, and exhibition design.

That said, it seems art museums situated within academies should be the most willing to share their curatorial voice, to challenge longstanding museology traditions, and to experiment. University and college art museums enjoy academic freedom and, to varying degrees, significant institutional expertise and financial support.

The importance of faculty-inspired exhibitions to the Snite Museum of Art has led us to include a "University gallery" within our architectural program for a new art museum building. This space will be dedicated solely to exhibitions organized to support teaching and research at Notre Dame: I imagine exhibitions curated by students, faculty, guest curators, and Snite Museum curators. The University gallery will be one space within a zone dedicated to university audiences; additional spaces will include a lecture hall, classrooms, seminar rooms for the close examination of artworks, intern offices, the Museum library, and a café.

The University of Notre Dame's relative distance from national cultural centers coupled with its responsibility to engage students and faculty in the most pressing, difficult, and controversial contemporary ideas indicates that the museum should offer more provocative and challenging exhibits. Risk taking and a sense of experimentation should characterize museum programs. In the Snite Museum's case, it is the museum's obligation to engage students in the debate of contemporary, and often controversial, ideas within Notre Dame's supportive community of faith. Students who are protected from challenging ideas at the university may be at a disadvantage when they encounter these ideas on their own in the "real" world.

It is for these reasons that I am so grateful to Professor Douthwaite for having shared a healthy dose of the greater world with our faculty, staff, and students—many of whom come from privileged backgrounds that fortunately do not include hunger, disease, inferior housing, and political oppression. At Notre Dame we hope to instill a sense of social responsibility within our students—either as a faith-based value or as a core expression of essential humanity. It was truly gratifying to see that so many within the Notre Dame community were moved by what they saw within the DIGNITY exhibition and by what they heard from guest speakers.

The exhibition and associated programs were evidence of the Snite Museum of Art operating at its highest level—within a realm that can create positive change within individual lives and within the world.

CONTRIBUTORS

We have included the ages of scholarly and artistic contributors, as was done for sitters in the DIGNITY portraits, to retain the democratic spirit of this volume. (Ages of all other contributors, when available, are listed with their names in the Teach This! section.)

THE DIGNITY TEAM

Thanks go to YVES PRIGENT of Amnesty International, the original curator of *DIGNITÉ: Droits humains et pauvreté*, for the inspiration behind this project, for funding it, organizing it, and making it come to life.

PHILIPPE BRAULT. Born in 1965, Brault works on violence as it is involved in the civil and environmental consequences of political conflict. His exhibits include *La Mémoire serbe du Kosovo* (2008) and *Scènes de crimes à Guatemala City* (2008). He has published series in newspapers such as *Le Monde, Libération*, and *Télérama* in France, and English-language publications such as *Time* and *Vanity Fair*. In 2010, he created a documentary for the French channel Arte, *Prison Valley: L'Industrie de la prison*.

GUILLAUME HERBAUT. Born in 1970, Herbaut has received numerous awards for his work, including the Lauréat of the Fondation de France, the Lucien Hervé prize, and he took second place in the World Press Photo competition of 2009 ("contemporary issue" division). His work *Tchernobylsty* won the Kodak prize for photographical criticism in 2001 and the Fuji prize of 2004. Other works include *Oswiecim* (2005) and a project on the consequences of the bombing in Nagasaki. His work has been exhibited in France, Spain, and the United States (Gallery Silverstein, NY).

JEAN-FRANÇOIS JOLY. Born in 1961, Joly has won the Alpa prize from the city of Vevey and a fellowship from the Grand Duchy of Luxembourg for works such as *Naufragés* and *Roms*, both of which focus on people who live on the margins of society. He has published two books, *Naufragés de la ville* (1994) and *Résonances* (2005), and exhibits his work regularly in France and abroad.

JOHANN ROUSSELOT. Born in 1971, Rousselot's work is frequently published in newspapers such as *Le Monde* and *Le Courrier international* in France, *El País* (Spain), and *Newsweek* (United States). Some of his work has been published in books such as *India Now* (2007) and *This Day of Change: Kodansha's 100th Anniversary Photo Book Project* (2009). He received the Kodak prize (2003) for a series entitled *Balkans: Les Belles, la bête*.

MICHAËL ZUMSTEIN. Born in 1970, Zumstein works on conflicts in Africa and the relations between Africa and the West, with a special focus on human rights, ecology, and the consequences of the global economy. His work has exposed abusive situations endured by miners of the coltan mines (the Democratic Republic of the Congo) and the pollution caused by mining for the minerals used in manufacturing computer technology. He was hired by *Le Monde* in 2007 to cover the presidential campaign and follows French news for several newspapers at present. He also holds photographic workshops in Africa for World Press Photo.

SCHOLARLY CONTRIBUTORS

ANDREW BILLING. Born in 1972, Billing is currently associate professor of French at Macalester College. He came to Macalester in 2008 as a Mellon Postdoctoral Fellow and was previously a visiting assistant professor at the University of Missouri–Kansas City. He completed his Ph.D. in 2007 from the University of California Irvine with a specialization in the fields of eighteenth-century French literature and political theory. He is the author of articles published in journals such as *French Studies* and *Romanic Review*.

JULIA V. DOUTHWAITE. Born in 1958, Douthwaite is professor of French at the University of Notre Dame. She was the curator and organizer of the Amnesty International DIGNITY exhibit at Notre Dame. Her most recent books are *The Frankenstein of 1790 and Other Lost Chapters from Revolutionary France* (2012) and *The Wild Girl, Natural Man and the Monster: Dangerous Experiments in the Age of Enlightenment* (2002), both published by the University of Chicago Press. She has received grants from the John Simon Guggenheim Memorial Foundation, the National Endowment for the Humanities, and the Lilly Foundation. She is currently writing a book called *Financiers We Have Known*, which combines her interest in myths of economics with the study of French fiction and popular art, 1719–1843.

ESTHER DUFLO. Born in 1972, Duflo is the Abdul Latif Jameel Professor of Poverty Alleviation and Development Economics at the Massachusetts Institute of Technology and a founder and director of the Abdul Latif Jameel Poverty Action Lab (J-PAL). Duflo has received numerous academic honors and prizes, including the David N. Kershaw Award, the CNRS Médaille de l'Innovation, the John Bates Clark Medal, and a MacArthur Fellowship. Her most recent book, with Abhijit Banerjee, is *Poor Economics: A Radical Rethinking of the Way to Fight Global Poverty* (2011). Duflo currently serves as the founding editor of the journal *AEJ: Applied Economics*.

FAYÇAL FALAKY. Born in 1977, Falaky completed his Ph.D. in 2008 from New York University. He is currently associate professor of French at Tulane University, where he specializes in eighteenth-century French literature, culture, and politics. He has published articles in journals such as *Forum for Modern Language Studies*, *Journal of Eighteenth-Century Studies*, and *European Journal of Political Theory*. He is also the author of *Social Contract, Masochist Contract: Aesthetics of Freedom and Submission in Rousseau* (2014).

GABRIELLE GOPINATH. Born in 1976, Gopinath teaches modern and contemporary art history at Humboldt State University in Arcata, California. She received her Ph.D. from Yale University, where her dissertation addressed the theme of bodily absence in multimedia art of the 1970s. She has published articles on video, graffiti, sound art, and new media. Her current book project addresses euphoric and dysphoric metaphors of containment in postwar American art.

CHRISTOPHER KELLY. Born in 1950, Kelly is professor of political science at Boston College, and has also taught at the École des Hautes Etudes en Sciences Sociales, Paris, and Dartmouth College. He is co-editor of the authoritative *Collected Writings of Rousseau* (1990–2010; see citations throughout the present volume), and *Rousseau on Women, Love, and Family* (2009). Among his many writings are *Rousseau as Author: Consecrating One's Life to the Truth* (2003) and *Rousseau's Exemplary Life* (1987), as well as articles in journals such as *Modern Intellectual History*, *Polity*, and *Interpretation*.

CHARLES R. LOVING. Born in 1957, Loving is director of the Snite Museum of Art at the University of Notre Dame and curator of the George Rickey Sculpture Archive. He has contributed to numerous publications featuring the collection of the Snite Museum, including: *Artist in Residence: Working Drawings by Luigi Gregori*

(1819–1896) (2011), *Eighteenth- and Nineteenth-Century British Drawings from the Collection of Mr. and Mrs. Allan J. Riley* (2002), and *A Gift of Light: Photographs in the Janos Scholz Collection* (2002).

SERGE MARGEL. Born in 1962, Margel is professor in the History and Philology Department at the University of Neuchâtel (Switzerland) and at the Geneva School of Art and Design (Cinema Section). Member of the Academia Europeae, he is also a researcher at the Swiss National Science Foundation. He is the author of more than twenty books, including *L'invention du corps de chair* (2016), *La Societe du spectral* (2012), *Alienation* (2008), and *De l'imposture* (2007; English translation forthcoming).

CHRISTIE McDONALD. Born in 1942, McDonald is Smith Professor of French Language and Literature and Comparative Literature at Harvard University. She is the author of *The Extravagant Shepherd: A Study of the Pastoral Vision in Rousseau's "Nouvelle Heloise"* (Studies on Voltaire and the Eighteenth Century, repr. 2007), *The Proustian Fabric: Associations of Memory* (1991), and articles such as "Hommage to Jacques Derrida," *PMLA* (March 2005). She is also the editor, with Stanley Hoffman, of *Rousseau and Freedom* (2012, 2010), with Susan Suleiman, of *French Global: A New Approach to Literary History* (2011), *Painting My World: The Art of Dorothy Eisner* (2008), *Images of Congo* (2008), and of Jacques Derrida, *The Ear of the Other: Otobiography, Transference, Translation* (1988), as well as numerous other publications.

DELPHINE MOREAU. Born in 1978, Moreau is the co-founder and a member of the production company Cinésphère. She has made films such as *Kumpo & co* (with Gabrielle Gerll), *Marmites Khmères*, *La Société des Arbres*, and *Quatre Saisons en forêt*, this last film for the TV station France 3. She is particularly interested in creating films that explore the ties between humans and the earth, such as *Initiation Andalouse* and a work-in-progress, *Les gens du sucre, deux siècles d'histoire*.

DANIEL PHILPOTT. Born in 1967, Philpott is professor of political science and peace studies and director of the Center for Civil and Human Rights at the University of Notre Dame. His scholarship focuses broadly on religion and global politics and more particularly on reconciliation in the aftermath of genocide, civil war, dictatorship, and other forms of violence and injustice. He is co-author with Monica Duffy Toft and Timothy Samuel Shah of *God's Century: Resurgent Religion and Global Politics* (2011) and is author of *Just and Unjust Peace: An Ethic of Political Reconciliation* (2012). He has pursued an activist dimension of his interest in reconciliation in Kashmir and in the Great Lakes region of Africa under the auspices of the Catholic Peacebuilding Network.

ALISON RICE. Born in 1973, Rice is associate professor of French and Francophone studies at the University of Notre Dame. She is the author of *Time Signatures: Contextualizing Contemporary Francophone Autobiographical Writing from the Maghreb* (2006) and *Polygraphies: Francophone Women Writing Algeria* (2012). Her current book project, inspired by a series of filmed interviews she conducted in Paris, explores the present proliferation of women writers of French from around the world.

PHILIP STEWART. Born in 1940, Stewart is Benjamin E. Powell Professor Emeritus of Romance Studies and Literature at Duke University. He is author of eight books including most recently *L'Invention du sentiment: Roman et économie affective au XVIIIe siècle* (Studies on Voltaire and the Eighteenth Century, 2010) and *Éditer Rousseau: Enjeux d'un corpus (1750–2012)* (2012). He has done translations of Rousseau's *Julie* and several other works, and produced critical editions of *Le Philosophe anglais* (1977, 2003), *Les Heureux Orphelins* (1995, 2001), *Lettres persanes* (2004, 2013), and *Rousseau juge de Jean-Jacques* (2012). Among volumes he has edited are *Interpreting Colonialism* (with Byron Wells, 2004), *Du genre libertin au XVIIIe siècle* (with Jean-François Perrin, 2004), *Le Second Triomphe du roman du XVIIIe siècle* (with Michel Delon, 2009), and *Les "Lettres persanes" en leur temps* (2013).

MONICA TOWNSEND. Born in 1990, Townsend is a 2012 graduate of the University of Notre Dame and currently enrolled at the University of Connecticut Medical School. While at Notre Dame, Townsend founded a chapter of "She's the First," a nonprofit organization that raises funds to promote education for girls in developing countries, and participated in an International Student Summer Learning Project for pre-med students in India.

STUDENTS AND SCHOOLCHILDREN IN THE USA

Notre Dame Students

> Alexa Craig
> Kathleen Ginty
> Ryan Koter
> Lea Malewitz
> Darsie Malynn
> Amie Wei
> Lauren Wester

Students and Children from the South Bend Community

Riham Abu-Gdairi
Kasey Bridges
Tamera Bruce
Damaris Buendio Escobedo
Daniela Buendio Escobedo
John "Jack" Driscoll
Raini Fleming
Alice Goulding
Mateo Graubart
Jack Griffin
Joseph Habimana
Maximiliana M. Heller
Michael Kirbie
Patrick Kline
Sofia Lora
Kieran McKenna
Ruben Velazquez
Sydney Weber
Sophia Zovich

PARTICIPANTS IN THE *ENTRE NOUS JEAN-JACQUES* DOCUMENTARY

The documentary was filmed in Compiègne, France by the Cinésphère team: Delphine Moreau, Oona Bijasson, Marie Famulicki, and Corinne Sullivan.

The Literacy Class

Arnaud
Esma
Fatimata
Maïmouna
Partha
Sulasemi
Zeliha

The Nursing Home Residents

>Lucienne Calleja
>Andrée Doucet
>Noélie Lafon
>Gilberte Vidal

The Teenagers

>Alexandre
>Luc
>Mona
>Quentin

The Children

>The CM2 class at l'École Hammel, Compiègne

INDEX

University of Notre Dame (*cont.*)
  students
  —activities and ambitions of, 3, 15–16
  —contributors to this volume, 21–29,
    231–34
  —responses to DIGNITY exhibit, 3–4,
    10–11, 254
  —supported by Snite Museum of Art,
    249–50
  See also teenagers
Upward Bound program, 15–16

Velazquez, Ruben, 228
Vidal, Gilberte, 241–42
video letters
  epistolary form, 32–33
  genre, 5, 32–34
  three styles (discourse, reverie, and
    confession), 32
  See also Cavalier, Alain; Cinésphère group
    and productions; Erice, Victor;
    Godard, Jean-Luc; Kiarostami,
    Abbas; Moreau, Delphine
violence
  in DIGNITY exhibit, 45
  domestic violence and rape, 174, 217, 235
  domestic violence in Rousseau, *Julie*,
    139–44 (fig. 3), (fig. 4)
  against non-Catholics during Inquisition,
    61
  against Rousseau, recounted in auto-
    biography, 104–6
  in South Bend, Indiana, 15, 17n14
  See also military vs. citizens; murder;

police vs. refugees; Revolution, French;
    rights, human
Voltaire, 122–24, 127–28, 137
  See also under Rousseau, Jean-Jacques,
    author of: "Letter to Voltaire"
voting, Rousseau's view on, 6

Warren, Elizabeth, 145
Weber, Sydney, 229–30
Wei, Amy, 233–34
Wester, Lauren, 17n13
Whitman, Walt, 39
Will, George, 145
Wolmar, Monsieur de, in *Julie*, 139–40
women. *See* children and childhood;
    Levasseur; mothers and motherhood;
    rights, human; violence; *see under*
    Rousseau, Jean-Jacques, author of:
    Emile, or, On Education and *Julie, or,*
    The New Heloise
work. *See under* economics
"Write YOUR Story" program, 15–16

Yugoslavia, 210
  country of origin of Esma, 238
  war and exile of inhabitants, 210–12,
    238
  See also Macedonia

Zeliha (*Entre nous Jean-Jacques*), 240
Zovich, Sophia, 229
Zumstein, Michaël, photographer of
    DIGNITY exhibit (Nigeria), 4, 7
  definition of dignity, 158

CPSIA information can be obtained
at www.ICGtesting.com
Printed in the USA
LVOW06*1958091216

516441LV00012B/24/P